A Guide to Opera
for the Perplexed

Bravo!

Barrymore Laurence Scherer

With Illustrations by the Author

INTRODUCTION BY THOMAS HAMPSON

A DUTTON BOOK

DUTTON
Published by the Penguin Group
Penguin Books USA Inc., 375 Hudson Street,
New York, New York 10014, U.S.A.
Penguin Books Ltd, 27 Wrights Lane, London W8 5TZ, England
Penguin Books Australia Ltd, Ringwood, Victoria, Australia
Penguin Books Canada Ltd, 10 Alcorn Avenue,
Toronto, Ontario, Canada M4V 3B2
Penguin Books (N.Z.) Ltd, 182–190 Wairau Road, Auckland 10, New Zealand

Penguin Books Ltd, Registered Offices:
Harmondsworth, Middlesex, England

First published by Dutton, an imprint of Dutton Signet,
a division of Penguin Books USA Inc.
Distributed in Canada by McClelland & Stewart Inc.

First Printing, December, 1996
10 9 8 7 6 5 4 3 2 1

REGISTERED TRADEMARK—MARCA REGISTRADA

LIBRARY OF CONGRESS CATALOGING-IN-PUBLICATION DATA
Scherer, Barrymore Laurence.
    Bravo! : a guide to opera for the perplexed / Barrymore Laurence
  Scherer : with illustrations by the author : introduction by Thomas
  Hampson.
        p.   cm.
    Includes index.
    ISBN 0-525-94248-3
    1. Operas—Analysis, appreciation.   I. Title.
  MT95.S465   1996
  782.1—dc20   96-28304
                                                                      CIP
                                                                      MN

Printed in the United States of America
Set in Century Expanded
Designed by Eve L. Kirch

This book is printed on acid-free paper. ∞

For Michelle

Great men might envy me
the great woman who stands at my side.

Contents

Introduction by Thomas Hampson   **xi**

An Invitation to the Opera   **1**

It Doesn't Start Till *Somebody* Sings   **12**

    Hitting All the High Notes: The Soprano   *14*
    Mezzos and Altos: The Marvelous Middle Ground   *18*
    The Well-tempered Tenor   *21*
    The Lowdown on Low Voices   *26*
    Altered States: The Castrato   *31*
    Airs and Graces: What Is an Aria?   *35*

    Interludes: In Praise of Divas and Prima Donnas   *40*
                Icons of an Age—Caruso and Callas   *43*
                The Conductor—Holding It All Together   *54*

Italian Opera: The Source   **58**

    Monteverdi, the First Master   *63*
    Opera Seria   *66*
    Toward a New Aesthetic: Mozart   *68*
    Rossini: A Bridge to the Romantic Era   *72*
    Romantic Bel Canto   *74*
    Verdi: The Glory of Italy   *77*
    Puccini and the New Century   *83*
    A Dagger in Every Plot: The Pulse-Pounding World of
        Verismo   *86*
    Further Adventures in Italian Opera   *92*

French Opera: *Vive la Différence!*   **93**

Voilà Lully   *94*
Rameau: Controversy, Baroque Style   *97*
From Baroque to Classical   *98*
Romanticism Arrives   *100*
Grand Opera: Bigger Is Better   *101*
A Fork in the Road: Gounod, Bizet, Massenet   *107*
Into the Twentieth Century: Debussy, Ravel, Poulenc   *110*
Further Adventures in French Opera   *114*

German Opera: *Was Ist Das?*   **116**

Going for Baroque   *117*
Singspiel   *119*
Mozart   *120*
Revolutionary and Romantic: Beethoven and Weber   *123*
Wagner Without Tears   *128*
The Once and Future Richard Strauss   *136*
The Roaring Twenties: Berg and Weill   *140*
Further Adventures in German Opera   *143*

Interludes: Death, Be Not Loud   *145*
                Sheer Madness!   *151*

Russian Opera: East Meets West   **158**

Glinka: Father of It All   *161*
The Mighty *Kuchka*   *164*
Tchaikovsky: French Wine in Russian Bottles   *170*
Seeing Red: The Soviet School   *175*
Further Adventures in Russian Opera and Czech
   Opera, Too   *178*
And to End, a Hungarian Opera   *181*

English Opera? It's Actually Jolly Good   **183**

Masques and Marvels   *184*
Purcell: Interrupted Melody   *186*
Eighteenth-Century Developments   *188*

Contents

Nineteenth-Century Operas: Too Long Overlooked   *191*
Victorian Opera: Dead, or Just Sleeping?   *193*
Twentieth-Century Masters   *196*
Further Adventures in English Opera   *203*

Operetta, or Sleeping Beauties   204

American Opera: Cinderella Was a Stepchild, Too   212

Italian Opera Emigrates to America   *214*
Americanism   *216*
American Opera Takes Wing: Virgil Thomson   *217*
Great American Classics   *219*
On the Cutting Edge with Philip Glass   *223*
Rubbing Elbows with Broadway   *227*

**Getting Your Feet Wet: An Introduction to
the Opera Experience**   229

Beginner's Luck   *235*
Learning What's Around   *241*
When in Rome, or A Little Bit of Opera Etiquette   *243*
Making a Production of It   *248*
Why We Say "Bravo!"   *253*

Postlude: If Music Be the Food of Love ... Let's Eat!   *255*

Coming to Terms with Opera: A Concise Glossary   261

Acknowledgments   283

Index   285

Introduction

by Thomas Hampson

$\mathcal{T}$ he world of opera is as passionate as you are!
Essentially, opera is the art form that excites our passions and sensibilities to the most euphoric—and sometimes ultimate—degree. It offers a world of myriad descriptions and emotions, which are, in fact, the very descriptions of our personality itself—simply because opera is all about LIFE.

Opera re-creates that intoxication of head and heart, reason and feeling, as it blazes through the prism of passion we call personality, slinging words with catapults of music until our senses ultimately harmonize, and recognize a fuller meaning to what we call *being alive*.

This little book is about *being alive*. Whether you are just awakening to the pleasures of opera, or as the philosopher Joseph Campbell so aptly put it, "following your Bliss," *Bravo!: A Guide to Opera for the Perplexed* will guide, beguile, amuse, and inform you, thus enhancing your enjoyment of opera and, by extension, your enjoyment of being alive.

Barrymore Scherer's own contagious passion and his amazing ability to communicate a wealth of information through a narrative that is at once personal and disarming will seduce the neophyte and challenge the learned. Scherer arms you with reasons and facts. He lets you explore the development of opera during the past four centuries. He conjures up the personalities of the

composers, librettists, conductors, singers, and stage directors
who have contributed to that development. He investigates the
differences between opera and operetta. And he examines
issues, such as the use of surtitles, which modern opera houses
must confront in order to keep the tradition freshly evolving. In
a straightforward, highly readable manner, he offers guidance
for experiencing opera on stage and on disc, pausing along the
way to encapsulate what each opera is about. For the curious
and for those seeking a better understanding of the medium,
Scherer's extensive references will provide a treasure trove of
history, anecdote, and explanation that enlivens, connects, and
contributes to building a working knowledge about opera.

It seems that today we measure knowledge more and more by
bits, bytes, and spreadsheets and less and less by questions, dialogue, and reason—which has made the humanities, in general,
and cultural, artistic, and musical studies, specifically, increasingly
rare or increasingly sterile. But, in fact, it is from the humanities,
which serve as a forum for the imagination, that we can celebrate
the efforts of the human spirit and appreciate more deeply its
search for communication and for the clarification of life.

Passion thrives on understanding and enlightenment. How
full is your passion? How big is your world of opera? Read on!
Search on! BE ALIVE!

Editor's note: *The American baritone Thomas Hampson is
one of the most distinguished singers of the present day. In addition to making regular appearances at the Metropolitan Opera,
the San Francisco Opera, Covent Garden, Salzburg, and other
international theaters, he is among the world's chief song recital-
ists, acclaimed for his musicianship and interpretive sensitivity
in a variety of languages.*

*His work has garnered him an array of prizes as well as
induction into the Royal Academy of Music, London.*

An Invitation to the Opera

One goes to see a tragedy to be moved; one goes to the Opéra either for want of any other interest, or to facilitate digesting.

—VOLTAIRE

The great American humorist Robert Benchley reputedly observed that "opera is where a guy gets stabbed in the back, and instead of dying, he sings." Even the most rabid operaphile would have to admit that there's more than a little truth to Benchley's quip, at least on the surface. And certainly a lot of people think opera a bit crazy. In opera the most private moments of a character's existence—the contemplation of love, or death,

religious ecstasy or deep sadness—are expressed in song. More often than not, the more intense, the more intimate the emotion, the stronger its musical profile. This can mean anything from Canio the clown's full-throated cry of sorrow in Leoncavallo's *Pagliacci* to the comparative whisper at the moment that Debussy's lovers, Pelléas and Mélisande, kiss for the first and last time.

But opera, if you look at it from the right angle, is not all that far removed from more common expressions of popular culture. The first is the Broadway musical, which is a direct descendant of opera anyway. Can you imagine a successful musical in which the dramatic high points were *not* expressed through song? From *Show Boat* to *Sunset Boulevard*, that's how it's done. Moreover, both *Sunset Boulevard* and Andrew Lloyd Webber's finest work, *The Phantom of the Opera*, are virtual operas in their emphasis on musical continuity and minimum spoken dialogue—not to mention the visual spectacle, which, most appropriately for their highly emotional sub-jects, is operatic. So, even if you don't think you like opera, you are already well on your way to appreciating it if you are amongst the many fans of those shows.

Even real life has its operatic moments—ceremonial rites of passage such as one's graduation or wedding, and more intimate moments like a dance between lovers or a candlelit seduction. Either way, these moments would be completely empty without the right musical underpinning. That's what opera is all about.

In September 1995 the *New York Times* reported that opera is the fastest-growing performance art in the United States, with an audience rise of 35 percent over the last decade. This must surprise the many pundits who have cried for years that "Opera is dead."

But why should this be? Why, in the age of the multiplex and the Internet, should increasing numbers of people concern themselves over Puccini's Madam Butterfly waiting for her ship to come in? Why should they be touched as Verdi's Aida and Radamès prepare for eternity with a final embrace? Why should spirits soar when Siegfried finally makes his way through the Magic Fire and into Brünnhilde's waiting arms? Why should anyone at the end of the twentieth century care about an entertainment devised in the sixteenth century, and care about it passionately?

Simply, because no popular film, no best-selling novel or even hit play can duplicate the sheer emotional high that opera can offer. That's why those who love opera love it with a particular intensity. Nevertheless, ask ten opera lovers how they fell in love, and you'll get ten different answers. Some people are hooked while attending their first opera; others take their time, progressing from an aria or two to complete works.

As I remember my first operatic exposure, I must have been five, and it was purely accidental. We were visiting my grandparents one Sunday, and as usual, the television was on. Instead of *Meet the Press*, however, there was a live telecast of an opera, performed, I believe, by the NBC Opera Company. I remember that the opera was Puccini's *Madama Butterfly*, for I fully expected to see a real winged insect. There was none. Instead, everyone was singing. I would certainly like to report that the experience transformed me like St. Paul on the road to Damascus. But in truth I was *bored!*

When did the opera bug finally bite? I must have been around seven or eight when I began to notice that certain cartoons on television had particularly catchy music. One favorite opened with Porky Pig working in a blacksmith shop, hammering an anvil to an exceedingly infectious tune. In another that I always anticipated with great pleasure, Sylvester Cat took a final pratfall followed immediately by the ascent of his nine lives accompanied by another piece of music that hit home. In a third, Mickey Mouse skippered a tempest-tossed ship, to music that I found not only infinitely appropriate to the imagery of pounding ocean waves but impossible to forget. Later on I began to discover that the sources were operatic: Porky hammered to the "Anvil Chorus" from Verdi's *Il Trovatore*, the feline ascension was accompanied by the Sextet from Donizetti's *Lucia di Lammermoor*, while Mickey's gale raged to the opening measures of Wagner's overture to *The Flying Dutchman*, an opera drenched in salt water and grog.

Little by little I was feeling my way. By the time I had entered the High School of Music and Art in New York, opera was a vital part of my existence. Moreover, at Music and Art—where I had gone to study art, and ended up taking music courses as well—I met one of the greatest influences on my musical development, Rudolf Cooper, who taught English there. Though I never took a course with him, providence had put me in his homeroom class. One morning shortly into my first semester at "the Castle," I noticed, with wide eyes, a pile of 78s on the floor of Mr. Cooper's wardrobe closet. "Where did you get all those?" I asked. "So you like that old stuff, too?" he responded. "Would you be interested in doing any trading?"

I told him I'd give my eyeteeth for the opportunity.

Unfortunately, the handful of 78s I owned at the time contained nothing of interest to a connoisseur. And, as I was to learn, Rudolf Cooper was indeed a connoisseur. It was certainly his generosity of spirit and his essential fineness as a teacher that led him to encourage my interest despite my lack of anything to trade.

Instead of records, he suggested trading me batches of 78s in return for reels of blank recording tape. I got the best of a splendid bargain, for not only did Mr. Cooper expand my awareness of Golden Age singers, he began to broaden my taste in vocal music. From obvious starting points such as Enrico Caruso's recordings of "Vesti la giubba" and "Celeste Aida" we moved into increasingly sophisticated fare.

One day he presented me with a recording of the trio "Qual voluttà" from Verdi's early opera *I Lombardi*. I was already fascinated by "forgotten" operas, and I will never forget the effect it had on me. The melody of this piece is one of the sweetest in the entire Verdi canon, and at the climax of this performance, the voices of Caruso and Frances Alda rise higher and higher until they hit a series of repeated high Bs. As I listened for the first time, I was rooted in place, with a lump in my throat the size of an egg. It still has the same effect on me, and I have yet to hear a better recording or performance of this trio, let alone one to equal it.

While I was at Music and Art, I made my first visits to the Metropolitan Opera, during the final season of the old house on Broadway and 39th Street. I bought a seat in the Family Circle for a Saturday matinee performance of Donizetti's *L'Elisir d'Amore* (The Elixir of Love). When the great day came, I arrived at the house to discover that I could not enter through the front door—the Family Circle had its own dingy entrance on the north side of the house. Breathless from a climb up endless iron stairs, I found myself in a dim corridor. As I walked through the doors into the auditorium, my temples were pounding from the exertion and excitement. Before my eyes was a vision I can never forget: the beautiful gold proscenium, the ornate ceiling with its painted cloudborne putti, the wine-colored sea of mohair seats, the great gold curtain, and the stage. There the greats had sung, the greats I was collecting on my 78s—Caruso, Melba, Ponselle, Pinza, Chaliapin. In the pit, Toscanini and Gustav Mahler had conducted. At that point in my life there was no place more hallowed.

By the time I had left Music and Art I was determined to be an opera singer myself. However, though my tenor voice was said to be pretty, it was also pretty small. While I enjoyed my training years as a performer, I'm glad that I eventually realized when to throw in the towel and pick up the pen. Nonetheless, those years behind the footlights were not wasted, because they instilled in me a sympathetic understanding of what it takes to stand before an audience and face the music.

As a critic, few art forms have given me so much pleasure as opera. And though it isn't necessary to listen to a performance or recording as intensively or as comprehensively as a professional critic, it remains that the more you understand, the deeper your enjoyment.

That said, I listen to a variety of elements. I listen to the melodic lines, of course, and follow the story. I listen with a critical ear to the singing and to how it expresses the composer's intentions. On another level, I listen to the components of complex musical sound: to the harmony and the rhythm and to the orchestration, the beguiling combinations of instruments that clothe the music in a lustrous aural fabric of ever-changing color and weight that conveys an expression of its own. I listen to the way the composer works with his thematic material within a single aria or an entire act, repeating it, altering it—in musician's terms, developing it. I listen to the musical architecture of a scene, and to the way each scene relates to the entire act, and each act to the whole opera.

When I am viewing an opera on stage or on video, I watch the acting, the direction, and the physical production just as anyone would at a theatrical presentation. From its inception, opera was theater above all, theater enhanced by music that often expresses what mere words cannot.

Whether a critic or not, when an opera lover listens to an opera, be it a familiar favorite, a brand-new work, or an old one heard for the first time, he or she hopes to be moved by the music, by the story, by the performance. One hopes to be moved to the very marrow of one's bones, for there is no high comparable to the emotional high that comes of a glorious opera wonderfully performed. Your pulse quickens, your muscles tighten, you feel yourself uplifted, occasionally with the happy sting of tears in your eyes. And you can feel that sensation more than once during the course of an opera, for the best operas—dramas and even comedies— are full of these moments.

The key to learning about opera is not to fear what you don't yet know. One of the greatest pleasures of opera is the sheer amount available—in the opera house, on records and video, and on radio and public television. If you haven't heard a particular opera, or even heard of the title, don't be afraid to try it. If you don't want to buy a ticket, or can't find one, there is probably a recording or a video. If you don't want to buy the recording, look for it at your public library, or persuade the librarian to acquire it. If you don't want to take the whole opera in at the first try, go for the highlights. A good way to acquire a broader knowledge is to listen to some recital albums, in which the featured singer performs scenes and arias from a variety of operas. When you hear excerpts you particularly enjoy, you can explore the complete opera later on.

Regardless of whether it is an old or a new work, not every opera appeals to every listener. Moreover, your discernment develops as you go along; you may outgrow some operas that appeal at first, while others will start to attract you as your taste develops. Still others will remain close to your heart forever. But above all, the happiest opera lover is open to everything. If you keep listening, if you remain curious about the unknown, your confidence will grow in leaps and bounds. And the payback in pleasure will be infinite.

Opera is an enormous subject, and there are obviously a great many books available on it, from scholarly histories and surveys like the Norton/Grove *History of Opera* and the magnificent encyclopedic *Viking Opera Guide*, *The Oxford Dictionary of Opera*, and the monumental *New Grove Dictionary of Music and Musicians* to very handy references such as John W. Freeman's two volumes of *Metropolitan Opera Stories of the Great Operas*, which contain the plots of the works currently performed in the major opera houses. In writing this book, I have consulted such reference works repeatedly, and with pleasure. My own aim, however, has been to distill the vast amount of material within these and other references into a reasonably thorough introduction to opera without overwhelming the reader. In doing so, I have tried to strike a balance between a discussion that is too sketchy and one that is too richly detailed. For you who have just come to opera and want to know more about it, I hope this book will make you conversant enough to go on learning and enjoying. I also hope that it will offer a clear and orderly discussion of the diverse facets of opera for those who already enjoy it but who require a convenient tool to brush up on the background.

In writing I have been guided by a single thought: What do most people want to know about opera?

First, the operas themselves: What is the repertoire, who are the primary composers, when were they active, and how did opera develop as an international form? Though I have not given detailed plot synopses of the many operas covered in the discussions of the various national categories, I have tried to characterize each work with a sentence or two telling what the story is about. Unless noted otherwise, the parenthetical dates following the first mention of an opera are those of the first performance.

I have divided each of these historical surveys into brief subsections concerning a specific composer or group of contemporaries. So you have in each instance the choice of reading, say, the complete chapter on Italian opera from end to end, or dipping into the subsection on Verdi or Monteverdi as you need to. (Certain composers made important contributions to the development of more than one national school. Therefore you will find specific discussions on Handel and Mozart in the Italian and German sections, and on Rossini in the Italian and French sections.)

The "Further Adventures" at the end of each historical

survey gave me the chance to mention works that may fall outside the meat-and-potatoes repertoire, but are well worth looking into as you gain experience. In my attempt to cover a lot of ground without swamping the reader, I have had to leave out many operas from my discussion, especially in the Italian repertoire. This is not intended as a dismissal, and the fact that they aren't included here should not dissuade you from listening to them or attending a performance when the opportunity presents itself.

I have tried, also, to highlight the operatic voices. How does a coloratura soprano differ from a dramatic soprano, a heldentenor from a countertenor, an alto from a contralto? And what exactly was done to create the extinct species of singer called *castrato*? You'll find complete discussions of each major voice group in a section at the start of the book. In addition, I singled out for more detailed examination two singers whose reputations have transcended the bounds of the opera world to secure their places as icons of culture: Enrico Caruso and Maria Callas.

And because any discussion of opera entails the use of a variety of musical terms and foreign words, you'll find a brief glossary, "Coming to Terms with Opera," as well.

I have sprinkled throughout the book brief "interludes" on curious and even humorous aspects of opera, from the traditions and significance of the cry "Bravo!" and the variety of ways that many opera characters either die or go mad to the rich world of operatic cuisine and the grand tradition of the prima donna.

Therefore I extend the invitation to dip into this book to those who have heard some opera and are really curious to discover what all the fuss is about. I also invite those who are developing an increasing taste for opera but want to know how all the parts fit together and those who already love the music, but still find the background a bit too daunting to discuss easily. And, of course, I welcome readers who have forgotten more than they can remember, and would just like to brush up their working vocabulary.

Those of you who have already made a reconnaissance trip through opera's garden of earthly delights may nurture a hearty appetite. To those of you who have just begun the journey, I say, welcome aboard. Are you in for a good time!

It Doesn't Start Till Somebody Sings

Whether it's a Bach or Mozart violin concerto, a Beethoven or Dvořák string quartet, or a Mahler symphony, the great works of classical music often make their strongest initial impression through the memorable quality of their melodies—a strong theme grabs the ear and plants itself in the memory. In opera, the melodies often make their point because they are *sung*, and for many opera lovers the heart and soul of an opera are embodied in its most fundamental element: the voice.

No instrument is more personal than the human voice. Regardless of how deeply felt the performance of the finest pianist or the greatest cellist, an instrumentalist always produces a sound that is by definition at a remove from the actual player—that is to say, outside his or her own body. Only the singer produces music physically from within. Indeed, regardless of quality, anyone who can speak can sing in one way or another—even the most raucous monotone is a form of singing.

We listeners hear every singer's performance not just as song but as something far more primal, because however refined, however cultivated, singing is still a basic human ululation, a mating call, a cry of pain, of ecstasy or sadness. And our response to a voice is as basic a reaction as our response to someone's face or figure. When we comment on the way a violinist plays, we are considering externals—musicianship, skill, but not an instrument made of flesh and blood. Commenting on a singer's voice, however, is the equivalent of talking about the size of his or her nose.

Singing itself is elementally physical—even sexual—in a way common to no other musical performance. It is also the only truly articulate musical expression, for the singer alone combines tone with speech.

Opera couldn't exist without singers and their myriad voices, from the airiest coloratura soprano to the deepest basso profundo. Thus the ideal way to begin our discussion of opera is with a quick breakdown of the kinds of singers that make up the vocal panoply.

Hitting All the High Notes: The Soprano

They are the highest of the female voices, and as such they make the most brilliant sounds of all singers. Sopranos. The word itself puts those whom it describes at the top of the vocal heap, for it is derived from the Latin root *supra*—"over" or "above."

Evidence of the earliest period of female singing in Europe is fairly scarce. On one hand, women were officially banned from performing ecclesiastical music because of the Church's overzealous interpretation of the biblical command that women should "keep silence" (a command that pertained only to speech rather than song, according to modern interpretation). On the other hand, women took part in secular court entertainments in a more or less unofficial capacity. Nonetheless, while every high-born young lady was expected to have a smattering of musical training, the most accomplished women musicians of the Middle Ages were courtesans, whose talents, musical and otherwise, were intended primarily for the entertainment of men.

Because of this double standard, music expressly intended for women singers didn't appear until the mid sixteenth century, when Italian composers published volumes of madrigals (songs for multiple voices) in which the top line was written for a soprano. Moreover, to improve the female musician's social standing, influential patrons like the powerful Alfonso d' Este, Duke of Ferrara, began to invite female singers from other towns, give them honorary titles, and even arrange the occasional marriage between them and his noble courtiers (given these women's extra-musical gifts, it wasn't a bad deal for the selected husbands).

During the seventeenth century, the soprano "diva" achieved cult status—composers wrote reams of music for them, including important roles in the new entertainments called operas. Though sopranos sang the heroines in eighteenth-century *opera seria*, they were often overshadowed by castratos, who customarily played the heroes. Still prima donnas enjoyed considerable celebrity—witness Sir Joshua Reynolds's elaborate portrait of the London favorite, Elizabeth Billington, as St. Cecilia. However, it was only after the vogue for gelded male singers passed at the beginning of the nineteenth century that sopranos truly came into their own as popular idols.

A perfect example is the "Swedish Nightingale," Jenny Lind, who maintained the image of an earthly seraph of unparalleled charm, despite the fact that she was smug and bigoted in private. When P. T. Barnum (long before his circus days) brought Lind to America in 1850, her tour sparked a fashion blitz that yielded everything from "Jenny Lind" hats to the "Jenny Lind" beds that still turn up in antique shops. Hans Christian Andersen was among her rejected suitors; Felix Mendelssohn composed the soprano part in his oratorio *Elijah* with Lind's voice in mind.

As the nineteenth century progressed, the building of increasingly larger opera houses, and the trend toward an increasingly dramatic style of opera that emphasized orchestral volume, led to the demand for louder singing. In addition, as highly ornamental bel canto opera gave way to the more declamatory styles of nineteenth-century grand opera and music drama, the variety of roles and styles demanded a variety of soprano categories that have long since entered the standard opera parlance. Some pundits use the terms to describe voices; others use them to define the character of a particular role rather than the actual voice that sings it.

Highest and most brilliant of these categories is the *coloratura*, or *soprano leggiero* (i.e., light or buoyant soprano). Sometimes referred to as a soubrette, her voice, variously described as silvery or bell-like in quality, is often called upon to sing elaborate florid passagework (*fioritura*), not to mention numerous brilliant notes high above the staff. Typical coloratura roles include the Queen of the Night in Mozart's *Magic Flute*, Zerbinetta in Richard Strauss's *Ariadne auf Naxos*, Marie in Donizetti's *Daughter of the Regiment*, and the title role in Léo Delibes's *Lakmé* (from which British Airways has adopted the Act I duet as its theme song).

Because of the essentially decorative quality of their singing, coloratura sopranos as a genre have gone in and out of fashion more frequently than other voice types. Adored in the Victorian era, they underwent an eclipse after World War II, dismissed as mere songbirds by more rigorous postwar palates. The work of Maria Callas, and later of Beverly Sills and Dame Joan Sutherland, however, focused serious attention on the florid romantic style (though both Callas's and Sutherland's extraordinary coloratura virtuosity was an extension of instruments whose rich, dramatic tone was hardly typical of the soprano leggiero). Today, singers like Edita Gruberova, Luciana Serra, Ruth Ann Swenson, and Sumi Jo are performing this graceful repertoire with the persuasive style and vivaciousness of coloratura sopranos a century ago and more.

Like coloraturas, *lyric sopranos* are characterized by a bright silvery vocal quality and the ability to tackle music that lies along a fairly high *tessitura* (range). But although lyric sopranos often sing coloratura repertoire, their voices are a shade mellower in quality, with a touch of additional heft that often contributes a note of poignance to their delivery. Mimì in Puccini's *La Bohème* and Marguerite in Gounod's *Faust* are ideal lyric soprano roles, while Barbara Bonney, Sylvia McNair, Renée Fleming, and Barbara Hendricks are prime examples of the voice type.

Slightly richer and more vigorous in quality, but still characterized by the ability to soar with a limpid purity, the *spinto soprano* (*lirico spinto*, literally, "pushed lyric") is often a more dramatic singer—Leontyne Price, Mirella Freni, or Dame Kiri Te Kanawa, for example. The spinto repertoire typically embraces roles like Madam Butterfly, Desdemona in Verdi's *Otello*, Elsa in Wagner's *Lohengrin*, and the title role in Richard Strauss's *Salome*.

Finally, the *dramatic soprano* is, to many listeners, the most commanding of all sopranos. This is the soprano voice of almost metallic heft and power, able to tackle the staggering demands of Wagner and Strauss. To the dramatic soprano go such roles as Wagner's Brünnhilde (the *Ring*) and Isolde *(Tristan und Isolde)*, Leonora in Beethoven's *Fidelio*, the title part in Strauss's *Elektra*, and the icy heroine of Puccini's *Turandot*.

Kirsten Flagstad is probably the most venerated of the earlier-twentieth-century dramatic sopranos, though even her admirers admit that for all the extraordinary beauty of her singing, there is rarely a sense that she cared a fig about acting. Flagstad's successor was undeniably Birgit Nilsson, whose vocal projection, like burnished steel, can still raise gooseflesh on recordings. Among those who have inherited their mantle are Dame Gwyneth Jones, Eva

Martón, Hildegard Behrens, and their younger American colleague Deborah Voigt.

The lines between adjacent soprano categories can be very fine indeed, and many sopranos perform roles in several categories. The chief example among today's singers is perhaps Cheryl Studer, whose versatility is astonishing. Having started her career as a Wagnerian (her Elsa and Elisabeth are resplendent), she now performs a repertoire that embraces everything from Salome and Desdemona to Marguerite and Lucia, not to mention a Merry Widow that is the best on record.

Mezzos and Altos: The Marvelous Middle Ground

Say "opera," and most people think immediately of high voices and high notes. Lower-registered singers are usually an afterthought. Nevertheless, if opera singers are rare birds, the rarest of them is probably the true contralto, the lowest pitched of the female voices. Though they are often an acquired taste amongst listeners, in fact no less a connoisseur of vocal art than Gioachino Rossini preferred their wine-dark tone, and he composed many of his greatest female roles not for high-flying coloratura sopranos, but for the meatier sound of mezzo-sopranos and contraltos— among them Cinderella in *La Cenerentola* and Rosina in *The Barber of Seville*. The contralto is the female equivalent of the Rock of Gibraltar. Ideally, she sings with a round and powerful tone that evokes the rich colors of sunset and twilight; not usually showy, but mellow and expressive.

The term itself originated during the sixteenth century as

contr'alto, an abbreviation of the earlier term *contratenor altus*, which denoted a high *(altus)* male part lying just above the tenor line in fifteenth-century choral music. During the later sixteenth century, the Latin word *altus* and its Italian form, *alto*, were often printed in choral part-books to denote the same voice line, sung by a male most of the time, and by a woman only in secular music. In modern usage, alto and contralto are interchangeable, though British musicians often simplify the matter by reserving alto for male singers of this range (both boys and adults) and contralto for females.

Early Baroque opera composers tended to reserve the true contralto voice for more or less comical old women hot on the trail of younger men, a stock situation perpetuated two centuries later by Gilbert and Sullivan in such roles as the formidable Katisha in *The Mikado*. From Handel onward, however, composers learned to savor the deep, autumnal contralto sound as a vehicle for serious emotion, and to deploy it in dramatic contrast to the soprano.

Beginning with Rossini, nineteenth-century composers exploited the contralto voice—if not with great frequency, then with profound insight into its evocative qualities of age, wisdom, or supernatural power. Operatic contraltos are often cast as oracles (Erda, the Earth Goddess in Wagner's *Das Rheingold* and *Siegfried*), sorceresses (Ulrica in Verdi's *Un Ballo in Maschera* [A Masked Ball]), or sympathetic mother figures (Mamma Lucia in Mascagni's *Cavalleria Rusticana*).

A number of contraltos have been among the most beloved singers in history, among them the English singer Kathleen Ferrier, whose career was tragically cut short by cancer, and the American Marian Anderson, the first black singer to appear at the Metropolitan Opera. Both not only possessed exceptionally powerful singing voices, but as true contraltos their glory was in their lowest registers, rich, round, and penetrating to the furthest row of the largest auditorium. In the case of the *mezzo-soprano*, however, the vocal characteristics are often a little more difficult to isolate. The term itself means "half-soprano" in Italian, and the mezzo voice lies midway in quality between the contralto and the soprano—lighter than the former, darker or richer than the latter. Indeed, the mezzo-soprano voice is distinguished more by its quality than by its range, and numerous roles that lie in the upper reaches of the mezzo, such as Bizet's Carmen, Purcell's Dido *(Dido and Aeneas)*, and Wagner's Kundry *(Parsifal)* are often sung by sopranos as well as mezzos.

Mezzos are also the gender benders of the opera world, for in addition to singing roles originally composed for castratos, such as Gluck's Orfeo *(Orfeo ed Euridice)*, they often play as many adolescent boys (the "trouser" parts)—like Mozart's Cherubino *(The Marriage of Figaro)* and Richard Strauss's Octavian *(Der Rosenkavalier)*—as they do female temptresses like Saint-Saëns's Dalila *(Samson et Dalila)* and Bizet's Carmen.

The past half century has been rich in fine mezzo-sopranos, from Risë Stevens to Maureen Forrester and the great Marilyn Horne. Grace Bumbry, Shirley Verrett, Christa Ludwig, and the matchless Dame Janet Baker are among the leading mezzos of the postwar era, each distinctive in her own way. Happily this golden line of mezzos has continued into the present, represented by such artists as Frederica von Stade, who has been singing with flawless elegance for over twenty years, and a young international quintet of beauties, the Italian Cecilia Bartoli, Americans

Jennifer Larmore and Susanne Mentzer, the Swedish Anne Sofie von Otter, and the Russian Olga Borodina.

The Well-tempered Tenor

Plácido Domingo, Luciano Pavarotti, and José Carreras are without a doubt the three most famous opera singers in the world today. To popular culture they are The Three Tenors. But more important, they are the three TENORS. Opera without tenors is as inconceivable as the Kentucky Derby without thoroughbreds, for the sound of a tenor—rarest of mature male voices—produces an excitement unmatched by any other vocal range. Is it any wonder that when Rodolfo, in Puccini's *La Bohème*, reaches the climactic high C in his aria "Che gelida manina," throats in the audience tighten in gratified response. And he sings that note, appropriately, on the word *speranza*, hope, because that's what every tenor feels as he approaches the clarion tones at the top of his range.

The word "tenor" is rooted in the Latin verb *tenere*, to hold, and its earliest use, in the writings of Cicero, Virgil, Livy, and other classical authors, implied the idea of holding fast to a course or a career, which ironically anticipates what tenors have to do nowadays to stay on top of the competitive heap. "Tenor" meant a variety of things to medieval theorists. For our purposes, however, the most important use of the word was to indicate the fundamental vocal line in polyphonic music (i.e., ensemble writing usually for four or more voice parts): The tenor line was usually written in notes of relatively long values, around which the other voices wove their intricate patterns of counterpoint in more rapid notes of shorter duration.

During the sixteenth century the tenor was the dominant solo voice in Church music, while much secular Renaissance music for male voice and lute accompaniment was
probably sung by tenors, most of them amateurs, for this
was the era when secular music was primarily sung at
home. With the invention of opera at the end of the century,
some tenors began to enjoy fame that went beyond their
hometowns. Nonetheless, though the tenor was usually
cast as the romantic lead in early Baroque opera—e.g.,
the title role of Monteverdi's *Orfeo* (1607)—tenors were
shunted into second place by the end of the seventeenth
century as the hero-lover roles went increasingly to the
castrato. Indeed, apart from playing old men and comic
roles in opera, and singing the important narrative parts in
oratorios and Passion music (e.g., the Evangelist in J. S.

Bach's *St. Matthew Passion*), the tenor was relatively overshadowed through the beginning of the nineteenth century.

He came fully into his own with the rise of nineteenth-century Romantic opera. Instead of a hero-lover singing with the castrato's soprano voice, the tenor offered a high male voice pitched roughly an octave below that of the soprano. It was the ideal musical foundation for countless amorous couples, who could blend their voices sweetly in parallel melodic lines that are the musical equivalent of an embrace: Listen, for example, to the glorious effect of the love duet "Verranno a te" (My ardent sighs will reach thee), which ends the first act of Gaetano Donizetti's *Lucia di Lammermoor*.

While Rossini's tenor roles still demanded extreme vocal flexibility to negotiate florid passagework, the tenor parts in operas by Donizetti and Bellini increasingly emphasized the ability to sing long, arching melodies that are a hallmark of the Romantic *bel canto* style. Yet the tenor role of Rossini's final opera *William Tell* (1829) also set the stage for the kind of heroic singer who could combine lyricism with the virility implied by greater power and volume. This kind of tenor was to become the foundation of the Verdi repertoire, in which high notes were not sung in a light "head tone," but full force from the chest.

Rossini himself didn't like the sound of this new kind of singing. On one occasion, after the tenor Gilbert Louis Duprez demonstrated one of his specialty high Cs in Rossini's Paris apartment, the composer pointedly checked to see if any of his Venetian glass had been destroyed, claiming later that the tone struck him "like the squawk of a capon whose throat is being cut."

Nevertheless, the die was cast, and with the move toward greater dramatic heft in mid- and late-nineteenth-century opera, with its increasingly heavier orchestration, came the demand for a generally more robust tenor style that capitalized on what the Italians call *squillo*, literally, pealing, the ringing brilliance that we now identify with a fine tenor. Though roles like Bizet's Don José *(Carmen)* and Verdi's Alfredo *(La Traviata)* are still essentially lyrical, Wagner's Siegfried, Verdi's Otello, and Puccini's Calaf *(Turandot)* exemplify the opposite end of the spectrum, demanding not only volume and an almost baritonal weight to the voice but virtually superhuman stamina to sing them well: Ludwig Schnorr von Carolsfeld, the burly, bearded tenor who created the role of Wagner's Tristan in 1865, died a few weeks after the premiere—he was twenty-nine, done in largely by his dedication to this grueling *heroic tenor* part.

Although most singers perform roles in several categories, tenors can be grouped by the overall character and quality of their voices. Among these groupings are the *lyric tenor*, distinguished by a lightness of tone, and often an extended top register needed to tackle the stratospheric range of some early-nineteenth-century bel canto works. For example, the role of Tonio in Donizetti's *Daughter of the Regiment* contains a string of high Cs, while the role of Arturo in Bellini's *I Puritani* (one of the young Queen Victoria's favorite operas) is asked to sing a written high F. The lyric coloratura tenor of Rossini not only needs sweetness but extensive vocal flexibility in order to execute trills, turns, and rapid scale passages.

The heroic tenor (Italian, *tenore di forza*; German, *Heldentenor*) often begins his career as a baritone, and even after taking on the heavier tenor roles in Wagner (Siegfried, Tristan, Tannhäuser), Verdi (Radamès in *Aida*, Otello), and Puccini (Calaf in *Turandot*), his middle and lower registers still retain a dark, baritonal hue, while his top high B-flat and C will often peal forth with the power of a trumpet.

Among early-twentieth-century tenors, three almost legendary names easily characterize the chief tenor categories. The first, Enrico Caruso, was the exemplary Italian *tenore*, whose ringing tone and seamless line remain touchstones of romantic sound and style to this day. The second, John McCormack, was the supremely sweet-voiced Irish tenor whose almost whispered *pianissimo* top notes are still in a class of their own. The third was the Danish Lauritz Melchior, who began his career as a baritone and developed into a matchless heldentenor, an exponent of Wagner almost unrivaled in his day.

We should acknowledge that the second half of the century has been rich in magnificent tenors: Franco Corelli, for example, could not only strike listeners speechless with the arresting beauty and urgency of a single note, but with his Italian good looks. His contemporary, Mario Del Monaco, a resplendent Otello, was equally gifted. He could even strip to the waist to play the Indian chieftain in Antonio Carlos Gomes's *Il Guarany*—no mean accomplishment for a tenor in any era. The Canadian Jon Vickers might be likened to the Marlon Brando of the opera world. Notoriously temperamental, he suffered fools badly because he was dead serious about his work. A superb heroic tenor in German and French repertoire, his voice was like a thunderclap in a role like Saint-Saëns's Samson *(Samson et Dalila)*. Moreover, he was a truly effective actor, and his portrayal of the brutish, outcast fisherman Peter Grimes in Benjamin Britten's eponymous opera was one of the high points of any season.

On the current scene, while Plácido Domingo and Luciano Pavarotti have long since moved from the essentially lyric repertoire of their younger days into dramatic roles like Parsifal or Otello, they are continuing to sing with power and beauty that testify to their rock-solid vocal technique. And we have other stars as well, like John Aler, Richard Leech, Ben Heppner, Roberto Alagna, Francisco Araiza, and the splendid Siegfried Jerusalem.

Rossini may have deplored the move away from florid bel canto in his own time, yet the renewed interest in his music has fostered a literal rebirth of the coloratura tenor after a long fallow period. To listen to the work of tenors like the Argentine Raúl Giménez and the American Stanford Olsen is to realize how thrilling this intricate, highly ornamented music must have sounded during the so-called Golden Age.

The Lowdown on Low Voices

Ironically, the *baritone* is the most common voice in adult males, most of whom speak in this middle range. But mere talk is very different from a baritone or bass voice of musical distinction. The term "baritone" derives from the Greek *barytonos*, or deep-sounding, and was first used in Western music toward the close of the fifteenth century in various forms—*baricor, barisonans, bariclamans, baritonans*—all of which described the lower parts in polyphonic music (i.e., music with several voice parts rather than the unison voice writing of Gregorian chant).

The Italian word *baritono* appeared in the seventeenth century, but still as a designation in choral music rather than for a soloist in opera. Indeed, until the later eighteenth century the baritone was virtually ignored by opera seria composers, who favored high voices suited to the highly ornamented singing then in vogue. German and Austrian composers were first to exploit the baritone in solo roles, especially Mozart, who astounded the rest of Europe by writing principal baritone roles in his operas—Count Almaviva in *The Marriage of Figaro* and the rakish title character in *Don Giovanni*.

The decline of florid opera seria and the parallel rise of the Romantic school, with its more varied character types, brought the baritone voice increasingly into its own as the tenor's equally virile foil—as rival lover, friend and confidante, father or brother figure, or bold-faced villain. It was Verdi, however, who created the demand for a particular type of high, powerful baritone.

The "Verdi baritone" must have a reasonably large voice, its middle rich and dark-hued, capable of a seamless *legato* (smooth vocal movement from note to note of a melody) as well as infinite variations in color. Most of all he must have solid top notes.

Once established, the "Verdi baritone" became the baritone of choice in the opera house, from the wicked Barnaba in Ponchielli's *La Gioconda* and Tchaikovsky's coolly self-destructive Eugene Onegin, to Tonio in Leoncavallo's *Pagliacci* and the villainous Baron Scarpia in Puccini's *Tosca*. To be sure, the light Mozartian baritone retained his place, especially in the French school. He is characterized by such roles as Lescaut in Massenet's *Manon* and by Debussy's enigmatic Pelléas *(Pelléas et Mélisande)*, whose range and luminescent texture allow him to be cast with high baritones and lyric tenors alike.

Historic recordings preserve the voices of great baritones from the beginning of the century, singers like Titta Ruffo, the only baritone to rival the fame of Caruso, and Riccardo Stracciari, whose middle range was like melted chocolate.

The 1930s through the 1960s saw the heyday of such baritone stars as Americans Lawrence Tibbett and Nelson Eddy—who enjoyed radio and screen careers in addition to stage and concert work—and Robert Merrill; the magnificent Italian singing actor Tito Gobbi; and German artists like Dietrich Fischer-Dieskau and Hermann Prey, who excelled as much in *lieder* (art song) as in opera.

After a relatively fallow period during the late sixties and seventies, we seem to be enjoying a new golden age of baritones, whose leading lights include: the Americans Thomas Hampson and Dwayne Croft, the Canadian Gino Quilico, the suave Englishman Thomas Allen, the Welsh Bryn Terfel, the Italian Lucio Gallo, and the Belgian veteran José Van Dam. Surprisingly, two Russians, Vladimir Chernov and Dmitri Hvorostovsky, have raised hopes of new blood in the elusive category of the Verdi baritone, though they are neither of them slouches in Russian repertoire.

Pitched slightly lower in range than the baritone, the *bass-baritone* typically sings the roles of Wotan in Wagner's *Ring of the Nibelungs* cycle, Hans Sachs in *Die Meistersinger*, and the title role in *The Flying Dutchman*. Names to note include Americans James Morris and Simon Estes and New Zealander Sir Donald McIntyre.

Moving downward in range, we come to the lowest of all male voices: the bass. Even among actors true bass voices are less common than baritone voices, hence the enormous effect made when dramatic texts, and even television commercials, are rendered by such resounding *basso* speakers as James Earl Jones and Geoffrey Holder.

Given the striking depth and power of the natural bass voice, however, it is surprising that so little attention seems to have been paid it in ancient times. Medieval and early Renaissance composers were less concerned with the bass sound as a color for solo song and more concerned with the bass as a foundation for harmony in choral music—often referring to it by the Greek *basis* (foundation) rather than the medieval Latin *bassus* (low). However, during the sixteenth century basses themselves began to take increasing interest in improvising the same kind of elaborate ornamentation that was being cultivated by high-voiced singers.

The dramatic potential of the bass voice was explored almost from the earliest days of opera, and Claudio Monteverdi assigned two forbidding roles to basses in his *Orfeo* (1607): Pluto, god of the Underworld; and the sepulchral Charon, who rows dead souls across the River Styx. Yet by the middle of the century it was in French Baroque opera rather than Italian opera seria that serious roles were being written for basses.

Mozart, again, helped considerably to establish the operatic bass on two fronts, in comedic roles like the blustering Osmin in *The Abduction from the Seraglio* and the overworked servant Leporello in *Don Giovanni*, and in patriarchal figures like Sarastro in *The Magic Flute*. The bass as comedian was further exploited in eighteenth- and nineteenth-century Italian *opera buffa* (comic opera), where such roles as Doctor Bartolo *(The Barber of Seville)* and Donizetti's Don Pasquale emphasized the contrast between an imposing tone and the lightness of rapid patter singing.

By the nineteenth century, basses were being divided into several categories beyond buffo: The *basso cantante* or French *basse chantante* were still weighty but somewhat lyrical, "singing" basses who were assigned such roles as the toreador Escamillo in Bizet's *Carmen*. The *basso profondo* or French *basse-noble* possessed deep, heavy voices that vividly suggest a wide range of qualities: For Berlioz *(La Damnation de Faust)* and Gounod *(Faust)*, the *basse-noble* embodied the supernatural *diablérie* of Mephistopheles. For Verdi, the basso profondo was ideally suited to regal authoritarian figures like King Philip II and the Grand Inquisitor in *Don Carlos*. For Wagner, the basso profondo could represent the villainy of Hagen *(Götterdämmerung)* and the terrifying immensity of Fafner, the giant-cum-dragon in *Das Rheingold* and *Siegfried*. In his comedy, *Der Rosenkavalier*, Richard Strauss wrote one of the greatest of all bass roles, the boorish Baron Ochs. Meanwhile to the east, Russian basses, noted for the uncommon richness and power of their extreme lower register, enjoyed particular favor at home, inspiring most notably the title role in Mussorgsky's masterpiece *Boris Godunov*.

The Russian Fyodor Chaliapin was one of the first basses to enjoy an international reputation, as much for his acting as for his singing. Similarly, Ezio Pinza, who possessed one of the warmest *basso cantante* voices in history, was among the few basses to achieve the kind of stardom reserved for sopranos and tenors during his tenure at the Metropolitan Opera (1926–48). And his matinee idol looks didn't hurt when he opened on Broadway in the first run of Rodgers and Hammerstein's *South Pacific*.

Truly fine basses are still rare, but the best of today's crop include the German Kurt Moll, whose voice is like black velvet; the Finnish Matti Salminen, who can project fearsome power in Wagner; Enzo Dara, Italy's leading buffo bass; and the American Samuel Ramey, whose roles encompass the grandeur of Verdi and the florid vocal acrobatics of Rossini.

Altered States: The Castrato

The need for male sopranos and altos to sing in ecclesiastical choirs rose from the Roman Catholic Church's too-literal interpretation of St. Paul's exhortation to "Let your women keep silence in the churches." Paul only meant that women should not take part in theological disputation, but the Vatican took his words at face value, forbidding women not only to speak in church but also to sing. As soon as opera houses were opened in Venice (1637) and other cities, this taboo was extended to them as well.

The prohibition led to a nice dilemma, however: The complex polyphonic style of sixteenth- and seventeenth-century sacred choral music demanded treble voices to execute the top lines. Unfortunately, by the time choirboys had mastered their music after years of practice, they were usually adolescents whose voices had cracked. For a time, male falsettists were imported from Spain—they sang in *falsetto*, an artificially produced high voice comparable to the upper tones in yodeling. Then in 1599 the first two Italian *castrati* were admitted to the Sistine Chapel Choir.

Castration was nothing new, having long been employed in China and Turkey as a punishment or to transform slaves into suitable guards for the harem. In the most dramatic instances the entire male organ was removed and replaced with a wooden or bamboo tube (if the victim survived the blow). In the case of singers, however, only the testicles were cut away, usually when the boy was between six and eight years old. This preserved the youthful high voice, a beardless face, and often the capacity to engage in some form of unfruitful sexual intercourse.

Naturally the practice was forbidden by the Church, and officially punishable by death and excommunication. Nonetheless, surgical preservation of treble and alto voices had been practiced since the mid-sixteenth century, and rather than cry over spilt milk, as it were, the Church didn't let good voices go to waste. With the introduction of castrati in the Sistine Chapel Choir, a black market for gelded singers rose. Worse, hundreds of orphans and sons of indigent parents were put under the knife whether they had singing voices or not. Obviously, in a culture that valued male virility, even the most admired castrato was often regarded as less fortunate than his uncut brethren, and the terms *musico* and *evirato* (unmanned) were used as castrato euphemisms by more delicate sensibilities.

Castrati were employed in opera right from the start, included in the casts of Peri's *Euridice* (1600) and Monteverdi's *Orfeo* (1607). They sang female roles in towns where women were forbidden on stage, but even where female singers flourished, the castrato most frequently sang the heroic roles. Indeed, composers of seventeenth- and eighteenth-century Italian opera seria, from Cavalli and Handel to Gluck and Mozart, cast their heroes as castrato sopranos, mezzo-sopranos, and altos (which is why these parts are sung today by women, or by ungelded counter-tenors and male altos).

During their heyday, between 1650 and 1750, castrati were among the greatest, most highly paid stars. Their flamboyant behavior was notorious—for his first entrance in an opera, the castrato Luigi Marchesi demanded to be mounted on horseback, wearing a helmet with plumes at least a yard high. Their amorous escapades, real and fabricated, were the stuff of gossip. But it was the beauty of their voices and the exceptional strength and virtuosity of their florid technique that made household names of singers like Handel's favorite, Senesino (born Francesco

Bernardi), and certainly the great Farinelli (born Carlo Broschi). Indeed, Farinelli was something of a living legend.

Born into an important but apparently shady political family (the Farinelli nickname applied to the Broschi clan came from the word *farinello*, or rogue), Farinelli made his debut at fifteen in Naples, in 1720. Within two years his reputation was clinched by his appearance in an opera by his teacher, Nicola Porpora, in Rome. Porpora, whose showmanship anticipated that of Barnum, included an aria with trumpet obbligato for Farinelli, which evolved into a nightly competition that had the audience taking sides. Farinelli would hold a note, swell on it, trill on it, all the while accompanied by the trumpet in thirds. The audience grew increasingly excited, waiting to see who would run out of breath first. Each night, the trumpeter would give up, sweating and flushed, whereupon Farinelli, still trilling away on the same breath, would smile at his rival and bring down the house by breaking into further ornaments and scale passages without stopping for air.

After touring Europe in clouds of glory for the next fifteen years, Farinelli retired from the stage upon his engagement as court singer to King Philip V of Spain in 1737. His assignment was to ease the king's melancholy, no easy task since Philip was not just a depressive but a slob who refused to bathe, and reportedly wore and slept in the same clothes and sheets for a year and a half. Worse, he was nocturnal. Hence every night, from midnight to 5:00 A.M., Farinelli would stay in the king's fragrant bedchamber, converse with him, and sing him the same four songs (possibly a few more, according to modern hypothesis). And he did this for almost ten years, until Philip's death in 1746.

Castrati remained in demand through the end of the eighteenth century, though the vogue for them in opera quickly faded as neoclassical opera seria was superseded in the nineteenth century by Romantic opera, with its tenor heroes. Production of castrati continued for the papal choirs until the dissolution of the Papal States in 1870. Domenico Mustafà, one of the last of them to enter the Sistine Chapel Choir, served as its director from 1860–1898. However, it was the last known castrato, Alessandro Moreschi, a member of the Sistine Choir between 1883 and 1913, who actually made some recordings in 1902–1903. Though he was at best a mediocre singer, Moreschi's primitive records at least serve as tangible evidence of the ethereal sound produced by the great castrati of the past. Ironically, there is also a sense of urgency about these particular vocal documents, for in 1903 Pope Pius X formally banned castrati from the papal chapel, thus ending an admittedly curious three-hundred-year-old legacy.

With the tremendous reawakening of interest in Baroque opera, many of the old castrato roles are now taken either by female sopranos and mezzos or by physically unaltered male altos and high countertenors. Of these, such current exponents as the German Jochen Kowalski and his American colleagues, Derek Lee Ragin and Drew Minter, sing magnificently with highly cultivated falsetto registers.

Airs and Graces: What Is an Aria?

The word *aria* means "air" in Italian, which makes perfect sense since it takes a lot of air to sing one. Fundamentally, every aria is a song, though not every song is an aria.

An aria is a particularly elaborate song for solo voice with instrumental accompaniment, and as such it is one of the traditional building blocks of opera from the seventeenth through the end of the nineteenth centuries.

An aria is usually longer in duration than an ordinary song or air. Simple songs tend to be written in strophic form, that is, one strophe, or stanza, after another, which is the form of folk ballads such as "My Darling Clementine" and patriotic songs like "The Star-Spangled Banner." Strophic songs can go on at great length in this way; moreover, the words of each strophe are fitted to the same melody regardless of whether the mood or meaning of the strophe differs from the one before. But because expression of deep emotion through refined and eloquent melody is one of the primary purposes of an aria, an aria is usually written in a more elaborately developed musical design. Ideally, the music is more closely related to the meaning of the text, and the melody changes to reflect the shifting mood. For instance, where the character changes from describing happiness to doubt, the melody might shift from a major key to a minor one.

From a dramatic point of view, the aria is the counterpart of the soliloquy in a Shakespearean play. In both cases, the forward motion of the drama, which is carried on in dialogue, slows down or stops completely while the individual character reflects upon the situation at hand, and considers the next course of action, as in Hamlet's "O, what a rogue and peasant slave am I!"

Both the soliloquy and the aria allow their respective artists to take the stage entirely alone, but with subtle differences between them. The dramatic actor makes his point by expressing the playwright's text with poetic feeling, directly playing off the beautiful sounds of the words themselves and their imagery. The quality of the actor's voice is only of secondary importance, though a fine speaking voice is an asset to a classical actor. The aria, on the other hand, is directly concerned with the voice. It affords the singer a vehicle for displaying tonal beauty and individuality. But equally important, the aria provides distinct lyrical episodes in the course of a drama, melodic interludes to be savored in their own right.

Because an aria places emphasis on melodic outpouring, the text often takes a back seat to purely musical considerations. This is especially so in the case of Italian and Italian-style arias written from the Baroque through the early Romantic era, in which the melodic line is often highly ornamented with coloratura and passagework, which tends to be sung as a *melisma* (a long passage sung continuously on a single open vowel). In their operas and oratorios, Handel and other Baroque composers often wrote extended arias to a very few lines of text, repeating words and phrases several times if necessary to allow themselves time to spin out the melodic line:

Handel's aria "Ev'ry valley shall be exalted," which opens his oratorio *Messiah*, exemplifies this procedure. At the start of the aria, the tenor sings:

Ev'ry valley—[he pauses while the orchestra plays a phrase]— ev'ry va-alley sha-all be ex-a-al-ted—[another orchestral phrase]—shall be-e-e-e-e ex-a-a-a-a-a-a-a-a-a-a-a-a-a-a-a-a-a- a-a-a-a-a-a-a-a-a-a-a-a-a-a-a-a-a-a-a-a-a-a-a-alted.

And so on.

Even in nineteenth-century opera, the text of an aria is

usually subjected to word and phrase repetitions employed
by the composer to give himself sufficient length to spin out
his melody, but which we would never use if we were
merely reciting the words.

The aria underwent many changes as opera developed. In
Baroque opera, where purely vocal display was paramount,
the usual form was the *da capo* (from the beginning) aria,
with three parts, the opening section, reprised at the end of a
second section in a contrasting mood. At the time, composers
wrote distinct types of arias to fit all kinds of stereotyped
manners and moods, with melodic and harmonic styles immediately recognized by their sophisticated audiences. They
wrote entrance arias, to be sung when an important figure
made his first entrance on the stage, and exit arias *(aria di
sortita)*, after which the singer was obliged by strict convention to leave the stage. Anger was vented in the *aria
infuriata* and the *aria agitata*, deep feeling in the *aria di sen-
timento*. Expressive moments were delivered in an *aria di
carattere* (character); mourning in the *aria di lamento*. And
for unabashed vocal display, composers supplied their prima
donnas and castrati with a whole variety of showpieces from
a fiery *aria di bravura* (bravery or skill) to the long and
solemn phrases of an *aria di portamento* (fine bearing).

As composers like Gluck and Mozart moved away from the
formalities of Italian opera seria, they wrote arias with
increasing freedom, putting their desire for intensely dramatic expression ahead of the old rules governing the hierarchy of singers and the number and type of arias each could
perform within a single act (so many for the *prima donna*, so
many for the *primo uomo*, so many for the *basso*, etc.). This
tendency was continued by composers in the next century,
especially as opera moved from neoclassical libretti, which

were mainly a succession of arias, to romantic interpretations of history and legend, in which the focus broadened from the single aria to the whole scene: An aria or an ensemble occurred because the drama warranted it, not because of conventions that stipulated when a certain singer was supposed to sing one.

Wagner's music dramas completely integrated arias and connecting recitative into a continuous unit that flowed without stopping from the beginning of an act to the end. Even so, the lyrical nature of his work is signaled by his own term, "infinite melody," which he coined to define passages that are constantly expressive of thoughts and emotions and not merely filler. In opera, the importance of the voice, and its expression of emotion through melody, remains paramount even in much contemporary work, where composers are reinvestigating the lyrical traditions that gave rise to the aria in the first place.

Arias are often known by the first few words of text, e.g., "Che gelida manina" (What a frozen little hand) from Puccini's *La Bohème*, or "Salut, demeure chaste et pure" (Greetings, chaste and pure dwelling) from Gounod's *Faust*. They are also referred to by recognizable types, such as the *brindisi* (drinking song), the *buffa* aria (humorous), the *cantabile* aria (lyrical), and even the isolated *aria concertante* or *aria da concerto* written for nondramatic use in concerts. The most important thing to do when confronted with an aria is to sit back and enjoy it.

Interlude: In Praise of Divas and Prima Donnas

It is a title shared in recent history by Joan Sutherland, Maria Callas, and Renata Tebaldi, by Golden Age singers like Maria Malibran, Nellie Melba, and Rosa Ponselle, and by such contemporary stars as Cheryl Studer, Dame Kiri Te Kanawa, and Jessye Norman: Diva. In Italian, the word means "goddess" (as in the aria "Casta [chaste] Diva" in Bellini's *Norma*), "lady love," or "fine lady." Divas have their etymological roots in the Latin *divus*—divine or deity—and stretch even further back to the *div* or demonic spirit of ancient Persian mythology and the *deva* or gods of old Sanskrit.

Indeed, the connection is obvious between goddesses and operatic sopranos, whose ability to mesmerize audiences with their florid song can certainly be called divine. And certainly an impresario having a bad day with a touchy diva might well dream of sending her somewhere into the clouds. "I loathe Divas," complained the composer Hector Berlioz. "They are the curse of true music and musicians."

Although the title is very much a compliment accorded by the public to its favorite stars, the related term *prima donna* (Italian for "first lady") has a technical root. It entered common usage to denote the leading lady of an opera troupe after public opera houses opened in Venice and other Italian cities during the seventeenth century. Commercial rivalries between the several theaters that normally operated in one town led their managers to promote their respective prima donnas to attract audiences. Needless to say, the singers themselves enjoyed all the ego massage, and during the eighteenth century, audiences developed a full-blown prima donna cult.

Moreover, once a singer achieved prima donna status, she milked the title for all it was worth, usually demanding that no other singer in the company share it. Faced with frequent conflicts between rival prima donnas engaged during the same season in the same house, impresarios often had to perform incredible flights of euphemistic fancy, according their temperamental stars such alternative titles as *altra* (other) *prima donna, prima donna assoluta* (absolute), or the unequivocal *prima donna assoluta e sola* (absolute and only).

During the early nineteenth century, opera production in Italy was governed by *convenienze*, strict rules of theatrical etiquette by which singers were accorded specific kinds of roles and specific amounts of music according to their rank. Thus codified, the *prima donna* was specifically the leading female singer in an opera or the leading soprano of an opera company. She sang the heroine's part opposite the hero, sung by the *primo uomo* (or first man, which meant the tenor). Both the *prima donna* and the *primo uomo* were accorded solo arias and scenes as well as ensembles. According to the *convenienze*, the secondary parts—such as nurses, confidants, and faithful retainers—were given to the *seconda donna* and *secondo uomo*, who sang in ensembles but had no solo arias of their own. And while we're on the subject, let's not forget the *comprimario* (from the Italian *con prima*, or "with the principal"). Ranked between the prima and seconda personnel, the *comprimario* took part in ensembles, could sing a duet with one of the principals, and was also allowed a simple aria, though not a full scene.

Admittedly the opera business will more often than not overexploit any talented artist given the chance, and such a

competitive world is no place for misguided good nature.
Therefore stars have often been demanding, just to make
sure an unscrupulous manager wouldn't take advantage of
them. Nonetheless, history is full of prima donnas who
made it their business to be difficult, indeed adding to their
allure. A century before Kathleen Battle reportedly drove
her colleagues to distraction with demands about everything from album-cover photos to the length and color of
her stretch limousines, Adelina Patti, one of the greatest
divas of the Victorian age, not only insisted that her con-
tracts include the stipulation that her name appear on
posters in letters at least one-third larger than those used
for other singers, but also a clause excusing her from
attending rehearsals! Her younger rival, Nellie Melba,
demanded the right to approve of other cast members in
any opera she sang at Covent Garden, and to approve or
veto the engagement of new artists to the company. And
she got it.

Certainly, Patti's nonrehearsal clause would be dismissed
as unprofessional today. Moreover, now that international
singers jet from one house to another in a single week, the
terms "diva" and "prima donna" are purely complimentary,
and they no longer refer to any strict company hierarchy. In
fact, they can often be distinctly *un*complimentary.

Nevertheless, in a denim-clad world increasingly de-
void of genuine glamour, our delight in divas and
prima donnas still bespeaks our fundamental need for
the radiance a great singer's presence can bestow on a
performance through the power and beauty of her vocal
artistry.

Interlude: Icons of an Age—
Caruso and Callas

Not, perhaps, until the arrival of The Three Tenors have opera singers had such a visible presence in popular culture, for it is often the case with opera that it appeals only to those who take the time to understand it. And yet, before our current age, two historic figures, the tenor Enrico Caruso and the soprano Maria Callas, achieved a level of celebrity that transcended the boundaries of the opera world and made them cultural icons of the world at large. Through the power of their voices and the force of performance, they came to define the role of the opera star and added as much to social history as they did to their extravagant art.

Enrico Caruso (1873–1921) went from the slums of Naples to supremacy in the operatic world on the strength and beauty of his matchless voice. And this was no mean accomplishment in an era that boasted other Italian tenors such as Alessandro Bonci and Giovanni Martinelli, as well as non-Italians like Dmitry Smirnov, Leo Slezak, and Edmond Clément. They were all famous, but with the exception of the Irishman John McCormack, Caruso alone was the operatic icon familiar even to those who knew little or nothing of opera or classical music in general.

For nearly two decades, starting in 1903, Caruso was the chief ornament of both New York's Metropolitan Opera and the Victor Talking Machine Company in Camden, New Jersey. Because that voice was providentially suited to the requirements of the acoustical recording horn, he was one of the earliest musicians to develop a symbiotic relationship with the budding record industry. When he made his first recordings for the Gramophone & Typewriter Company of London in 1902, the phonograph was still regarded as something of a toy—those typewriters were a stopgap in case the gramophones didn't pan out. But the compelling quality of Caruso's initial discs helped legitimize the phonograph as a serious musical medium.

Moreover, in the days before radio, the single-sided Victor Red Seals made Caruso's voice familiar even to those who lived well off the route of his personal tours. And because people everywhere bought Caruso's recordings of arias, Italian *canzoni*, and a surprising number of popular American songs, the originals have survived in countless attics and basements. Hence, more than seventy years after his death Caruso's name is still a household word, and the sound of his voice still makes your pulse quicken.

To call that voice "beautiful" scarcely does it justice. In his most famous recording, the 1907 "Vesti la giubba" (Leoncavallo's *Pagliacci*), it not only rings with a clarion brilliance but with a heartbreaking pathos. Yet even in its most anguished moments, Caruso's Canio never overdoes the tear-jerking, for no matter how heated the emotional content of the music, Caruso always sang like a gentleman. Nor did he always belt his high notes. The 1906 "Salut, demeure chaste et pure" (Gounod's *Faust*) is a sterling example of this. Where most tenors—including many French ones—would attack the climactic high C in full voice, Caruso follows Gounod's markings, beginning softly in head voice and swelling to a robust tone. Then he crowns the final cadence with a beautifully articulated *portamento* (vocal slide) on the descending perfect fifth at the final word. Artistically, as well as from a purely vocal standpoint, the performance is a magnificent achievement.

Few tenors then or now could match his command of legato and portamento—the incredible smoothness with which the notes flow from his throat, connected to each other like a shining liquid band—or the almost playful ease with which he sings and shapes a melodic line, or his ability to balance brazen tones with a velvet *mezza voce* always with subtlety and consummate good taste. And few could command the breadth of color in Caruso's voice. The golden top is complemented by a warm middle, and a dark, baritonal low register. Indeed, Caruso's baritonal quality was so pronounced that after he had made his first duet recording, "Solenne in quest' ora" (Verdi's *La Forza del Destino*), with the baritone Antonio Scotti in 1906, Victor eventually issued the single-faced disc with an explanatory label on the blank side to end confusion over who sang the first line. As he matured, Caruso's voice took on added weight, and the singing became increasingly heroic; yet while he could manage the blockbuster effects demanded of Radamès *(Aida)*, Samson *(Samson et Dalila)*, and Alvaro *(Forza)*, he still maintained a light touch for Nemorino *(L'Elisir d'Amore)* and Lionel (Flotow's *Martha*).

Caruso was not only blessed with the right voice to take center stage in the opera world of his time, he also had the looks and personality of a leading figure. By looks, one doesn't mean those of a matinee idol. But his dark, expressive eyes, bulbous nose, and ready smile lent vitality and distinction to a large, open face that was easily remembered. In addition, despite his humble Neapolitan roots, Caruso was endowed with an innate dignity, reflected in the many photographs of him in stage costume. He also acquired a polished sense of style. After his best friend and fellow Neapolitan, Scotti, brought Caruso to his London tailor, the tenor learned to wear his beautifully cut suits, his suede-topped shoes and fine hats with an easy elegance. From his thirties on, Caruso always presented an image of fashionable affluence without ostentation.

If he was ostentatious in any direction it was with his good nature. Caruso's generosity and sense of humor were extolled in his own day, and at a time when opera singers were notorious for their temperamental personalities, he was universally liked as a man as well as an artist. "His company was a tonic for all ailments," according to the coloratura soprano Luisa Tetrazzini, with whom he often sang in Europe. Geraldine Farrar, the beautiful American diva who was often his stage partner at the Met—though not always a docile one—declared that "His was a simplicity which sprang from innate kindness." As gifted a caricaturist as a singer, Caruso once moved the composer Victor Herbert—who, like Caruso, enjoyed good food and lots of it—to remark gratefully that "Even in his caricatures he shows the sweetness of his nature. He has never drawn me as fat as others have."

But aside from the pictorial images and written memories, what lives today is Caruso's voice, tragically silenced by his early death. He was only forty-eight when he died in great suffering in a sweltering Naples hotel room. Popular opinion has often attributed his death to cancer, but Michael Scott's thoroughly researched biography *The Great Caruso* (1988) makes it clear that he died of a resistant infection that was abetted by medical incompetence, and by the wear and tear of Caruso's own career, until it overwhelmed and poisoned his constitution.

The news of his death was received like a thunderclap. And the response was equivalent. When Giuseppe Verdi had died twenty years earlier all Italy draped itself in mourning, and at his final interment the official procession included members of the Italian royal family. However, it seemed that not just Italy but the whole world mourned Caruso's passing, and at the tenor's funeral the king himself opened the church doors.

Although thinning hair and a portly figure added at least ten years to Caruso's appearance, to judge by his last recordings, made in September 1920, his voice was still in top form, the sound velvety, rich, bronze-toned, and virile. How many who have listened to various examples of his later recordings—the 1917 version of the *Rigoletto* Quartet (with Amelita Galli-Curci), the heroic selections from Saint-Saëns's *Samson et Dalila* recorded in 1916 and 1919, and certainly the famous 1920 recording of "Rachel, quand du Seigneur" from Halévy's *La Juive* (erroneously believed to have been Caruso's last record)—how many who have listened to these and other Caruso records on the original shellacs or on CD transcriptions have thought, what if he *had* lived? The electrical recording process was introduced by Victor less than four years after his death. How much more extraordinary might his voice have sounded at fifty-two if it could have been captured through a microphone instead of a recording horn, in the more ambient acoustic made possible by the electric method, and with a real orchestra instead of the dry, scrappy little bands necessary for the old process.

Had Caruso lived out his full threescore and ten, he might have gone on singing into the 1930s. Quite possibly he would have made a few sound films, which would have given us the chance to see him in action as well as hear him. (McCormack, Martinelli, and certainly Beniamino Gigli all made feature films and shorts in the '30s, and Caruso himself did make two silent films, the first, a comedy, failing so badly in the theaters that the second was never released.)

Yet electrical recording and even film might well have captured the decline of his powers, as it did McCormack's. Furthermore, had Caruso lived into the flapper age and beyond, his historical identity would have been somewhat dissipated. The fact that Caruso died when he did has only strengthened his position in the public mind. "They Needed a Songbird in Heaven (So God Took Caruso Away)" was the bathetic title of a Tin Pan Alley commentary. But however morbid or mawkish, such a perception proves how Caruso's tragic end, like that of Rudolph Valentino, has etched his memory that much more vividly upon ours.

Caruso began his career while Verdi was still alive, yet he predeceased Puccini, his elder by two decades. Caruso's America spanned only three presidencies—Theodore Roosevelt, Taft, and Wilson—his seasons at Covent Garden were within the reigns of only two English kings—Edward VII and the first half of George V's. Therefore Caruso has come to symbolize almost all that was best about a distant operatic era that we like to consider "golden"—a sumptuous musical age, generously endowed and vastly appealing. Yet such is the immediacy of his singing that the *Chicago Tribune* music critic Claudia Cassidy could write many years after his death, "Caruso is as urgent in communication as if he had closed the door of a room, not of life." And therein lies the secret of his immortality.

In the late Gerald Fitzgerald's seminal iconography *Callas, the Great Years* (published in the same volume with

John Ardoin's equally valuable essays on Maria Callas's art and life), there is a photograph of Callas as Violetta in Act II of Luchino Visconti's 1955 La Scala production of *La Traviata*. She sits at a table, having written her farewell note to the man she loves. Her posture bespeaks her sorrow: She leans her head in her right hand, and although she wears a formal Victorian afternoon gown, her hair cascades wildly down her back and sides, a typical theatrical metaphor for innocent childhood or madness. Above all it is her face that tells the story, the eyes narrow as if blinded with tears, the brows arched, the wide mouth contorted with weeping. It is a stricken expression of anguish that cries out to the viewer as if this desperate woman were actually present. Even printed in a book, this black-and-white photograph resounds almost as vividly as an actual sound recording.

That was the miracle of Callas.

Now, twenty years after Maria Callas's death, her name, like Enrico Caruso's, is a household word familiar even to people who have little interest in opera. She has been the subject of several biographies that achieved a commercial interest beyond the musical and operatic sphere, including one by her former husband, the Italian industrialist Giovanni Battista Meneghini, whom she deserted for the Greek shipping magnate Aristotle Onassis. In addition, Callas's work has inspired two Broadway plays by Terrence McNally, *The Lisbon Traviata*, about a man's obsession with her performance, and more recently *Master Class*, a dramatization of the celebrated series of open teaching sessions she held at New York's Juilliard School in 1971–72.

Few singers have been so controversial in their time as Callas. Her voice struck many as ugly. It still does. In fact, her recordings prove that her voice is unique among sopranos. At its best, the middle range is rich, almost like that of a mezzo, often smooth with a velvety sheen, yet just as often it is produced with a timbre that specialists refer to as "covered." Indeed, at times it seems that the voice is curling itself through a metallic hood.

Callas's lower register can be dark and booming, her top notes brilliant, ringing. It is a "close-grained" voice; that is to say, the vibrato is satisfyingly rapid, and imparts an urgency to the sound. Callas's voice is as distinctive as a fingerprint. Unique. Unmistakable. "Generally I upset people the first time they hear me," Callas once said, "but usually I am able to convince them of what I am doing."

But inherent in that distinctive timbre is an edge, a husky quality that offends some listeners. Imperfections in her vocal technique that emerged by the middle of her career become increasingly apparent in her later recordings. The low notes harden, slicing the air like knives. Though her middle register remains vibrant and compelling, her top notes can turn shrill in the later recordings, especially when pressed by the demands of a dramatic moment. Worse, they are often marred by an intrusive wobble.

Those who preferred the aural purity of a Renata Tebaldi or the plush richness of a Joan Sutherland tended to dismiss Callas's voice as flawed. Admittedly the Callas sound has always been an acquired taste. But for the legions who acquire it, the so-called flaws are akin to the natural occlusions in a fine emerald, and as with an emerald, the flaws actually define the gemlike quality of Callas's voice. Allied with its extraordinary color is an aural sense of vulnerability that emphasizes the feminine nature even of her strongest characters and captures our sympathy. On disc her Lucia di

Lammermoor, her Norma, her Tosca are landmarks in the history of singing. On disc even her Rosina in *The Barber of Seville*, widely regarded as a fiasco—a Carmen played for comedy—when she sang it at La Scala in 1956, is splendidly fluent and fiery to a new generation of listeners.

The wonder of Callas lies not just in the sound of her voice; it lies in the extraordinary way she uses it. At a time when acting was too often barely a consideration in opera, Callas proved that a singer could portray roles as convincingly as any actor on the stage or screen. If her recordings provide ample evidence of the way she makes music speak to the listener by giving every note and every word an interpretive purpose, her precious few appearances on film and kinescope are even more emphatic. On stage, even in concert, her every movement is meaningful. Her famous second act of *Tosca* at Covent Garden in 1964 provides a case in point, as does the same act performed at the Paris Opéra to celebrate her debut there in 1958. In both performances her Scarpia is the baritone Tito Gobbi, a superb singing actor in his own right, and together they set fire to the stage. Toward the end of her singing career, Callas made a nonsinging film of *Medea*, adapted and directed by the poet Pier Paolo Pasolini, which forms a vivid document of her acting, if an imperfect one.

Of supreme importance to the operatic repertoire, Callas, who had been trained to sing dramatic soprano roles such as Turandot, Aida, and Wagner's Isolde, turned her attention early in her career to the works of Vincenzo Bellini and Gaetano Donizetti, some of which had largely been forgotten by the late 1940s. She learned the role of Elvira in Bellini's *I Puritani* in five days, and thereafter continued to undertake other such parts—Bellini's Amina in *La Sonnambula*, the title role in Donizetti's *Anna*

Bolena, Fiorilla in Rossini's *Il Turco in Italia*. At the time, these and other bel canto roles had long been shelved as empty showpieces for old-fashioned songbirds. Callas, however, imbued each one with a vividness and dramatic depth that prompted a complete reevaluation of the repertoire, and that led to what we now refer to as the bel canto revival. Not only did Maria Callas's work in this area pave the way for subsequent bel canto exponents like Joan Sutherland, Marilyn Horne, and Luciano Pavarotti, but to a great degree her pioneering interest in the special demands of these operas laid the groundwork for the "authentic performance" or "original instruments" movement that has brought the operas of Handel, Lully, and Rameau back into the opera house, and by extension, to the screen: Without Callas, the film *Farinelli* might never have been made.

Unlike Caruso, whose tragedy it was to be cut short in the prime of his vocal and personal life, Maria Callas's tragedy was of her own making. First, because she brooked no opposition where her art was concerned, her career was marked by continual struggles with those who opposed her. Battles with managements and rivalries with other singers made better copy than discussions of her artistic goals. Hence Callas the media figure often eclipsed Callas the singer. Second, she interrupted her career at its high point to pursue her liaison with Onassis. When she returned to the stage, she was out of practice and out of voice.

Only in her late forties, Callas was destined to live beyond the point at which she could contribute to the art that was her very *raison d'être*. And once the affair with Onassis dissolved, she found herself an outsider in the profession on which she had turned her back.

Like a rudderless ship, Callas searched for a way to

remain active. She tried directing, but as an intuitive actress she was unable to convey to other singers the interpretive subtleties that came naturally to her. Her Juilliard master classes (selections from which are now available on compact disc) revealed her keen musical intellect, her assured command of her own stage technique, even her sense of humor. But they also revealed that same inability to teach what to her was instinctive. Her attempt at straight acting, in the film of *Medea*, proved interesting but ultimately unsatisfying—she needed music as a vehicle for complete self-expression.

Accustomed to the public limelight, she turned inward, especially after an extended concert tour with the tenor Giuseppe di Stefano proved even to a public that didn't want to believe it that her singing days were over. Suffering a heart attack, Maria Callas succumbed as well to a broken heart. She died alone in Paris in 1977.

Thanks to those recordings, however, she lives on. Like Caruso, she remains the standard by which dramatic singing is measured. But even more than Caruso, Callas remains the standard by which the singing *actor* is measured.

Interlude: The Conductor — Holding It All Together

In an art whose practitioners vie to keep their faces in the spotlight, conductors are the only major players who keep their backs to the audience. Yet conductors have achieved enormous stardom in the contemporary opera world, and names like Sir Georg Solti, Daniel Barenboim, Claudio Abbado, Riccardo Muti, James Levine, and the late Herbert von Karajan often carry as much weight with fans as the singers themselves. This wasn't always so, for the conductor's position as ultimate musical authority over a production, let alone as a box office attraction, took a long time to evolve.

Early opera performances were usually directed, or at least held together, by the keyboard *(cembalo)* player—often the composer—who became known as the *maestro al cembalo*. As eighteenth-century Italian and German orchestras grew in size, the keyboard player—who accompanied the recitatives—tended to direct the singers, while the instrumentalists looked to the principal violinist (ancestor of the modern concertmaster) to set their tempos. Although such divided leadership often resulted in disagreements that could send a performance reeling in confusion, the custom was maintained on the Continent into the early nineteenth century and even longer in England. In Louis XIV's France, however, the sheer number of performers in an opera required stronger measures to keep soloists, chorus, dancers, and orchestral musicians together. Thus the conductor (though not called that specifically) beat audible time either with a stick against a table on the stage or with a heavy staff thumping on the floor.

Either way, the effect was akin to a giant metronome beating loudly through the music, and it would certainly be exasperating to modern listeners.

During the nineteenth century, the rise of the large Romantic orchestra and the concomitant decline of the keyboard continuo shifted the balance of divided leadership away from the old *maestro al cembalo* and toward the concertmaster—often known as the *primo violino direttore* (first violin director)—who would frequently stop playing to stand in front of the orchestra and beat time with his violin bow. Given the increasing musical complexity of nineteenth-century opera scores, the concertmaster spent less time playing and more time coordinating the singers and musicians. Thus the conductor began to emerge as an officiating musician who didn't actually play in the orchestra.

Composers like Berlioz and Weber were among the first of this new breed to have a major impact on orchestral and operatic performance. To facilitate leading the musicians without resorting to a bow, the earliest conductors in the modern sense often waved a rolled-up sheet of music to make their tempo indications more visible. Several drawings exist of Weber, for example, using this method to conduct rehearsals of his last opera, *Oberon*, in 1826. Rolled music was soon replaced by a baton, at first a fairly sturdy one, often grasped in the middle and waved crisply about in the manner of a military bandmaster. Batons later were more slender and were held at one end to create a pliant extension of the conductor's hand.

Contemporary illustrations also show that opera conductors in the first half of the nineteenth century normally stood in the orchestra pit, directly at the apron of the stage, which put them close to the singers but left the orchestra to play *behind* them in the pit. Later in the century the pit conductor moved to the now customary position, which allows eye contact with the players as well as the singers.

Even in earlier times, composers who took charge of their own works had exerted a good deal of authority over the interpretation of their music—Lully, Mozart, Beethoven, and the aforementioned Berlioz and Weber were adept at instructing the players and singers on just how to shape their parts and balance them in relation to each other. Nevertheless, it was Richard Wagner who essentially created the image of the professional conductor that we recognize today—the authoritarian figure who is supposed to be all-knowing about matters musical and whose interpretative decisions are law.

Following Wagner's footsteps, the professional opera conductor developed from a time-beater—who merely accompanied the singers and ensured that the orchestra started and ended together—into a subtle interpreter of the score. Yet even with Wagner as a model, the average opera house conductor had no easy time exerting his authority in an era when the singer still ruled the roost. Indeed many of the leading singers in those days considered it their prerogative to instruct the conductor on how *they* wanted their arias to go, how long they would prefer to hold their high notes, and even what favorite aria or song they might want to insert into another opera: A century ago, Rossini's music for the "Lesson" scene in *The Barber of Seville* was usually replaced with whatever showpiece the prima donna fancied, from Johann Strauss's "Voices of Spring" to Sir Henry Bishop's "Home Sweet Home."

By the beginning of the present century conductors like Gustav Mahler and Arturo Toscanini had turned the tables completely, placing the conductor at the top of the musical heap with no questions asked. Certainly Toscanini is widely regarded as the first twentieth-century conductor to become a cult figure whose magnetism as a musician and as a personality was sufficient to bring in an audience.

In a modern opera company the chief conductor is often called the music director and is in charge of all matters relating to the musical performance, from overseeing the selection of repertoire, singers, and orchestral personnel to directing musical rehearsals and performances. Depending on the size of the company, the music director may appoint additional conductors to the roster and divide productions and performances with them. Though music directors often work with assistants in major opera companies, the music director of a small company may also rehearse the soloists and chorus as well as the orchestra, and in very small groups that perform without an orchestra the music director often conducts from the piano.

Conducting has long been a man's world—other prime names at present include Americans James Conlon and Kent Nagano, England's John Eliot Gardiner, and elusive Austro-Argentine Carlos Kleiber—but since the 1960s, when pioneers like Boston's Sarah Caldwell (first woman to conduct at the Met) and New York's Eve Queler made the first serious attempts to wrest the podium from total male domination, women have been entering the ranks. Resistance, which has more to do with societal views than musical ones, remains strong, but the sterling work of conductors like Jane Glover, Sian Edwards (first woman to conduct at Covent Garden), and Australian Simone Young (with a winning Met debut in 1996) is helping to break down the barrier for good.

Italian Opera: The Source

I have adored this art, and I adore it still. And when I shut myself alone with my notes, my heart beats, the tears stream down my face and my emotion and pleasure are indescribable.

—Giuseppe Verdi

To many people, "opera" is synonymous with "Italian opera." The word itself is Italian, and it was in Italy that opera began. You well might ask why Italy, rather than England, France, or Germany.

Not only was Italy the center of artistic and musical activity at the end of the Renaissance; more important, the Italian language lent itself to the development of a sung drama because of its inherent

musicality. The language emphasizes vowels over consonants, open vowels that voice teachers often refer to as pure: A (ah), E (eh), I (ee), O (oh), U (oo). Most Italian words end in a vowel—*bella, Roma, Venezia, gondola, Non posso mangiare più!* This emphasis makes Italian naturally singable because even to speak all those vowels, you must keep your mouth and throat open in a different way than you would to speak the present sentence, or to declaim something in German, such as, *Ich bin ein Berliner!*

Indeed, those sustained vowel tones actually lend a melodic quality to Italian speech patterns. Anyone who has visited Italy has heard the songlike character of Italian speech. The clarity of the voices, the emphatic rise and fall of the spoken lines, even the body language are all, in a word, operatic.

To investigate the development of Italian opera is to investigate the development of all opera, for it was from the Italian root that French, German, Russian, American, and all other national schools of opera sprouted. After nearly four hundred years of development, however, it might come as a surprise to realize that Italian opera actually began as a mistake!

To be sure, opera didn't spring out of thin air, for there was always a natural attraction between drama and music. Medieval liturgical dramas such as *The Play of Daniel* proliferated between the eleventh and thirteenth centuries. Performed in churches as illustrations of biblical tales, they sometimes combined monophonic (i.e., one voice line) chant with the action.

Between the fourteenth and sixteenth centuries, liturgical dramas grew into "mystery" plays ("mystery" being a corruption of the Latin *ministerium*, or service). Unlike the liturgical dramas, which were performed in Latin, mysteries were played in the local tongue, and staged on outdoor platforms. The stories were drawn from a wider range of material than those of the liturgical dramas, and because they could encompass such broad subjects as the Life of Christ or the Creation, they sometimes lasted for a week or more. Despite their length, these mysteries were rarely boring. Staging was elaborate, with Heaven, Earth, and Hell represented by platforms of graduating heights. And not only were settings like the Garden of Eden or Noah's Ark shown, but all miracles, visions, calamities, and torments took place on stage. Music played an incidental role, including fanfares, dances, processions, and occasional bits of plainchant and popular song.

Performed throughout Europe, mystery plays were called by various names depending on the country—*mystère* in France, *auto* in Spain and Portugal (whence they were also transported to the new colonies in Latin America), *sacra rappresentazione* (sacred performance) in Italy. Meanwhile, between the sacred mysteries and their secular counterparts, dramatic performance moved from the church to the market square, and thereafter to the nobleman's banquet hall and court. The scene was thus set for something new, and sixteenth-century Italy was primed for it to appear.

An overriding theme of the Italian Renaissance was the increasingly widespread interest in the culture of classical Greece and Rome. In late Renaissance Florence, around 1580, a group of scholars, poets, musicians, and wealthy amateurs formed an academy, or philosophical arts club, dedicated to classical study. Their membership included the poet Ottavio Rinuccini, the composers Giulio Caccini and

Jacopo Peri, and the singer-composer Vincenzo Galilei (father of Galileo).

Known as the Camerata (from the Italian *camera* meaning "chamber" or "room"), the club met in the home of Count Giovanni de' Bardi, a leading Florentine patron of the arts, and concentrated on ancient Greek music. At least they did this in theory, for although theoretical writings on the subject existed at the time, actual examples of Greek music did not.

The dominant style of Italian Renaissance music was the madrigal, in which a text was set polyphonically, for many voices in counterpoint, each voice singing a different melody in different rhythms. One scholar, Girolamo Mei, therefore suggested that composers write songs in monody, for a solo voice, supposedly imitating the Greeks. Vincenzo Galilei took up the cause, arguing that madrigals had reached a stage in which complex vocal counterpoint made a mess of the words, and instead of expressing the poetry, served only to display the composer's ingenuity for the pleasure of a sophisticated "in" crowd.

At the same time a new cycle was beginning as a direct result of the mannered tendencies of contemporary composers: While the amateur Galilei dabbled at strict—and rather dull—note-per-syllable settings of passages from Dante's *Inferno*, his professional colleagues Peri and Caccini were composing monodies embellished now and then with vocal ornaments that made things a bit more entertaining. In 1594, Peri and Rinuccini collaborated on an experimental merging of drama and music intended to reproduce their hypothetical idea of classical Greek tragedy. The work, *Dafne*, related the story of the beautiful nymph who escapes being raped by Apollo by having Zeus transform her into a laurel tree. It was first staged in 1598, and several more times over the next few years. Although only a few fragments of the music have survived, Peri's *Dafne* is traditionally regarded as the first opera (the word is actually short for the original generic term *opera in musica*, or work in music).

In 1600, Peri wrote a new opera, *Euridice*, for the wedding festivities of King Henri IV of France and Maria de' Medici. The *libretto* (book) by Rinuccini was another neo-classical pastorale based on the tragic legend of Orpheus, but supplied with a happy ending to suit the nuptial occasion. Meanwhile, Peri's rival, Caccini, a shady creature who had been dismissed from the Medici court because of his scheming, sought to ingratiate himself again by writing music for his own dramatic spectacle to be given as part of the same celebration. In addition, Caccini contrived to introduce portions of his own music into the performance of Peri's *Euridice*. Apparently the audience preferred the spectacular scenic effects to the music. Nevertheless the slippery Caccini rushed his complete setting of *Euridice* into publication weeks before Peri's was ready.

Peri and Caccini cast their music primarily as recitative—monodic declamation without vocal ornamention—but though they proudly called their novel musical manner the "theatrical style" *(stile rappresentativo)*, it was pretty thin stuff. Even the original audiences considered it rather dull: When Caccini's *Euridice* was performed complete in 1602, the Florentines were apparently unimpressed, though they presented the cast with a roasted boar for their troubles. Indeed, infant opera might have been a victim of crib death were it not for someone at that first performance of the Peri-Caccini collaboration who was inspired to try his hand at his own setting of the same story, and who came up with the first opera still worth hearing today: Claudio Monteverdi.

Monteverdi, the First Master

Claudio Monteverdi (1567–1643) was a court musician to the Duke of Mantua, and had made his name as a composer of madrigals, when he embraced the ideas of the Florentine Camerata. His first opera, *Orfeo*, a "musical fable," was produced in 1607 at the duke's private theater in Mantua, after which it was given private performances in other towns.

Monteverdi's operatic style emphasized rich harmony to underscore the intensely emotional story of Orpheus, the legendary musician, who loses his beloved wife Euridice to a snakebite, and travels to Hell and back again in an unsuccessful attempt to retrieve her from death. Monteverdi also specified elaborately detailed instrumentation, which was to become a principal characteristic of the emerging Baroque musical style: Renaissance composers had concerned themselves primarily with an instrument's range instead of its color or timbre (e.g., flutes were interchangeable with high strings, low strings could serve as well as low brasses). But Monteverdi and his generation showed a new concern for particular instrumental colors to underscore a character's mood or temper. Moreover, they began to exploit the colors of instruments and instrumental combinations for their own sake, to add variety to the overall sound of a musical score (an important principle of orchestration to this day).

In *Orfeo*, we hear how Monteverdi improved on the monodic recitative style: As before, solo voices are accompanied by the *continuo* (continuous bass) a supporting line of keyboard and viola da gamba (an ancestor of the cello). But the vocal line is much more tuneful than the Peri-Caccini brand. A sense of form is also created by alternating the solo passages with instrumental refrains, called *ritornelli*. Monteverdi also expanded the use of the chorus, which he accompanied by the full orchestra.

In 1637 the world's first public opera house, the Teatro San Cassiano, opened in Venice, bringing opera out of the private theaters with their invited audiences, and making it available to a paying public. Monteverdi, who had been appointed music director at St. Mark's Cathedral there, was among the many composers who wrote for Venice's new house, but of the several works he contributed to the repertoire, only two survive. The first, *Il Ritorno d'Ulisse in Patria* (Ulysses' Return to His Homeland, 1641), is based on the final episodes of Homer's *Odyssey*, and reveals a greater ornamental richness in the vocal lines than *Orfeo*. Moreover, there are more arias and songlike passages in *Ulisse* than in *Orfeo*. Not only does the score boast a love duet of supreme tenderness, sung by the reunited Ulysses and Penelope at the opera's close, but *Ulisse* also has its lighter side, especially the comical fight between Ulysses and one of Penelope's suitors.

L'Incoronazione di Poppea (The Coronation of Poppea, 1643), Monteverdi's last and finest opera, is the first known opera founded on historical fact. The libretto dramatizes the sordid machinations of the emperor Nero to divorce the empress Octavia and have his mistress Poppea crowned in her place. Written when Monteverdi was seventy-three,

Poppea is a work of extraordinary vitality and tunefulness. Nero and Poppea sing love music that exudes genuine passion, Octavia's Act III lament touchingly expresses the deepest grief of the abandoned wife, and the comedic characterizations establish what was to be a long and happy tradition in Italian *opera buffa*.

Though they were neglected for over two hundred years after their initial heyday, all three Monteverdi operas are now firmly back in the early Baroque repertoire, and aside from live performances, they are widely available on recordings and video.

With the opening of the Teatro San Cassiano, opera as a popular entertainment rapidly spread throughout Italy and beyond. But with the rise of the public audience came the increased demand for scenic extravagance. Then as now people enjoyed a good show, replete with earthquakes, naval battles, fire-breathing sea monsters, and cloudborne celestial visions, in which gods descended from the painted canvas heavens on pulleys and ropes (the *deus ex machina*, or "god from the machine") to resolve the tangled plots of the mortals on stage.

Florentine opera had begun with the idea that music was to serve the drama. The theatergoing public in Venice and elsewhere changed this priority as the audience focused its primary interest on the music and clamored for more tuneful, showier melodies than the neo-Greek recitative devised by the Florentines.

The resultant style, which by the nineteenth century came to be known as *bel canto* (beautiful song), capitalized on the fundamental traditions of Italian singing. A beautiful tone was paramount, along with *legato* (smooth) phrasing, and a thorough vocal technique and flexibility that would enable the singer to execute rapid repeated notes, trills, florid passagework, and a variety of other embellishments. Supported by the work of composers like Francesco Cavalli (1602–1676) and Antonio Cesti (1623–1669), Italian opera moved into its high Baroque stage.

Opera Seria

The high Baroque period in Italian opera was dominated by the elaborate form known as *opera seria* (serious opera), the standard operatic genre through the end of the eighteenth century. Troops of Italian composers, from Antonio Vivaldi and Alessandro Scarlatti in Italy to those like Nicolò Jommelli who traveled through Europe, spread the demand for opera seria as far afield as Russia, while non-Italians from George Frideric Handel to Wolfgang Amadeus Mozart went to Italy to learn the operatic craft and bring it back home.

The literary foundation of opera seria rested on the work of Europe's two most influential librettists, the Venetian Apostolo Zeno and the Roman Pietro Metastasio. Apart from Metastasio's smaller dramas, his twenty-seven large-scale heroic libretti were variously set over eight hundred times between the eighteenth and early nineteenth centuries.

The primary concerns of the dramatists were twofold: First was the presentation of polished verses that clearly expressed a variety of emotions that were codified according to an aesthetic theory that prevailed at the time. This theory, termed the "doctrine of the affections" by twentieth-century musicologists, not only specified "affections"—hatred, jealousy, sadness, love, etc.—but prescribed specific methods for expressing them in music.

The second concern of the two librettists was to provide in every opera a definite number of arias in which the solo singers could display their respective vocal abilities.

Opera seria plots of Zeno, Metastasio, and lesser authors often revolved around a conflict between love and duty and were inspired by serious themes in classical mythology or episodes in ancient history. In addition, these courtly entertainments generally had an underlying mandate to compliment and flatter the noble or royal patron whose treasury footed the bill. The deeds of the magnanimous Roman emperors, mythological gods, mighty warriors, and faithful lovers who warbled their way through hundreds of *opere serie* were meant to reflect and enhance the reputations of the princes who built the elaborately decorated court theaters where they were performed.

Opera seria plots could often be interpreted as allegories of current events, as in the case of Johann Adolf Hasse's *Arminio*, which dramatized the military exploits of the ancient German prince Arminius (Hermann), and was therefore produced for Frederick the Great's celebration of the Peace of Dresden, which ended the Second Silesian War in 1745. Similarly, Mozart's *La Clemenza di Tito* (The Clemency of Titus) was written to celebrate the coronation of Emperor Leopold II as King of Bohemia in 1791, and it was meant to reflect in the titular emperor's mercy a similar quality that the good Bohemians might hope for in their new king.

Strict formalities govern the structure of opera seria. Stage action moves forward in *recitativo secco* ("dry" recitative), in which dialogue is sung as in earlier operas over a continuo accompaniment. Later opera seria composers also wrote particularly dramatic passages in *recitativo accompagnato*, accompanied by strings. Recitative passages, which serve as operatic speech, link the all-important *da capo* arias (the song passages), in which each character expresses his or her emotions at the moment, one emotion to an aria. (In its simplest form, the da capo aria has three sections, the middle contrasting musically with the first section, the third section repeating the first, usually with the melody elaborately ornamented by the singer.)

During the seventeenth and eighteenth centuries, highly trained singers effectively ruled opera seria, and their ability to perform exceedingly difficult vocal acrobatics (rapid scale passages, long-held notes, trills, turns, wide leaps between notes) added to the fun. By the mid-eighteenth century the emphasis on these flourishes (known as *fioritura*) had reduced opera seria to a showpiece for singers.

Then along came Christoph Willibald von Gluck (1714–1787), who decided to reform opera seria by bringing it back to its roots as the servant of the drama. In 1762, he exemplified his new concern for dramatic truth with his version of the perennial Orpheus theme, *Orfeo ed Euridice*, in which he kept vocal embellishment to a minimum in favor of a more straightforward melodic line. Operatic change was in the wind.

Toward a New Aesthetic: Mozart

Gluck meant business. So did his chief successor, Wolfgang Amadeus Mozart (1756–1791).

Fictitious as it is, Peter Shaffer's ingenious play *Amadeus*, and its subsequent film treatment, have stripped away the powder-puff image of Mozart invented in the nineteenth century and perpetuated on Austrian chocolate boxes to this day. To be sure, Mozart was hardly the grotesque monkey in a fright wig portrayed on the screen. True, he was a boy genius who had performed like a traveling sideshow for crowned heads. True, as an adult he had a taste for dirty humor (his published letters are liberally sprinkled with scatology). True, he died tragically young, though he wasn't poisoned by the rival composer Antonio Salieri (Beethoven's revered teacher). But he was certainly *not* the broken-down failure of romanticized legend.

Indeed, modern scholarship has shown that once Mozart was settled in Vienna after his departure from Salzburg in 1781, he was not only among the first genuine freelance musicians—as opposed to one more commonly employed at a salary by a noble or princely patron—but he was successful at it. His performance receipts, teaching fees, and publication royalties netted him a relatively high income. The problem was that Mozart had expensive tastes and had put nothing aside for the lean periods that are a fact of freelance life. Unfortunately, he was in just such circumstances when his final illness struck.

Though Mozart wrote opera serias through the end of his life, his three greatest Italian works—*The Marriage of Figaro* (1786), *Don Giovanni* (1787), and *Così fan tutte* (loosely translated as "Women are like that," 1790)—are not in the opera seria style. Written to libretti by Lorenzo da Ponte, they abandoned mythological subjects in favor of more contemporary plots, thus presenting audiences with flesh-and-blood characters rather than stereotypical gods.

At the risk of overgeneralizing, Mozart's da Ponte operas

probe the eternal war between the sexes. *Figaro* and *Don Giovanni* depict women acquitting themselves admirably against men whose libidos are always in high gear. In the former we see the lusty Count Almaviva, hankering to bed his wife's maidservant on her own wedding night: The opera's title refers to Figaro's wedding, but in fact the action unfolds in a single day that represents a crisis in the marriage of the Count and Countess Almaviva. In *Don Giovanni*, the hero (or anti-hero, given his habits) is the rapacious Don Juan, who exists in a state of perpetual tumescence, and brings little lasting pleasure to the women he tumbles with.

In *Così fan tutte*, however, it's the women who fall from the pedestals their men have placed them on: Two sisters are lured by their servant girl into a game of switcheroo with each other's disguised fiancé, who have bet an older friend that their women are both paragons of virtue. In fact, *Così* is probably the most timely of Mozart's operas from both the licentious eighteenth-century and the liberal twentieth-century viewpoints, because it candidly depicts the erotic susceptibilities of human nature without unrealistic idealism. But as the eminent scholar H. C. Robbins Landon observes, Mozart has balanced da Ponte's undeniable cynicism with music that flows from "the deepest love and the deepest forgiveness of which human beings are capable."

In his da Ponte operas, Mozart moved away from the static da capo aria, toward more flexible musical scenes that convey a less formalized expression of the dramatic situation at hand. The degree of formality is relative, of course, comparable to the relative informality of Bernard Shaw's finely honed dialogue next to Shakespeare's blank verse.

Moreover, though Mozart did not live into the Romantic era of the nineteenth century, he made definite strides toward a liberated Romantic idiom in these scores. For example, the overture to *Don Giovanni* opens with a terrifying passage that returns later when the ghostly statue of the Commendatore (Donna Anna's father, whom he killed in the opening scene) stalks into Don Giovanni's palace. Thus, instead of simply calling the audience to order—as overtures traditionally did—this one actually sets the mood for the action to come. The first-act finale opens with a soft, atmospheric trio of masked conspirators—all whispering and shadow, like a moonlit canvas by Caspar David Friedrich. And during the finale itself—which revolves around a ball at Don Giovanni's palace—three groups of guests dance to three different orchestras simultaneously playing music in three different tempos, while the protagonists carry on their woven texture of conversational lines. It's a bit of contrapuntal virtuosity on paper that brings a heightened sense of realism to the proceedings on stage.

Most important, from our modern viewpoint, the richness of Mozart's melody and harmony, his vocal writing and instrumentation, are on a plane of their own. Mozart's music conveys with immediate naturalism every emotion, every dramatic feeling, from the bitter comedy of disguised lovers in *Così* and the revolutionary situation of servants confronting their masters in *Figaro*—pretty explosive stuff in 1786—to the Gothic horror that culminates *Don Giovanni*, in which the lustful and unrepentant Don Juan is dragged off to Hell by demonic forces.

Rossini: A Bridge to the Romantic Era

Mozart's death at thirty-five in December 1791 left succeeding generations guessing at where he might have taken opera had he lived another twenty years or more. They pondered the same question about Gioachino Rossini (1792–1868). Born in Pesaro, Italy, ten weeks after Mozart died, Rossini lived well into his seventies. Nonetheless, having written thirty-nine operas by the time he was only thirty-seven, he then stopped composing them altogether, and divided the rest of his life between periodic nervous breakdowns and gourmandizing. Rossini is the chief bridge between the eighteenth- and nineteenth-century Italian traditions, one of the last major composers to write opera seria, but the first after Mozart to write comedies that are still regularly performed—among them *The Barber of Seville* and *La Cenerentola* (Cinderella).

Several recognizable features characterize Rossini's work in comedy, which is known by the Italian term *opera buffa*. First (though by no means his invention) are the patter songs, in which the words are sung with lightning speed (as in Figaro's famous entrance aria, "Largo al factotum," in *The Barber of Seville*). Second is his use of the *crescendo* (literally, "growing louder"), in which he repeats a simple musical phrase several times, softly at first, and then increasingly louder, bringing successive layers of instruments to each repetition to add volume and weight to the sound. Though Rossini didn't invent this particular kind of crescendo—for the term is also used to describe any intensifying of volume in a musical phrase—he used it so often and so effectively in his first-act finales and in his overtures that it became identified with his style.

Rossini also codified, in effect, the move away from the aria to the scene, or *scena*, as the central building block of the action in an opera. In its simplest form, the scena consists of a slow, often meditative movement (*cantabile*), followed by a fast, showy *cabaletta*, in which the character moves into action. Having inherited the Mozartean convention of giving each principal singer in an opera at least one scena, Rossini expanded the form, often introducing it with an extended recitative, and inserting an additional section (*tempo di mezzo*, i.e., middle) between the cantabile and the cabaletta. Moreover, the scena form could be applied to duets and larger ensembles as well as solos.

In one sense the Rossini style is a throwback to the Baroque era, for his vocal lines are festooned with ornaments, trills, runs (rapid scale passages), and other bel canto decorations. Ironically, however, as singers still customarily added their own ornaments to a composer's music, Rossini attempted to reform opera in his own way by writing his fioritura directly in his scores to prevent this—a revolutionary idea at the time that offended many prima donnas. Nevertheless, if there is one outstanding quality to Rossini's music, it is the exceptional amount of ornament—which demands extraordinary technical facility on the part of female and male singers alike.

Moreover, because Italian audiences didn't demand that tragedy and comedy require strikingly different music, the abundance of major keys and tuneful vocal lines even in a Rossini opera seria like *Semiramide* (1823) sometimes strikes modern ears as slightly off base: To those of us nurtured, for example, on films, in which the mood of the screen image and the background music are closely related, the exciting but often jolly-sounding vocal lines of Rossini's characters might make one ask if the situation is supposed to be amusing rather than serious. You simply have to accept this as part of the Italian musical spirit of the time. Rossini's musical ambivalence toward comic and serious genres allowed him to use the same overture for more than one opera, especially when he was facing a deadline.

While looking backward toward Baroque vocal tradition, Rossini also helped to move serious Italian opera into the Romantic age. In *Elisabetta, Regina d'Inghilterra* (Elizabeth, Queen of England, 1815, whose overture he later "borrowed" for his *Barber of Seville*) he treated a subject from "modern" history rather than the usual ancient Greek and Roman lore. With *Otello* (1816), freely based on Shakespeare, he not only tackled a dramatist thought to be rather crude in early-nineteenth-century Italy but shocked his audience with a tragic ending (for all its strife, an opera seria customarily ended happily). *La Donna del Lago* (*The Lady of the Lake*, 1819) was the first important opera to treat the poetry of Sir Walter Scott, an architect of European Romanticism.

But Rossini's only true Romantic opera was also his last: *William Tell* (1829), which he wrote in French. As we will see later (in the French Opera section), Rossini's heroic swan song was a departure from all his previous operas.

Romantic Bel Canto

Though not much younger than Rossini, Gaetano Donizetti (1797–1848) and Vincenzo Bellini (1801–1835) head the next generation of bel canto composers. Donizetti, who was adept at drama as well as opera buffa, was a feverish worker.

Starting in 1816, he wrote twenty-nine operas with only moderate success before striking pay dirt with *Anna Bolena* (Anne Boleyn) in 1830. Thereafter, his reputation spread internationally, and his workload increased.

Over the next five years he composed seventeen more operas, including the second and third parts of his so-called Tudor cycle, *Maria Stuarda* (Mary Stuart, 1833) and *Roberto Devereux* (Robert Devereux, 1837), a fictional dramatization of the amatory relationship between Queen Elizabeth and the Earl of Essex. And of course there is *Lucia di Lammermoor* (1835, based in part on Walter Scott's novel, *The Bride of Lammermoor*), in which clan warfare and a brother's political ambition drive a young woman insane. Because of its glorious score (including Lucia's celebrated Mad Scene and the great Sextet in Act II), *Lucia* remained a standard even during the period when Donizetti's other dramas had passed from the scene.

Like Rossini, Donizetti was brilliant at comedy, of which *Don Pasquale* (1843), about a pompous old fool who takes a young bride and learns the folly of his ways, is probably his comic masterpiece. According to tradition, he wrote his most famous opera buffa in a few weeks: *L'Elisir d'Amore* (The Elixir of Love, 1832), about a timid country bumpkin who falls for a quack doctor's love nostrum. The composer acknowledged his predilection for haste, writing in 1843 that "what I have done that is good has always been done quickly."

Donizetti also traveled relentlessly from one Italian opera center to another, back and forth to Paris, for which he composed another delightful comedy, *La Fille du Régiment* (*The Daughter of the Regiment*, 1840), and to Vienna, where he was eventually appointed kapellmeister (music

director) to the Austrian court. No wonder he burnt himself
out; by the time he died, a pathetic victim of venereal disease, Donizetti had composed about seventy operas.

Such frenetic pace would not do for the Sicilian Bellini.
Handsome, vain, and fastidious, Bellini preferred to take
several months to write an opera, though he could write
quickly when he had to. Hence, in a career that lasted all
of ten years (he died at thirty-four of an acute attack of
the chronic amebiasis that had plagued him for some
time), he completed only ten scores, of which three have
remained standards, especially during the last four
decades. *La Sonnambula* (The Sleepwalker, 1831), is
about a village girl whose nocturnal wandering almost
ruins her wedding plans. *Norma* (1831) dramatizes the
emotional and moral conflicts that arise when a Druid
high priestess, who has secretly had children with the
chief of the hated Roman military forces, discovers her
Roman now loves another priestess. In *I Puritani* (The
Puritans, 1835), set during the English Civil War, a Royalist plot to sneak King Charles I's widow, Henrietta
Maria, out of Cromwell's England leads to a disastrous
misunderstanding between the daughter of a Puritan lord
and her Cavalier fiancé.

The most moving Italian composer of his day, Bellini had
a knack for writing extremely long, extremely tender
melodies, whose graceful languor is almost hypnotic. Their
arching, spun-out quality had a marked influence on one of
Bellini's great proponents, Frédéric Chopin, especially in
his nocturnes and ballades. Like most major composers of
the time, Bellini wrote for specific singers, and demanded
that they not only produce a beautiful sound but an expressive
one. The simple directness of his melodic outpouring was

considered novel at the time, a radical departure from Rossini's florid brilliance. Moreover, the finesse with which Bellini handled his texts, following with his notes the actual inflections of the words, resulted in an eloquence that astonished his listeners, who marveled at what they perceived to be the speechlike effect of his melodies. Bellini's melody even won the admiration of Richard Wagner, usually no fan of Italian opera.

Most important, where Rossini was primarily a classicist, whose music expressed generalized emotions in an easily tuneful manner, Bellini, like the mature Donizetti, was a true Romantic in that his music expressed realistic emotion: Tragedy sounds tragic in a Bellini score—for example, the deeply affecting finale of *Norma*, in which Norma and her forbidden lover, Pollione, go to their execution to music that could never be mistaken for comedy.

Verdi: The Glory of Italy

Musicians and scholars can discuss at length how Donizetti's handling of musical forms grew increasingly sophisticated as his career progressed. They could do the same in Bellini's case as well. Nonetheless, on the surface an early Donizetti opera sounds pretty much like a late one. How different, therefore, is the example of Giuseppe Verdi (1813–1901).

Today Verdi is to Italians what George Washington is to Americans, an icon, whose portrait is on the Italian equivalent of our dollar bill. No one would have imagined this at the start, however. Born in a small farming community in what was then the Duchy of Parma, Verdi started life in extremely modest circumstances. His first teachers were village organists, and when he tried to enter the Milan Conservatory he was denied admission, a rejection that gnawed at him for the rest of his life.

Having secured the patronage—not to mention the abiding paternal affection—of a wealthy merchant in his hometown, Verdi was able to study privately in Milan with a La Scala conductor. He also married the merchant's daughter, who bore him two children.

In 1839, Verdi's first opera, *Oberto, Count of San Bonifacio*, was staged at La Scala through the influence of a leading soprano who at the time was the mistress of the general manager: Giuseppina Strepponi, who would later become Verdi's second wife. Verdi's next opera, the comedy *Un Giorno di Regno (*King for a Day*)*, was a complete failure at its solitary performance in 1840. It culminated the lowest period in his career, his children and his wife having died one by one during the previous two years. Despondent, Verdi nearly gave up music altogether. Then the La Scala impresario literally shoved a new libretto into his hands and told him to get to work.

The piece was a fictional embroidery of biblical references to the Babylonian king Nebuchadnezzar and his conquest of the Hebrews. Its dramatic focus was a power struggle between the king and Abigaille, a formidable slavegirl presumed to be his eldest daughter. In his low state, Verdi might have ignored the impresario's urgings, had he not been impressed with the libretto's scriptural majesty. One passage in the middle of the book had especially moved him from the start: Inspired by Psalm 137, it was a chorus of Jews weeping in exile by the rivers of Babylon, "Va, pensiero, sull' ali dorate." (Go, thought, on golden wings).

By the autumn, the opera, *Nabucco*, was completed, and its production at La Scala in 1842 was a major triumph. Northern Italy was then under Austrian rule, and the population latched onto that magnificent chorus of hope, making it an anthem of the liberty they sought. Verdi's next opera, *I Lombardi alla Prima Crociata* (The Lombards at the First Crusade), boasted a similar chorus, and achieved comparable success at its premiere the following year.

Verdi's name quickly became a household word, but to the Austrians it was literally handwriting on the wall: During the uprisings that eventually led to Italian unification in 1860, the phrase *"Viva Verdi"* was adopted by Italian patriots as an acronym for their forbidden motto *"Viva Vittorio Emanuele Re D'Italia,"* and splashed as graffiti up and down the peninsula.

In the course of his career, Verdi was always expanding his musical and dramatic vision, searching for a new way to write opera, for novel, increasingly vivid ways to convey to his audience the lifeblood of his drama. Hence Verdi's genius is not just apparent in the irresistible beauty of his melody, or the vital eloquence of his musical language in each opera. It manifests itself in the incredible breadth of the overall canon of his works. Donizetti composed seventy operas in an active career that spanned about twenty-seven years. In fifty-four years Verdi composed a mere twenty-eight operas (as well as several revisions, and the towering Manzoni Requiem). However, this relative handful represents not just a steady advancement of Verdi's personal technique but an advancement of the fundamental idiom of Italian opera.

Early Verdi works like *Nabucco* or *Ernani* (1844) sound tunefully naive compared to the emotional intimacy of a middle-period work like *Rigoletto* (1851). But even the heartbreaking melodies of *Rigoletto* sound less modern, if you will, compared to the sophisticated grandeur of the exotic *Aida* (1871) or the explosive orchestral sweep of his *Otello* (1887), with its minute psychological introspection.

In Verdi's work there is a constant development away from what had been a series of self-contained "numbers" linked by recitative—each number, or scena, with an orchestral introduction and a full close signaling applause. Instead, Verdi moved toward a more sophisticated idiom, in which climactic solo and ensemble passages, with recognizable melodic profiles, flow without introductions or closes through a sustained musical texture. In effect, the music and the dramatic action no longer stop for explanations. With the premiere of *Otello*, the seventy-four-year-old Verdi could have been content to rest on his laurels. But at eighty he brought out his final word on the matter of a continuous musical drama: *Falstaff* (1893).

Based on Shakespeare's *The Merry Wives of Windsor*, with interpolations from *Henry IV, Parts I* and *II*, it is one of the happiest and most amazingly beautiful of all operatic comedies. In *Falstaff*, the musical pace is incredibly fast and the texture continuous, with glorious melodic moments rather than conventional arias. Suffice it to say, therefore, that if *Falstaff* doesn't grab you at first hearing, don't give up on it. By listening to it on record, from time to time, with a libretto in hand, you'll get to know it better, and the subtle wonders of the score will become more apparent.

As a musical dramatist Verdi constantly tackled increasingly bold subjects from which earlier composers would have shrunk: *Rigoletto* deals with human deformity—in the person of a hunchbacked jester—as well as rape. At a time when Italian opera meant epic historical costume pieces, *La Traviata* (The Fallen Woman, 1853) presented an intimate social drama about a courtesan and her bourgeois lover, scandalous stuff in its day, especially when performed in what was then modern dress. Likewise, the unfamiliar *Stiffelio* (1850) was another contemporary drama, treating the dilemma of the German pastor who discovers his wife's adultery and must grapple with vengeful instincts forbidden by his calling. A married priest was a disturbing enough anomaly to Verdi's audience, but a man who could forgive his adulterous wife was an impossibility, at least to Italian men of the time. Hence *Stiffelio* was heavily altered, and was lost in its original form until the rediscovery of two manuscript copies in 1968. Recent revivals, at Covent Garden and the Metropolitan Opera, have revealed the work to be a masterpiece worthy of inclusion in the regular Verdi canon.

Without a doubt, Verdi's work forms the bulk of the standard Italian repertoire, and the subjects reveal his broad literary interests, from the thundering melodramas of Victor Hugo—*Ernani* and *Rigoletto*—to the brooding darkness of Spanish literature—the incredibly tuneful *Il Trovatore* (The Troubador, 1853) and *La Forza del Destino* (The Force of Destiny, 1862, composed for the Imperial Opera in St. Petersburg); from the fictional treatment of historical events—*Les Vêpres Siciliennes* (The Sicilian Vespers, 1855, also familiar as the Italian *I Vespri Siciliani*) to contemporary fascination with Egyptology that inspired *Aida* (1871, commissioned to celebrate the opening of the Suez Canal as well as the Cairo Opera House).

Plays by the eighteenth-century German dramatist Friedrich Schiller served as the basis for Verdi's greatest

Parisian grand opera, *Don Carlos* (1867), as well as for his more intimate *Luisa Miller* (1849), a tale of love, intrigue, and suicide in a quiet Tyrolean village. Verdi's two final operas, *Otello* and *Falstaff*, fulfill a lifelong fascination with Shakespeare that began with the early *Macbeth* (1847).

Working at a time of widespread censorship in Italy, Verdi repeatedly had to contend with often ludicrous demands to clean up his act. For instance, because Hugo's play *Le Roi s'amuse* showed the Renaissance king François I in an unflattering light, Verdi was obliged to change the character of the king to the Duke of Mantua in his version, *Rigoletto*, to avoid besmirching the Hapsburg monarchy then ruling Venice. Moreover, in some theaters the final scene was altered because the image of a heroine dying in a sack was considered too sordid for genteel eyes.

But that was nothing compared to what Verdi and his librettist were put through during the preparations for *Un Ballo in Maschera* (*A Masked Ball*, 1859). Based on the actual assassination of Sweden's flamboyant King Gustav III at a masked ball in his own opera house in 1792, the opera was considered politically dangerous: Stage regicide might inspire a real assassin. So the whole story had to be transplanted to the American colonies. Gustav became Riccardo, governor of colonial Boston. The king's friend and murderer, Count Anckarstroem, became one Renato, a Creole adviser. To this day *Ballo* is still often performed in the "American" version, which Verdi himself approved.

Censors aside, for Verdi, a good opera upheld the classical Italian traditions of beautiful melody, no matter how advanced in technique or radical in subject. A good opera deployed poetry and music to probe human behavior in situations of profound stress. Above all, a good opera played to packed houses.

To a great degree, the same beliefs in the traditions of Italian melody and intimate character study that inspired Verdi also inspired his effective musical heir, Giacomo Puccini.

Puccini and the New Century

Born in the olive-oil capital of Lucca, Giacomo Puccini (1858–1924) came from a long line of composers starting with his great-great-grandfather, also named Giacomo. Yet, though even his father Michele was a composer, the youngest Giacomo exhibited no particular affinity for music. However, he *did* reveal an early affinity for the money his future work would earn him: In order to teach him the rudiments of the organ, Giacomo's patient father would put coins on the keys he wanted him to strike, and in grabbing for them, the boy would pound out a tune.

Unfortunately, this elementary form of subsidized musical education ended with Michele's sudden death, when Puccini was five. Puccini's mother nonetheless wanted her boy to carry on the family tradition, and formal music training commenced as soon as Puccini was old enough. There was a practical reason as well—as an adolescent, Puccini's earnings as a church organist and freelance pianist helped to piece out his widowed mother's minuscule pension.

Having started to compose at around sixteen, Puccini began to attract attention with his organ and choral pieces.

After trudging twenty miles to Pisa and back to hear a performance of Verdi's latest opera, *Aida*, he was bitten by the opera bug and determined to make his career in the theater. With assistance from a wealthy relation, and a stipend from the Queen of Italy, he applied to the Milan Conservatory. Unlike Verdi, he was accepted.

Puccini's chief professor at the conservatory was Amilcare Ponchielli, composer of *La Gioconda* (1876), and it was Ponchielli who later introduced him to his first librettist, and opened the way to Puccini's first opera, *Le Villi* (1884), a short piece that concerns a faithless lover who meets his end at the hands of the same dancing spirits—the *vilas*—who inhabit Adolphe Adam's ballet *Giselle, ou les Willis*.

Written for a competition, *Le Villi* failed to win the prize; however, it was subsequently produced in Milan, where Verdi's publisher Ricordi heard it and was impressed. Ricordi commissioned Puccini to write a full-length opera, and though *Edgar* was only moderately successful when it finally appeared five years later, Ricordi didn't lose faith. With his next work, *Manon Lescaut* (1893), Puccini became an international celebrity.

Puccini had first learned about opera through Verdi's work, and like Verdi he only succeeded with his third opera. Among Verdi's greatest contributions to operatic literature are his moving studies of father-daughter relationships—especially that of Rigoletto and Gilda (*Rigoletto*) and Simon and Amelia (*Simon Boccanegra*). In Puccini's operas, however, the emphasis is not on male-female relationships but on women, each with a tragic flaw that makes her plight that much more human, that much more unforgettable: Manon Lescaut, her bewitching loveliness sacrificed to her selfish love of pleasure and luxury; Mimì (*La Bohème*,

1896) already dying when she meets the poet Rodolfo; the obsessively jealous Floria Tosca (*Tosca*, 1900); and the innocent Cio-Cio-San (*Madama Butterfly*, 1904), faithful to the husband who abandons her.

To be sure, Puccini did create two extraordinary studies of men along the way: the sadistic Baron Scarpia, who actually tells Tosca that he likes it better when a woman puts up a fight; and the gritty bargeman Michele in *Il Tabarro* (The Cloak, 1918), in whose soliloquies we grow to understand the plight of a man whose younger wife no longer loves him.

Nonetheless it is the women who interest Puccini, and his remarkable gallery extends through the rest of his work: from the six-shooting Minnie in *La Fanciulla del West* (The Girl of the Golden West, 1910), who teaches Bible lessons to the gold miners in her saloon, but cheats at cards to save her man, to the icy Princess Turandot and the self-sacrificing little Liù (*Turandot*, 1926).

From the start of his career, Puccini, whose own marriage was far from idyllic, had confidence in his ability to move audiences through his musical understanding of women's varied stories. And he had a facility for sniffing out a good tale even in a foreign tongue: Puccini first saw the David Belasco dramatization of John Luther Long's novella, *Madame Butterfly*, in London, yet though he understood none of the English dialogue (fortunately so, for it contains some of the most ludicrous babble ever devised), the action was so apparent to him that he was immediately able to envision it as an opera. Moreover, he knew how to deploy Latin emotion to its best artistic advantage. A decade earlier, before embarking on *Manon Lescaut*, he dismissed any misgivings about tackling the same subject that Jules Massenet had already treated with tremendous success: Massenet's immensely popular opera, *Manon*, had chalked up two hundred performances in Paris during its first ten years. "Massenet feels it as a Frenchman with the powder and the minuets," wrote Puccini to his publisher. "I shall feel it as an Italian, with desperate passion."

And it is Puccini's ability to convey desperate passion, white-hot ardor, and moving personal tragedy through the intensity of his soaring melodic invention that makes his operas as popular as they are. Indeed, though Italian opera has maintained its vigor and novelty right up to the contemporary offerings of composers like Luigi Nono (1924–1990), Puccini is the last Italian composer whose work is substantially represented in the standard international repertoire.

A Dagger in Every Plot: The Pulse-Pounding World of Verismo

Cymbals crash, organs peal, blades flash, and the tenor dies, slashed in an offstage alley—and all in the first hour. That's not just *amore*; that's *verismo*. Pietro Mascagni gave birth to the genre in 1890; two years later, Ruggero Leoncavallo slapped the infant soundly on the rump. Since then, the lusty cries of their twins, *Cavalleria Rusticana* (Rustic Chivalry) and *Pagliacci* (Clowns), have echoed magnificently through the opera houses of the world. "Ridi, Pagliaccio!" sobs Canio. The show must go on even though his cuckold's heart is breaking. I have seen hard-boiled businessmen reduced to jelly by the time "the comedy is ended," for obviously the old story can still hit a nerve.

As an operatic school, verismo (literally, "realism")

aimed to treat common life, without the ostentatious trappings of traditional historic opera. Yet though it is generally identified with the period between 1890 and 1920, it neither sprang forth as suddenly as people tend to believe nor died out so soon thereafter. In fact, since music tends to lag behind the other arts, verismo's literary and artistic antecedents raised eyebrows and pulses long before Mascagni's Turiddu first serenaded his wanton Lola.

As far back as 1833 (when Chopin and Bellini were the rage), the genteel French scholar Prosper Mérimée wrote of murder, honor, and revenge among the hot-headed islanders of Corsica in his novella *Colomba*. He followed with *Carmen* in 1847, a study of lowlife among the Spanish Gypsies. During Europe's revolutionary year 1848, the French painter Gustave Courbet announced he would thenceforth paint only "modern and vulgar" subjects instead of romantic idealizations.

Following his lead, French authors adopted the new philosophy of *le réalisme*. Gustave Flaubert's *Madame Bovary* (1856) shocked (and titillated) Europe with its story of extramarital love. Emile Zola's *Thérèse Raquin* (1868) examined the guilt of a shopkeeper's wife who murders her husband with her lover's help, only to be driven to remorseful suicide. Shortly thereafter, Zola expanded *le réalisme* into *le naturalisme* by introducing a pseudo-scientific method of examining and documenting characters' emotions and motives in a series of novels—*L'Assommoir*, the story of an industrious laundress's descent into drunken poverty; *Nana*, the study of a slum girl turned courtesan; and *La Terre*, a brutal look at peasant life. Squalor was definitely hot.

Meanwhile Parisian theaters had been presenting

"realistic" dramas by Alexandre Dumas, *fils*, who created his first stir with the 1852 dramatization of his own novel, *La Dame aux camélias*, on which Verdi based *La Traviata*. Dumas subsequently produced a series of plays that provoked controversy by their comparatively unflinching look at subjects hitherto deemed unfit for discussion in polite society: *Le Demi-Monde* gave Bohemianism a new name; *Le Fils naturel* concerned an illegitimate son; *Un Père prodigue* presented a wayward father. By the 1880s, Victorien Sardou was taking Dumas's ideas even further with a series of full-blown melodramas on startling subjects as vehicles for the actress Sarah Bernhardt. The most famous of these—*Fedora*, *La Tosca*, and *Madame Sans-Gêne*—were later fashioned into veristic operas by Puccini and Umberto Giordano.

Operatically, Verdi's *Traviata* laid the foundation for operatic realism because it dealt seriously with the contemporary tragedy of a Parisian courtesan. Nonetheless, it was Bizet's treatment of Mérimée's *Carmen*, with its violent story and musical exploitation of Spanish local color, that proved the direct antecedent of what we now recognize as the verismo style.

Premiered in Paris in 1875, *Carmen* received its Italian premiere at Naples four years later, and by the time it was produced again at Turin in 1881, the Sicilian-born Giovanni Verga had published *Vita dei Campi* (Life in the Fields), a collection of stories of Sicilian peasant life, including a tale called "Cavalleria Rusticana," with its womanizing anti-hero, Turiddu Macca.

A Zola disciple, Verga probed what he called *i vinti*—the vanquished—people whose commonplace lives tend to go unnoticed by literature. In 1884 he rewrote "Cavalleria

Rusticana" as a one-act play, which became a great vehicle for the actress Eleanora Duse. Five years later, the twenty-six-year-old composer Pietro Mascagni (1863–1945), unknown but ambitious, set a libretto version of the play to music and submitted it to a publishing competition. Mascagni's score won hands down.

Produced in 1890 at Rome, *Cavalleria Rusticana* proved a bracing change to audiences grown tired of historical operas peopled by kings, princes, and knights. Its triumph unleashed a storm of veristic activity as Italian and other European composers turned to slums and basements for inspiration in their eagerness to beat Mascagni at his own game. Among them, Francesco Cilea, best known for the romantic *Adriana Lecouvreur* (1902), waded in with *La Tilda* (1892), about a vengeful street singer in a world of robber gangs. In 1892, Umberto Giordano wrote his first veristic essay, *Mala Vita* (Tough Life), in which a consumptive mechanic vows to marry and reform a harlot if the Virgin Mary will cure him: After finding Lola (always Lola!) in the gutter, their marriage doesn't quite work out, and he dies at her feet. Unfortunately, the notoriety *Mala Vita* achieved at its Rome premiere subsequently fizzled in Naples, where first-nighters rioted upon seeing a leading tenor dressed in overalls.

As for Mascagni, though he sired verismo, he hardly regarded it as a favorite child, and it was the tragedy of his career that the public continued to expect verismo from him whereas Mascagni himself strove to develop in more poetic directions. Meanwhile, *Cavalleria* found its perfect complement in a shattering drama of betrayal within a traveling theater troupe. Its composer, Ruggero Leoncavallo (1857–1919), a magistrate's son, claimed to have fashioned his libretto from one of his father's own trial cases, and the 1892 premiere of *Pagliacci* at Milan was a triumph Leoncavallo would never experience again.

By 1895 the characteristics of verismo were well established: Operas revolved around the violent, contemporary problems of commonfolk (usually equipped with daggers), with ample opportunity for ethnic local color, especially as dances and drinking songs. The music itself strove for relentless emotional impact, with soaring lyrical moments in rapid succession, emphasized by colorful, often noisy orchestration. "Artificial" operatic devices such as overtures were abandoned—the curtain usually rises quickly on veristic works—and the conventional progression of numbers linked by recitative gave way to a free-flowing texture in which arias were introduced only if they were natural soliloquies in the drama.

Nonetheless, the line between verismo and good old-fashioned melodrama was thin, and the delineation between them was clouded further once the first wave had spent itself. Composers and librettists began to find modern stories set amidst wet laundry, fish nets, and blood somewhat limiting. Hence they branched out into costume pieces, such as Giordano's *Andrea Chénier* (1896), and Puccini's *Tosca*, which blended the high tension of veristic musical speech with more conventional operatic trimmings. An alternative route was into the "modified verismo" of such works as *La Bohème* and *Madama Butterfly*, "modified" because while their plots are concerned with the tragedies of ordinary people, the action is hardly violent.

Still, the original strain of verismo continued to surface well into the new century. In 1911 the half-German, half-Italian composer Ermanno Wolf-Ferrari (1876–1948), who usually found inspiration in Goldoni's eighteenth-century comedies, wrote his solitary verismo shocker, *I Gioielli della Madonna (The Jewels of the Madonna)* to make money. And with its potent blend of striking music, thieves, religion, a hint of incest, and *two* (count 'em) suicides, that's precisely what the opera did. It is long overdue for revival, and anyone who has heard the throbbing intermezzo from that work has some idea why. Puccini wrote his one true veristic work relatively late in his career: The one-act *Il Tabarro* (The Cloak), a story of adultery and murder amongst the barge people of the Seine, forms the first part of his *Trittico,* premiered at the Metropolitan in 1918.

By the 1920s, verismo had not played itself out so much as transferred its energy to the newer medium of film, for the parallels are clear between such screen thrillers as *Fu Manchu* and an opera like Franco Leoni's one-act *L'Oracolo* (The Oracle), replete with opium addicts, kidnapping, and murder in San Francisco's Chinatown. Character actor Lon Chaney took his cue from *Pagliacci* in such silents as *He Who Gets Slapped* and *Laugh, Clown, Laugh,* while talkies like *Dead End* and *Tugboat Annie* contained enough tenements and squalor to delight the most rabid veristo. Of course, the most obvious cinematic reflections of verismo are found in Italian neorealism of the 1940s and 1950s, beginning with Luchino Visconti's *Obsession* and continuing with films like Federico Fellini's *La Strada,* Roberto Rossellini's *Open City,* and Vittorio de Sica's *Bicycle Thief.* Yet it is in the contemporaneous operas of Gian Carlo Menotti—*The Medium, The Consul,* and *The Saint of Bleecker Street*—that the grit, the melodrama, and above all, the powerful lyricism of old verismo enjoyed a final flowering.

Further Adventures in Italian Opera

Arrigo Boito, *Mefistofele* **(1868; revised versions, 1875, 1881)**
Boito, who wrote the libretti for Verdi's *Otello* and *Falstaff*, based *Mefistofele* on Goethe's *Faust*. Unlike Gounod, who concentrated only on the episode in which Faust romances and ruins Marguerite, Boito attempted to encompass more of Goethe's epic. Hence his opera is more like a series of tableaux than a continuously flowing drama.

Boito's score is immensely powerful, especially the towering chorus of angels that opens and closes the work. The love music is sweepingly melodic; the great basso solos for Mefistofele are shot with magnificent irony.

Puccini, *Gianni Schicchi* **(1918)** Puccini's only comedy, this one-act piece, based on Dante, forms the third part of his *Trittico* (Tryptich) and contains the irresistible aria "O, mio babbino caro" (O, Daddy dear), sung by Schicci's gentle daughter.

Puccini, *Suor Angelica* **(1918)** The second part of *Il Trittico*, in which an aristocratic woman is shut away as a nun in a convent by her family after she bears an illegitimate child. Upon learning of the baby's death, she takes poison but dies with a miraculous vision of the Virgin and her baby welcoming her to paradise.

French Opera:
Vive la Différence!

[Opera is] a bizarre affair composed of poetry and music, in which poet and musician, each obstructed by the other, give themselves no end of trouble to produce a wretched result.

CHARLES DE SAINT-DENIS, SIEUR DE SAINT-ÉVREMOND
(1613–1703), ESSAYIST

According to popular tradition, Catherine de Médicis, Italian-born queen of France, laid the groundwork for French *haute cuisine* when she arrived in Paris with her retinue of Florentine chefs. Modern scholarship largely refutes this; however, it seems apparent that she was at least instrumental in introducing "Italian ices" to the French court, her chefs having prepared a different-flavored ice for each day of her wedding

feast in 1533. A century later, Parisians were enjoying their fill of ices and sherbets, especially after another transplanted Italian, Signor Procopio, opened the Café Procope in 1660, specializing in the refreshment. By that time, the French court was enjoying another Italian confection, a good deal more substantial: opera.

In fact, Italian opera had taken a while to catch on in the France of Louis XIV. The first performances were staged in Paris around 1645, but the French were unimpressed. To them, the ballet and the spoken dramas of Racine and Corneille offered theatrical perfection. To add singing, they felt, would only muck up the words. Then from over the Alps came Giovanni Battista Lulli (1632–1687), a Florentine teenager brought to Paris to help the king's cousin, Mlle de Montpensier, practice Italian.

Voilà Lully

In 1653, Lulli entered the Sun King's service as a dancer, having also mastered the guitar and violin. At fourteen, Louis XIV was no mean dancer himself, and he often took part in the ballets performed at court. Hence it wasn't long before Louis and Lulli were jointly tripping the light fantastic in a whole series of court ballets. It also didn't take long for Lulli to establish himself as a ballet composer.

In 1661, Jean Baptiste Lully (his name gallicized to reflect his French naturalization) was appointed composer to the king. Three years later he collaborated with the dramatist Molière on *Le Mariage forcé* (The Forced Marriage), the first of their series of *comédie-ballets*, in which dance interludes were interpolated into a spoken comedy.

Modern stargazers would have had a field day with the performance, for the author himself played the lead role, Lully presided over the music, and His French Majesty danced the part of a Gypsy in the ballet.

Meanwhile, opera—though still mainly Italian—was catching on in France. In 1669 Lully's rivals, composer Robert Cambert and poet Pierre Perrin, received the exclusive license to establish the Académie Royale de Musique, ancestor of the present Paris Opéra. Their subsequent collaboration, *Pomone*, the first full-length opera written and sung in French, achieved a wild success at its 1671 premiere that goaded Lully into further action: When Perrin landed in debtors' prison the next year (embezzled by his unscrupulous business managers), Lully jumped at the opportunity to grab the Académie license for himself. With this monopoly on staged music production in his pocket, Lully reigned supreme in Paris, and embarked upon a long collaboration with the poet Philippe Quinault. Beginning with a *tragédie lyrique, Cadmus et Hermione* (1673), composer and librettist firmly established the French school of opera.

As defined by their eighteen joint works, French Baroque opera is distinguished from its Italian counterpart by several characteristics:

- The French wanted to understand what was going on. So texts, usually on classical subjects, were in French rather than Italian, and set to music with a consummate sensitivity to the distinctive spirit of the French language. "My recitative is meant for speaking," the composer himself declared, thereby emphasizing the importance of the words in relation to his music.
- The French did not share Italy's virtuosic singing tradition—

French voices tend to be less agile than Italian voices, and the French language is placed further back in the throat than Italian. Hence by comparison, the sung tone is darker, more veiled, and slightly nasal, all of which impart their own flavor to the most idiomatic French vocal music. Thus French opera emphasized the drama rather than florid singing.

- Because of the French love of dance, ballet was accorded tremendous prominence in French opera, a tradition maintained through the nineteenth century. So were massive choruses, which lent weight and majesty to the musical texture, as did purely orchestral movements, which showered the ear with a delectable array of instrumental color. Indeed, the variety and richness of French orchestral color was to remain a hallmark of French music into the present century.

- Because the French enjoyed visual spectacle as much as the Italians, cloudborne gods, sea beasts, and celestial visions also popped up at every opportunity.

Not only did Lully compose, act, dance, and play the violin, he also conducted. Unfortunately, conducting in his day was a less subtle affair than it is now; instead of directing the musical forces by waving a slender baton (a nineteenth-century invention), Lully customarily beat time by pounding the floor with a heavy staff. It was noisy. It was also dangerous: In January 1687, while leading his *Te Deum* (ironically to celebrate the king's recovery from an operation), Lully got so carried away with his music that he bashed his toe with the sharp point of his staff—right through the shoe. An abscess developed; Lully refused to let his physician amputate the toe—anesthesia was not yet invented—and within weeks he was dead of gangrene.

Rameau: Controversy, Baroque Style

Lully had firmly established French opera, but it was his chief successor, Jean-Philippe Rameau (1683–1764), who brought the genre into the full flower of late Baroque magnificence. Surprisingly, Rameau, a keyboard specialist and music theorist, didn't get into the opera game until he was fifty. Afterward, however, there was no stopping him, and he continued to write stage works right up to his death at eighty-one.

To Lully's essential tunefulness and dancy rhythmic vivacity, Rameau added revolutionary harmonic richness and instrumental color. His first opera, the tragedy *Hippolyte et Aricie* (1733), which treats the myth of Phaedra's love for her stepson Hippolytus, who loves the temple virgin Aricia, sent shivers of wonder down the spines of his audiences because of its unprecedented dramatic power and musical complexity. To be sure, critics and academics of the time argued that Rameau's emphasis on human emotion and characterization made his music too exciting to be artistically proper.

In this era when opera was a young art form that provoked lively debate, the Paris Opéra witnessed a face-off between the modernist Ramistes and the conservative Lullistes, which lasted almost twenty years. Moreover, just when the debate died down and Rameau was finally accepted by the French musical public at large, the arrival in Paris of an Italian opera buffa troupe in 1752 ignited the so-called War of the Buffoons. This time it was the supporters of Italian comic opera who hurled their barbs at the proponents of French tragic opera, targeting Rameau as the symbol of the musical establishment. But Rameau gave as good as he got, defending serious French opera, and emerging victorious from the fray. Even so, in his hilarious *Platée* (1745), Rameau had already revealed his brilliance as a composer of French comedy as well as tragedy. The opera dramatizes the god Jupiter's attempt to cure his wife's chronic jealousy by pretending to marry the vain but ugly marsh nymph Platæa and the cast calls for eight solo sopranos as well as a chorus of satyrs and frogs.

Indeed, a positive aspect of the War of the Buffoons was the development of native *opéra comique*, lighter entertainments in which spoken dialogue was interspersed with songs and airs. (More on that later in the operetta chapter.)

From Baroque to Classical

By the 1760s the elaborate decorative quality that characterized Baroque opera in Italy and in France had evolved into the clarity and balance propounded by the same eighteenth-century classicism that inspired architects like Ange-Jacques Gabriel (of Petit Trianon fame) and Robert Adam in England. As an art form, opera itself benefited from the increasing cosmopolitanism of its composers. Christoph Willibald von Gluck, whom we have already encountered in our look at Italian opera, is a prime example.

Born in Germany, Gluck spent four years in Italy, during which he made his successful debut in 1741 as an opera seria composer. After touring Europe, he settled in Vienna, where he continued to compose Italian opera. Gradually, however, he was exposed to the prevailing winds of French culture that started to blow in around 1750. With this

French influence, Gluck changed his tune: Reviving the elementary principle of the old Florentine Camerata, Gluck abandoned the current Italian manner in which the drama supported elaborate vocal music, and adopted the more straightforward melody of the French manner to express and support drama rather than merely decorate it. For his first new reform opera, Gluck returned—yet again—to the Greek myth that had inspired the earliest Florentine pioneers: *Orfeo ed Euridice* (1762).

Having enjoyed considerable success with his Gallic experiments, Gluck finally took his ideas to Paris itself. There during the 1770s he produced a series of new French operas, as well as French versions of his *Orfeo* and its successor, *Alceste* (Vienna, 1767; Paris, 1776). His arrival in Paris set off yet another controversy between partisans of the status quo and Gluckist reformers. The Gluck camp won. Henceforth France boasted two schools of opera: The first, *opéra* or *tragédie lyrique*, maintained classical plots, sung *récitatif*, and an emphasis on dignity and spectacle. The second, *opéra comique*, featured lighter, more sentimental music interwoven with spoken dialogue.

Gluck died of a stroke back in Vienna in 1787, a victim of his appetites for heavy work and heavier food. The very next year, in Paris, another foreigner tried his luck at capturing the French imagination. Like old Lully, Luigi Cherubini (1760–1842) hailed from Florence, and achieved his operatic immortality with a work that perpetuated the neoclassicism so dear to eighteenth-century hearts: his potent *Medée* (Medea). Premiered in 1797, the opera is based on Pierre Corneille's tragedy of the sorceress Medea's grisly revenge upon her husband Jason when he deserts her for another woman.

Napoleon found Cherubini's music too noisy. He preferred the work of another Italian émigré, Gaspare Spontini (1774–1851), whose most famous opera, *La Vestale* (1807), treats the old conflict between love and duty: The victorious Roman general Licinius returns from Gaul only to discover that his fiancée, Julia, has been forced to become a vestal virgin. Just why Napoleon found Spontini's music less noisy than Cherubini's is difficult to say, given that the score is loaded with grandiose choral scenes, stage bands, and general pomp. In any event, Spontini was famous as a great character in his own right, who received visitors to his home enthroned amidst portraits and busts of himself. He used to rehearse his own scores wearing full court dress, stiff with gold braid, waving a field marshal's baton and shouting over the orchestra as if leading them into battle.

Romanticism Arrives

While Spontini was overseeing the neoclassical glories of serious French opera, the lighter side—opéra comique—was moving healthily along. Instead of Greek and Roman plots, opéra comique looked to the Romantic movement for its subject matter. For example, in *La Dame Blanche* (The White Lady, 1825), considered the most revolutionary opera of its day, François-Adrien Boieldieu (1775–1834) and his librettist, Eugène Scribe, combined themes from two novels by Sir Walter Scott, whose work embodied the picturesque "Gothick Revival" that had swept through Europe. Its atmospheric Scottish setting, its old castle reputedly haunted by a beautiful ghost, and its extremely tuneful score added up to one of the most enduring hits of early French Romanticism.

Boieldieu's successor in the realm of opéra comique was Daniel F. E. Auber (1782–1871), who had a wonderful way with vivacious melody and piquant rhythms gleaned from the ballroom and parade ground. Given the effervescence of his music, it is surprising that the composer himself was so shy that he could never bear to conduct his own work, or even listen to performances of it. Of Auber's forty-seven operas, his chief success, *Fra Diavolo*, remained so familiar after its 1830 premiere that it served as the basis for Laurel and Hardy's 1933 screen comedy of the same name.

Scribe, Auber's longtime collaborator, modeled his dashing title character on the historical Italian bandit Michele Pezza, who as "Brother Devil" disguised himself as a nobleman in order to prey upon foreign travelers around Naples. The comedy is replete with bandits, country bumpkins, pretty women, and humorous caricatures of an English Milord and Milady, whose diamond necklace is Fra Diavolo's quarry.

Grand Opera: Bigger Is Better

Though Auber specialized in comedy, he and Scribe were responsible for the work that opened up a new genre of nineteenth-century dramatic spectacle that was to influence international opera composition for the rest of the century: French grand opera. Scribe based the libretto of *La Muette de Portici* (The Mute Girl of Portici, 1828) on the historic revolt against Spanish rule led by the Neapolitan fisherman Masaniello in 1647. Apart from Auber's zingy

music, the great novelty was its silent heroine—
Masaniello's sister Fenella, played by a ballerina—and her
ultimate suicide by leaping from a palace balcony as
Vesuvius erupts! Not only did the work catch on at its premiere in 1828, but when it was performed in Brussels two
years later its revolutionary sentiments inspired the revolt
that led to Belgium's independence from Holland.

To be sure, grand opera didn't spring from thin air. From
Lully to Spontini, France had enjoyed a more or less continuous line of spectacular lyric tragedies. French grand
opera—generously state-subsidized—took the old ideas
several steps further.

- To suit the taste of an age that enjoyed the romantic quality
  of Gothic, Renaissance, and Rococo design in everything
  from architecture to home furnishings, the plots of grand
  opera were taken from medieval and Renaissance history
  instead of classical mythology.
- Dramas, cast in four or five acts, often climaxed with a spectacular catastrophe—volcanic eruption, exploding palace
  (Meyerbeer's *Le Prophète*), battle or massacre (*Les Huguenots*), auto-da-fé (Verdi's *Don Carlos*), protagonists boiled in
  a cauldron (Halévy's *La Juive*).
- Elaborate, three-dimensional scenery was meticulously
  researched for historic authenticity, with a different set for
  each act, and often for each scene. There was much use of
  complex stage machinery and lighting, for shipwrecks,
  storms, fires, infernal apparitions, etc.
- In keeping with French love of dance (and the Frenchman's
  love of leggy dancers), a grand opera included at least one
  ballet sequence, and often several of them.
- As the Paris Opéra boasted the finest orchestra in Europe at
  the time, grand operas were characteristically scored for

large orchestras, with additional stage bands whenever needed.

- Large casts of soloists were employed, who sang not only elaborate arias but duets and ensembles. A massive chorus also played an integral part in the dramatic action, lending weight and sheer numbers to festival scenes, processionals, riots, battles, orgies, and especially prayer scenes.

The nineteenth century heartily enjoyed the sentimental implications of churchy trappings, and an operatic prayer, in which the chorus and soloists could belt a soaring melody over booming organs and pealing bells, always hit home inside and outside the opera house. If you're willing to be wowed, a good operatic prayer can still have that effect.

Having provided the Romantic grand opera archetype, Auber returned to more congenial opéra comique, leaving the way open for yet another Italian, Gioachino Rossini, to baptize the new infant with his final opera, *Guillaume Tell* (*William Tell*, 1829). Based on Friedrich Schiller's drama about Switzerland's fourteenth-century freedom fighter, *Tell* boasts one of the most familiar of all opera overtures— even before it was harnessed to "The Lone Ranger" it was an extremely popular concert piece. Like the overture, the musical style of the opera itself emphasizes an expansive melodiousness instead of ornamentation. With its forest scenes, storms, and glorious Alpine hymn to liberty (complete with chorus, rainbow, and sunset), *Tell* provides a musical counterpart to the sweepingly atmospheric imagery of Romantic artists like Gustave Doré or Frederick Edwin Church.

Scholars have long debated the reasons why Rossini

composed no more operas after *William Tell*. The pressure
of composing as rapidly as he did in Italy had exhausted his
health, and as a rich man he no longer needed to earn a living.
Moreover it is probable that having experimented with the
new operatic style, he found that he didn't like it, and shrank
from the idea of competing with composers who did.

Chief among them was another foreigner, Giacomo (born
Jakob) Meyerbeer (1791–1864). The scion of a German Jewish
banking family, he had first composed German operas, which
had failed, when Mozart's former rival, Antonio Salieri,
advised him to wet his feet in Italy. So it was off to Venice
in 1815, where Meyerbeer found that the only way to get
anywhere was to write florid opera seria à la Rossini. The
stratagem worked brilliantly.

His fame spread beyond Italy, until in 1825 Meyerbeer
went to Paris, where he was invited to produce a work for
the Opéra. The industrious Scribe supplied the libretto, and
in 1831 Meyerbeer's first grand opera, *Robert le Diable*
(Robert the Devil), created an unparalleled sensation.
Everything about it was irresistible to the audience: its setting in medieval Palermo, its Gothic supernaturalism
(Robert is the son of a mortal woman and a devil, Bertram,
who wants to win Robert's soul back). Meyerbeer's colorful,
often impassioned music moved their emotions and went to
their toes, especially a titillating moonlit ballet in which the
ghosts of nuns damned "for breaking their vows" (which
meant more than eating meat on Fridays) rise from their
graves in a ruined monastery to entice Robert to evil. That
scene in particular was subsequently immortalized on
canvas by Edgar Degas.

Robert was followed five years later by another triumph,
Les Huguenots, based on the bloody history of the Catholic

massacre of the Paris Protestant community on St. Bartholomew's Eve, 1572. Here Scribe and Meyerbeer brewed a potent mixture of love, religion, and political treachery that contains a plea for religious tolerance. Meyerbeer was only too familiar with anti-Semitism, which vented itself with increasing frequency as his successes attracted the envy of less fortunate composers, not the least vocal of whom was the polemical Richard Wagner, whose scurrilous essay "The Jew in Music" was aimed primarily at Meyerbeer.

Meyerbeer's third grand opera, *Le Prophète* (The Prophet, 1849), is his masterpiece. Loosely following the history of the Anabaptist revolt at Münster in 1534, Scribe's libretto focuses on the emotional relationship between the false prophet Jean of Leyden and his pious mother, Fidès. Jean, a visionary innkeeper, is persuaded by three rabble-rousing Anabaptists (one of many short-lived Protestant sects that emerged during the Reformation) that he is the Messiah. As their political dupe, he abandons Fidès. She goes off in search of him, only to meet up just as he is being crowned as a divinity in the Münster Cathedral. Scribe gave Meyerbeer opportunities for stirring crowd scenes and plenty of religious pomp during the Coronation Scene (source of the famous "Coronation March"). Keenly aware of popular taste, Meyerbeer even capitalized on the recent invention of roller skates by including a skating ballet, ostensibly on a frozen lake.

Indeed, Meyerbeer might be regarded from our viewpoint as the Andrew Lloyd Webber of his day. His spectacular operas were wild popular successes, but were disparaged by many critics and musicians. The disparagement was often unjust. Meyerbeer's finest operas—the three cited above plus the posthumously produced *L'Africaine*, a fictionalized account of the explorer Vasco da Gama—are best regarded as flawed masterworks. Rather than judge them against the greater psychological depth and musical complexity achieved by Verdi and Wagner, they are more fairly examined against the works of Rossini and Donizetti that preceded them. Better yet, just enjoy them for what they are, colorful, tuneful, and entertaining.

Meyerbeer was an architect of novel, often subtle instrumental effects—from pounding waves of full orchestra and brass band to the introspective combination of a single instrument and solo voice. His ear for sonority was virtually unrivaled in his time, except by Hector Berlioz.

During his lifetime, Berlioz (1803–1869) was one of the most magnificent failures in the whole of music history. Most widely known for his extraordinary symphonic works, he strove mightily to succeed as an opera composer as well. But though his greatest opera, *Les Troyens* (The Trojans, composed 1856–58), has become a fairly standard work today, it was too strange in concept, too high-toned, for Berlioz's audience. Even by then-current grand opera standards, it was just too big. Moreover, while he was ahead of his time in terms of rhythm, harmony, and his unwillingness to write songlike tunes, Berlioz was unfashionable in taking the classical opera of Gluck as his model. Berlioz wrote his own libretto, founded on Virgil's *Aeneid*, and cast the work in two enormous parts, of which only the second, *The Trojans at Carthage*, was performed during his lifetime. This fact ate at him continually.

He had better luck with his so-called *opéra de concert*, *The Damnation of Faust* (1846), based on the first part of Goethe's poem. Intending to dramatize the increasing void in Faust's soul as he is egged on to debauchery and wickedness by Méphistophélès, Berlioz ends it with Faust being dragged to Hell as Marguerite is redeemed. As a concert work, it was performed a number of times during Berlioz's lifetime, and was especially popular for the stirring Rákóczy March, which Berlioz adapted from the Hungarian piece named for the patriot Prince Ferencz Rákóczy. In 1893, it was first staged as an opera with sets and costumes at Monte Carlo, which started a vogue for it in this form.

A Fork in the Road: Gounod, Bizet, Massenet

Grand opera was holding its own, moving toward the biblical majesty of such works as Camille Saint-Saëns's *Samson et Dalila* (1877), with its famous "Bacchanale." Meanwhile, the more lightweight opéra comique arrived at a fork in the road around 1850. One path, taken by Jacques Offenbach, led to the deliciously uproarious genre of operetta. The other led to opéra lyrique. Where operetta laughs, lyric opera sighs and sheds a tear or two; where grand opera treats its heroic characters like figures in a vast historical fresco, lyric opera probes the hearts of its more human-scale protagonists to express their inward emotions through an outpouring of sweetly refined melody and lush instrumentation.

The chief composer of opéra lyrique was Charles Gounod (1818–1893), whose most famous opera, *Faust* (1859), treats the episode of Goethe's epic poem in which the old German philosopher Faust, made young again by the devil Méphistophélès, seduces the innocent Marguerite. In the end, Marguerite, imprisoned for drowning her baby, is borne to Heaven by a choir of angels after rejecting Faust's

ardent proposal to let him and the devil help her out. If this
bald description suggests a Hallmark card, Gounod's music
makes drama of it.

Modern critics often dismiss Gounod's "honeyed melody"
and "perfumed harmony" in this work and in his second
most popular opera, *Roméo et Juliette* (1867). In fact,
Gounod is not the most rigorous composer. At his best in
tender love scenes—e.g., the *Faust* Garden Scene and the
Balcony Scene in *Roméo*—he constantly wavers between
romantic eroticism and the more theatrical elements of
nineteenth-century piety. His essentially soft-edged music,
as comforting as a featherbed, perfectly mirrors the ideal-
ized imagery of French and English academic painters of
the time: smooth, solid, fleshly, and technically polished.

Gounod had first achieved distinction when he won the
Grand Prix de Rome upon graduating from the Paris Con-
servatoire. So had Georges Bizet (1838–1875), a composer
blessed with the French ability to get to the dramatic point
quickly and directly. He is universally known for his
Carmen (1875), one of the few operas that is virtually a
household word. The story was taken from Prosper Mérimée's novella about the ruin of a young Spanish officer
through his fascination with an amoral Gypsy woman.
Because of the overwhelming popularity of Carmen's
"Seguidilla" and her "Habañera," for which Bizet adapted a
song by his Spanish contemporary Sebastián Yradier—
apparently believing it an authentic folk song—Bizet is
often credited with writing a thoroughly Spanish score.
This was never his intention, however, and apart from its
more exotic moments, *Carmen* is a true French opéra
comique. Gounod's lyric sweetness pervades the Don
José–Micaela duet, Auber's vivacity bubbles through the

Smugglers' Quintet, and though the orchestral introduction to Escamillo's "Toreador Song" has a definite Iberian swing, the march refrain is as Parisian as the rue de Rivoli.

According to popular myth, Bizet died from the disappointment over *Carmen*'s failure. In fact, Bizet's publishers paid him well for the score, which chalked up forty-eight performances by the end of its first year. It is true that the opera was controversial, that the box office was initially poor, and that Bizet was stung by criticism from some quarters that the work was obscene: After all, the Théâtre de l'Opéra-Comique, which first produced it, was a rendezvous for middle-class parents and their marriageable children, and Carmen's torrid ways and violent end were hardly conducive to matchmaking.

Nonetheless Bizet's own rocky marriage, his susceptibility to persecution mania, and severe bouts of quinsy probably contributed to his fatal heart attack as much as anxiety over his masterpiece.

Through *Carmen*'s overwrought passions, violence, and focus on ordinary village folk, Bizet stands as a direct precursor of Italian *verismo*, and therefore an innovator. Jules Massenet (1842–1912) was happier to pursue more conventional paths to pleasing his audience. And he pleased them so well that he enjoyed one of the most successful careers of all time, which enabled him, like Verdi and Puccini, to live in regal splendor off his royalties.

A workaholic, Massenet was a fluent melodist, a compelling harmonist, and a fascinating orchestrator who could express passion, intimacy, pathos, and pageantry with equal verve. Moreover, he was able to discern in what direction the winds of fashion were blowing. Employing his personal style as a root stock, he grafted onto it Gounod's

sacred brand of eroticism, along with a few symphonic principles of Wagnerian music drama—adapted, of course, to
the French taste.

Massenet was fascinated by women, especially women
who were most charming when horizontal, including
Manon (1884), in which the Abbé Prévost's simple but
beautiful country girl is corrupted by her taste for high
living in Paris; *Hérodiade* (1881), based on Flaubert's
amorous biblical tale of Salome and John the Baptist;
and *Thaïs* (1894), based on Anatole France's novel of
the courtesan who captivates a holy man. But his operas
aren't entirely devoted to boudoir heat: *Werther* (1892),
based on Goethe's novel, is a remarkably sensitive portrayal of unrequited love—the poetic Werther loves Charlotte, who is honor bound to marry dull Albert; in despair
Werther finally shoots himself, but as he dies Charlotte
admits she loves him, and they kiss for the first time. *Cendrillon* (Cinderella, 1899) is a scintillating fairy opera
for adults; and in *Don Quichotte* (1910), Massenet provided
a nineteenth-century take on Cervantes' Knight of the
Doleful Countenance, full of boisterous humor but ultimately moving.

Into the Twentieth Century:
Debussy, Ravel, Poulenc

By the time Massenet died two years later, his extro-
verted, crowd-pleasing musical style was dismissed as
passé by younger modernists. One composer in particular
had set off along a more subtle path.

Claude Debussy (1862–1918) was inspired by the muted

tones and enigmatic dreamscapes of English Pre-Raphaelite painters like Sir Edward Burne-Jones and fin-de-siècle Symbolists like Gustave Moreau. He had declared his intention to create an opera like "two associated dreams: No place. No time." In the drama *Pelléas et Mélisande* by the Belgian Symbolist Maurice Maeterlinck, Debussy found the ideal vehicle for what would prove to be his only completed opera. From the moment the curtain rises, Maeterlinck's characters are wreathed in tantalizing mystery—Prince Golaud, lost in "a dark wood," finds Mélisande cowering and unable to articulate her nameless fears. After he takes her as his wife, she meets his younger half brother, Pelléas, and their mutual fascination eventually drives Golaud to jealousy and murder.

Passion runs high in Debussy's opera, but it is expressed in music of deceptive gentleness: Instead of belted top notes, the externals of conventional operatic lovemaking are replaced by a softly intimate expression that more closely approaches how real-life lovers would communicate in the still of the night.

Because it avoids catchy tunes, *Pelléas et Mélisande* (1902) is often regarded as an opera for connoisseurs. Nonetheless, anyone familiar with the sexuality implied by the intensely wordless moments captured in paintings like Burne-Jones's *Beguiling of Merlin* or *King Cophetua and the Beggar Maid* will understand what Debussy was after.

While *Pelléas* represents the darker Symbolist facet of early-twentieth-century French opera, two operas by Maurice Ravel, a composer usually linked with Debussy and the so-called Impressionist school, form that period's answer to opéra comique and fairy tale. Ravel (1875–1937), tiny, dapper, passionately fond of collecting music boxes and miniature objets d'art, is best known for his orchestral *Boléro*, whose immense popularity surprised the composer himself. His mother, a Spanish-speaking Basquaise, cultivated in him a love of Spanish music and folk culture that influenced several of his works, including his first opera, *L'Heure espagnole* (The Spanish Hour, 1911). Conceived in one act, this farce concerns the bored wife of a clockmaker (Torquemada), who spends an afternoon juggling a trio of lovers: a foppish poet, a banker with more girth than sense, and a dim but brawny muleteer. Guess who scores—offstage, of course.

If Debussy's characters flit through a shadowy world, paralyzed by their own inertia, Ravel's saunter through the cool shade of a summer day, their foibles weaving a cynical comedy of manners. Ravel's satin music tingles with Spanish flavor; sultry dance rhythms mingle with a beguiling array of horological jokes—the tightly wound clocks in Torquemada's workshop seem to mirror the over-wound libidos of the protagonists. In the end, we wonder in amusement if the mild-mannered clockmaker is really wiser than his clever wife suspects.

Ravel, a lifelong bachelor, had a great affection for children and for their world, which he channeled into his second opera, *L'Enfant et les Sortilèges* (The Child and the Enchanted Things, 1925). The libretto, by the novelist Colette, concerns a naughty boy whose temper tantrum leads to spiritual awakening when his broken, mistreated possessions come to life to teach him a good lesson. Ravel drew upon a variety of styles for his score, from the armchair's Baroque sarabande to the mock-Wagnerian cat duet to the jazzy fox-trot for the Wedgwood teapot and the china cup. Touching but never mawkish, Ravel's fanstasy refracts the essence of childlike wonder through the prism of Art Deco sophistication.

Both Ravel and Debussy were conservatory-trained, fastidious craftsmen. By comparison, Francis Poulenc (1899–1963) was a gifted dilettante. Born rich and well-connected, he was also a natural charmer. With minimal formal training, he started out by writing clever piano music, easy to play and to listen to, which found a ready market amongst fashionable amateurs. Though Poulenc hankered to compose serious opera, he didn't do so until he was in his forties, and then with a raffish, Surrealist romp, *Les Mamelles de Tirésias* (Tiresias' Breasts, 1947), about a woman who changes sex, and her husband who single-handedly produces over forty thousand children in a day. And they sing, too! Characteristically, Poulenc, who wrote the piece between 1940 and 1944, during the German occupation of France, concealed a sober message beneath the absurdity, namely, that war-torn France must renew and repopulate itself.

Moreover, beneath Poulenc's own lighthearted facade lurked the soul of anxiety, which vented itself in his *Dialogues of the Carmelites* (1957), deservedly the most frequently performed French opera of the post–World War II era. Based on an actual tale of martyrdom during the French Revolution, the story concerns the spiritual voyage of a neurotic young aristocrat, Blanche, who joins a Carmelite convent to escape the real world. Through her experiences there she learns that the only way to overcome personal fear is to face it head on—or in her case, head off, for in the end, after the convent is attacked by the revolutionaries, Blanche exults in her newfound courage and calmly joins her sisters in martyrdom.

Given the dissonance that was the common idiom of much music composed in the 1950s, Poulenc's score is courageously old-fashioned. Essentially melodic, it has scenic structures with their roots in Verdi. Its fluid, expressive recitatives are influenced by Debussy, its overriding sense of impending peril inspired by Mussorgsky's *Boris Godunov*. Intensely human, intensely moving, *Carmelites* is unforgettable.

Further Adventures in French Opera

Lully, *Atys* (1676) Derived from one of Ovid's less familiar mythological episodes, the opera deals with a classic love triangle: The beautiful youth Atys is loved by the goddess Cybèle and by Sangaride, who is betrothed to the King of Phrygia. Splendid choruses and an exquisite dream sequence are among the highlights of this majestic *tragédie*.

Rameau, *Castor et Pollux* (1737; revised version, 1754) Its focus on fraternal rather than romantic love sets this *tragédie* apart from the crowd. When his mortal twin Castor is killed in battle, Pollux agrees to sacrifice his own immortality to take his brother's place in Hades, and thus allow him to return to his beloved Télaïre, whom Pollux loves as well. The later version is one of the most vivacious and moving of Rameau's operas.

Bizet, *Les Pêcheurs de Perles* **(*The Pearl Fishers*, 1863)** This opera reflects the French fascination with the East. On the island of Ceylon, the rivalry of Nadir and Zurga over the priestess Leila leads to complications, tragedy, and heroic sacrifice. Bizet's lovely score includes the tenor-baritone duet, "Au fond du temple saint" (Within the sacred temple).

Ambroise Thomas (1811–1896), *Mignon* **(1866)** Brooding, bearded Thomas had a gift for charming melodiousness that touched the audiences of his time. *Mignon*, distilled from Goethe's *Wilhelm Meister's Apprenticeship*, upset German audiences because of its happy ending (Mignon dies in the book). Thomas obliged with an alternative tragic finale for the Germans. The sparkling overture contains two of the most popular melodies in the opera, Mignon's dreamlike "Connais-tu le pays" (Do you know the country) and the sprightly polonaise, "Je suis Titania" (I am Titania), sung in the opera by the flighty actress Philine, whose flirtation with Wilhelm lends tension to the plot.

Léo Delibes (1836–1891), *Lakmé* **(1883)** In Victorian India, an English officer falls in love with the beautiful daughter of a fanatical Brahmin priest. Love, alas, does not conquer all. Delibes, composer of the silken ballets *Sylvia* and *Coppélia*, loaded this score with music as richly fragrant as jasmine, including the famous "Bell Song," a coloratura show-piece, and the sultry duet, "Sous le dôme épais" (Beneath the dense forest vault).

German Opera: Was Ist Das?

German sounds a thoroughly respectable language, and indeed I believe is so.
—OSCAR WILDE, *THE IMPORTANCE OF BEING EARNEST*

A fair amount of opera was performed in seventeenth- and eighteenth-century Germany, but most of it was Italian. Moreover, the German nation we know today did not exist until 1871, when Otto von Bismarck achieved his aim to create a united Germany with the king of Prussia as emperor. When Italian opera first arrived along the Rhine, Germany was a loose confederation of several hundred German*ies*—principalities, duchies, free cities, and a host of petty holdings a few square miles in area. Vestiges of the Holy Roman Empire, they were bound by their common language, and ruled with absolute power by their respective princes, electors, margraves, and grand dukes, all of whom owed nominal allegiance to the emperor in Vienna.

Going for Baroque

It is easy to understand why Italian opera proliferated in the Austro-German lands. First of all, Italy, originator of the art form, produced the dominant repertoire. The leading opera singers were either Italian or Italian-trained. Italian composers and performers spread their influence as far off as England and Russia, while Italy was a magnet attracting non-Italian composers, many of them German or Austrian, who returned home to write operas in their acquired manner. Therefore, Italian opera was the brand-name product—regarded by cultivated, aristocratic German audiences as stylish and sophisticated.

One place that promoted opera in German, however, was the old Hanseatic city of Hamburg. In 1678, a group of musicians there, bucking fierce opposition from Church authorities, established Germany's first independent public opera house, unprepossessingly named the Theater at the Goosemarket. The repertoire consisted of operas written by Germans to German libretti, sung in German by German singers, none of them international stars. Goosemarket composers included such Teutonic worthies as Johann Kusser, Johann Krieger, Nicolaus Strungk, and Johann Förtsch; among the librettists were the mellifluously named local poets Christian Postel and Lucas von Bostel. Who says German is unsingable!

Hamburg's Goosemarket Theater remained active for sixty years, during which period several notable figures contributed to its repertoire, the most important one to emerge being George Frideric Handel (or to give the original German spelling, Georg Friedrich Händel), who cut his operatic teeth there. Handel (1685–1759) arrived at the Goosemarket at eighteen, having dropped out of law studies at the University of Halle, and was engaged as a second violinist in the orchestra. Two years later he composed his first opera, *Almira*, the only one of his three Goosemarket operas to survive in complete form. *Almira* was something of a shaggy mutt, with German recitatives and fifteen of the fifty-three arias in Italian. Nonetheless its vigorous, showy music and an entertaining plot proved so winning that it filled the house some twenty times in seven weeks.

Handel wrote two more German operas for Hamburg, but by the time the third was produced in 1708 he had long since gone south, to Italy, to refine his craft. When he returned to Germany in 1710 as Kapellmeister to the Elector of Hanover, Handel was a seasoned composer of Italian opera. The following year he was granted leave to travel to London, where he brought out *Rinaldo*, the first of a long series of Italian operas he would compose for the London stage. Back in Hanover, in 1712, he requested an extended leave of absence to travel to London again. Though he overstayed his leave, as luck would have it his patron, the stout Elector Georg Ludwig of Hanover, succeeded to the English throne as King George I in 1714, on the death of his distant cousin, Queen Anne, none of whose many children survived her. After winning his old patron's favor once again, Handel made London his professional base for the rest of his life.

Singspiel

The Hamburg vogue for opera in German was due in great measure to the fact that the city was not a royal seat but a mercantile one. The Goosemarket Theater was a people's theater, organized and supported by a prosperous middle-class audience, rather than by the private endowment of a royal or aristocratic purse. Even in German and Austrian cities that boasted court theaters playing a modish Italian or Italian-style repertoire, the good burghers wanted their own entertainments, and as in other countries, those entertainments often took the form of high spirited plays interspersed with songs. Instead of elaborate, formal poetry, these pieces featured simple, direct plots, with humor (often coarse), hummable tunes, and characters based on stereotypes long part of folk culture—Hanswürst, Pickelhäring, and the like.

Out of the medieval Church plays and mystery dramas, and the knockabout pieces put together by itinerant troupes at fairgrounds and public festivals, arose the German *Singspiel*, meaning "songplay," which is very much what these works are—plays interspersed with songs. As with French opéra comique, the mixture of talk and tune was especially suited to comedy, the spoken dialogue allowing the action and the humor to be plainly understood by the audience, the musical numbers contributing their vivacity and emotional appeal at the important points along the way.

Though singspiels appeared during the mid-seventeenth century, the term itself wasn't actually used until the early eighteenth century, as the genre developed into a standard form of German comic opera. Instead of the world of classical gods and heroes, singspiel dealt with ordinary folk, as implied by the titles of such works as *Der lustige Schuster* (The Merry Cobbler, 1766) by the Leipzig composer Johann Adam Hiller, and the Viennese comedy *Doktor und Apotheker* (Doctor and Apothecary, 1786) by Karl Ditters von Dittersdorf. Both were extremely popular throughout German-speaking countries, and continued to hold the boards there well into the nineteenth century. Nonetheless, the two finest singspiels were composed by Mozart.

Mozart

As we have seen, Wolfgang Amadeus Mozart (1756–1791) had already written a string of Italian opera serias by the time he tackled his first mature singspiel, *Die Entführung aus dem Serail* (*The Abduction from the Seraglio*, 1782). The commission had come from the National-Singspiel, a theater established in Vienna by the Emperor Josef II in 1777 specifically to promote German opera. The libretto, about two European women whose lovers contrive to rescue them from captivity in a Pasha's harem, capitalized on the eighteenth-century affinity for Turkish themes. As recently as 1683, the Ottoman Turks had besieged Vienna, and had remained a military threat to Europe until 1699.

Turkish operas had been composed by Gluck, Haydn, and even Mozart himself (his *Zaide*, left unfinished in 1780). The libretti are usually replete with fantastic locales and exotic pseudo-Turkish or Arabic decorations. Turkish stories allowed composers and librettists to explore the long-standing conflict between East and West, and to parody the arcane customs of foreign lands for comic effect. More important, these turbanned, pantalooned costume pieces with their "heathen" foreign potentates were usually not so scrupulously censored as those peopled with Western kings and emperors. Thus Turkish operas often served as subtle vehicles to spread liberal thinking, and perhaps enlighten modern rulers in the ways of benign despotism: In the last scene of *The Abduction*, Pasha Selim releases his four European prisoners precisely to prove that he is a merciful prince, unlike the European prince who robbed him of "my love, my wealth, my homeland."

In common with other Turkish operas, the score of *The Abduction* features colorful writing for instruments considered exotic at the time, especially the clangorous combination of cymbals, bass drum, and triangle. Played during the overture, and during the zesty choruses of Turkish subjects, this marvelously noisy rhythm section was intended to imitate janissary music (from the Turkish *yeniçeri*, or "new soldiers"), the band music that typically accompanied the Sultan's bodyguard.

Mozart, a Freemason, tackled another Eastern subject for his final singspiel, *Die Zauberflöte* (*The Magic Flute*). This time, however, the story was not a modern Turkish one, but a mystical fairy tale set in ancient Egypt, just the thing to entertain the Viennese crowd at a theater run by the actor-manager-playwright Emanuel

Schikaneder) in what was then considered a suburban district.

Schikaneder, a fellow Mason who created the role of the bird catcher Papageno in the premiere, had written the libretto and commissioned the opera. In fact *The Magic Flute* marked the first time that Mozart had composed for a "people's" theater rather than one under the auspices of the crown, and the premiere in September 1791 launched the most successful run of any of his operas—197 performances in two years.

Schikaneder's libretto lends a surprise twist to the rescue setup: Prince Tamino, assisted by Papageno, is charged by the Queen of the Night to free her daughter, Pamina, from the clutches of the sorcerer Sarastro. Soon, however, the conventional rescue evolves into an allegorical quest for love and virtue, and a contest between the powers of darkness and light, or in Masonic terms, despotism and reason. Tamino discovers that Sarastro is not Pamina's wicked captor but her wise protector, who puts Tamino through a series of trials to test his fortitude and worthiness of love. And by the end of the opera, the Queen of the Night is revealed as the villain.

Magic and the supernatural had long been exploited in singspiel, though usually with a comedic edge. Yet despite the comic tone of Mozart's opera, especially in the characters of Papageno and the grotesque little villain Monastatos, the shadowy remote setting, the arcane rituals of Freemasonry, and the vivid poignance of Pamina's aria, "Ach, ich fühl's" (Ah! I feel that love has vanished) anticipate the operatic rise of what we would come to know as German Romanticism.

Revolutionary and Romantic:
Beethoven and Weber

The words "romantic" and "romanticism" have been so overused that their artistic meaning has been clouded. In fact, the whole Rhine Valley, hoot-owl-at-midnight atmosphere we associate with operatic German Romanticism owes its existence to France.

Romanticism in the arts arose during the second half of the eighteenth century as a French literary movement. Led by the philosopher and composer Jean-Jacques Rousseau (1712–1778), it constituted a reaction against the cool formality of the classical tradition. Instead, the Romantic spirit called for a return to naturalism, to nature itself, and to its simplicity, concentrating on man's instincts and *feelings* rather than on intellectual reasoning.

In opera, the Romantic ideal led to a new emphasis on subjective emotional qualities, and to a new excitement that rose out of breathtaking situations rather than classical disputations between love and duty. Indeed, the tense rescue drama that so influenced German Romantic opera was fostered by the exciting climate of Revolutionary France.

This does not mean that Classical and Baroque opera lacked emotion. As we have seen, one of the predominant aesthetic theories of the eighteenth century was the so-called doctrine of the affections, which codified emotions according to a set of specific "affections," and prescribed specific methods of expressing them in music (see "Opera Seria"). Johann Mattheson, one of several musicians who published writings on the theory, instructed composers in detail how to express a catalogue of more than twenty affections: sorrow by a slow-moving, languid melody; hatred by "repulsive and rough harmony"; and so forth.

The difference between the Baroque-Classical approach to the emotions and the Romantic approach was their application. The earlier manner allowed only one affection—hatred, hope, anger—to be explored within a single aria or other self-contained scene. Romanticism prescribed a new freedom in this regard. Instead of the formal da capo aria, linked to specific musical devices that expressed a single affection, arias could take a variety of forms, from simple songlike ballads to increasingly complex structures utilizing fast and slow tempos in a succession of contrasting moods. This structural freedom also encouraged composers to write larger, more varied ensembles in addition to the solo arias and occasional duets of opera seria. Climactic moments of Romantic opera often occur in trios, quartets, and larger group numbers, in which several feelings and emotions are explored and contrasted within a unified musical framework. The sheer weight, energy, and variety of textures in these ensembles also serve the theatrical purpose of exciting the listener: A group of characters singing together provides aural pleasure for its own sake as well as the drama's.

Romantic freedom and its revolutionary implication of liberty for all appealed greatly to that most powerful and idealistic of German composers, Ludwig van Beethoven. Throughout his life (1770–1827) Beethoven wrote overtures and incidental music for plays such as Goethe's *Egmont*, and even music for a ballet, *The Creatures of Prometheus*. But despite his abiding love of theater, he wrote only one opera, *Fidelio*.

Scholars have long debated the reason why. Some feel

that Beethoven was simply not a born opera composer; others venture that *Fidelio*—its subtitle is *Married Love*— was the only subject that truly appealed to the lifelong bachelor. Yet although he wrote only one opera, Beethoven wrote it twice. The first version, usually called *Leonore*, was unsuccessful at its premiere, at the Theater an der Wien in 1805. A shortened version got a better response there in 1806, but because of a fight with the management, Beethoven himself withdrew it after only two performances. The opera went unperformed until 1814, when another theater inquired about reviving it. Beethoven consented, on condition that he could remodel his score completely.

The new version, *Fidelio*—tighter, leaner, musically finer—was a great triumph at its premiere in 1814. *Fidelio* is probably the only opera to boast four overtures: the brisk *Fidelio* overture, which precedes the opera, and the three symphonically expansive *Leonore* overtures, composed for the various stages of the earlier version of the opera (the third is customarily played between the final two scenes of *Fidelio*, though many Beethoven scholars feel that this is inappropriate).

Based on a play by the French dramatist Jean-Nicolas Bouilly, the story is a rescue drama. With its spoken dialogue and subsidiary comic touches, *Fidelio* is also a singspiel, but a heroic one. Despite the lighthearted overtones of the opening scene, Beethoven's opera is deadly serious. Its basic message deplores human suffering, exalts the ideal of beneficent humanity, idealizes marital devotion. And at a time when wives were supposed to prove their love by maintaining a docile nature, Beethoven dramatizes the courage of a woman whose conjugal devotion moves her to heroic action. In *Fidelio* it is the husband who is helpless—incarcerated in a Spanish prison for his liberal politics—and the wife, Leonore, who rescues him by infiltrating the prison disguised as a young man called Fidelio (a play on the Latin for fidelity). The prison setting could be a Piranesi etching come to life—dark, threatening, overshadowed by the tragedies of its forgotten inmates. The dungeon scene in which the prison governor prepares to murder his captive is the quintessence of the Romantic melodrama, an unparalleled thriller. And the final chorus of rejoicing remains a hallmark of the Romantic movement's espousal of personal freedom.

It is not Beethoven's French-inspired *Fidelio* that is the archetypical German Romantic opera, however. That distinction belongs to Carl Maria von Weber's *Der Freischütz*, the first and finest of Weber's three mature operas.

Like Beethoven and Mozart, Weber (1786–1826) was a virtuoso pianist; moreover, he was Mozart's cousin by marriage—Mozart had married Constanze Weber, much to the distress of his father, Leopold, who regarded the Webers as a raffish lot. Indeed, the "von" in Weber's name was a fraud, quietly inserted by Weber's father, an actor-manager and artist, who felt the baronial syllable would lend a touch of class to his enterprises. Carl Maria himself believed the "von" genuine, and went through life with an aristocratic air that compensated for his own liabilities—a limp resulting from a childhood mishap, and a speaking voice destroyed when he accidentally drank some etching acid his father had left in a wine decanter.

Der Freischütz is another serious singspiel—its title means "free shooter," or magic marksman, and refers to his use of *Freikugeln*, or magic bullets. Steeped in German folklore, the plot is as *alt-Deutsch* as a beer stein: In order to be eligible to marry Agathe, the huntsman Max needs to win a shooting match; however, he has lately been off his mark. A rival huntsman, who has sold his soul to the evil spirit Samiel, persuades Max to equip himself with a set of magic bullets from the same malevolent source. Soon Max is up to his ears in black magic that nearly costs Agathe her life.

Unlike *Fidelio*, which dramatizes a universal philosophy, and only nominally takes places in Spain (fandangos or other patches of local color would hardly suit the prison setting), *Der Freischütz* is specifically concerned with German folk life. It brims with hunters and forest horns, foaming tankards, jolly peasant dances, haunted glens at midnight, and other local touches that have endeared it to audiences since its premiere in 1821.

Yet Weber's masterpiece is more than just the operatic equivalent of a Black Forest cuckoo-clock: It is Weber's answer to the Gothic novel—to Horace Walpole's *Castle of Otranto* and Mary Shelley's *Frankenstein*. As in *Fidelio*, a life-and-death struggle takes place between good and evil. As in *The Magic Flute*, there are supernatural forces at play. But while Beethoven's evil character (the prison governor Pizarro) is purely human, and while Mozart's supernaturalism can hardly be called terrifying, Weber's opera deliberately plays up the qualities of true Gothic horror. The famous Wolf's Glen Scene, in which the magic bullets are cast to a chilling succession of disembodied voices and ghostly apparitions, was intended to be as hair-raising as a Stephen King novel is today. Even on recordings a good performance of Weber's score can send shivers down your spine because of the undiminished power of Weber's music to make that supernaturalism believable.

Der Freischütz represents a watershed in the development of German opera, as native composers continued to forge a distinctive style free of Italian influence. In part they accomplished this through their use of scenic and literary themes with a clear German identity: nature, supernaturalism, folk culture, medieval legend. Moreover, German composers strove to express increasing emotional and psychological depth in their characters—to make them more vivid, more believable, more human. The later singspiel tradition, with its essentially songlike musical texture and its spoken dialogue, is exemplified by such a tuneful, deservedly popular work as the Shakespeare-based *Die Lustigen Weiber von Windsor* (*The Merry Wives of Windsor*, 1849) by Otto Nicolai (1810–1849). Meanwhile, other composers sought to develop a more continuous dramatic texture, with lengthier, more sophisticated musical scene construction linked by true recitative instead of spoken dialogue.

Enter Richard Wagner.

Wagner Without Tears

Richard Wagner (1813–1883) was definitely an intellectual prodigy. As a boy, he translated twelve books of Homer's *Odyssey*; at fourteen, he wrote a bombastic and bloody Shakespearean tragedy. After hearing his first Beethoven symphony, he began what proved to be sporadic musical training. Yet by the time he entered Leipzig University in 1830, Wagner had composed a string quartet, a piano sonata, and an aria. Four years later he completed his first opera, *Die Feen* (The Fairies, based on one of the "fables" by the eighteenth-century Venetian Carlo Gozzi), which was never produced during his lifetime. In 1834 he became conductor of the Magdeburg Theater, where he composed the text and music of *Das Liebesverbot* (The Ban on Love, after Shakespeare's *Measure for Measure*). This was produced in 1836 by a troupe that went bankrupt, so Wagner lost money.

The exact contemporary of Italy's greatest nineteenth-century composer, Giuseppe Verdi, Richard Wagner was the most important opera reformer since Gluck. Not only did he alter the essential course of mid-nineteenth-century opera away from what he saw as empty show and intellectual shallowness; he changed its form, indeed, its name. Having begun writing German operas in the Weberian mold, his first great success, *Rienzi* (1842), based on a popular historical novel by Sir Edward Bulwer-Lytton, was modeled after Meyerbeer's French grand operas, with brilliant arias, powerful ensembles and choruses, ballets, and an overture that remains a wonderfully martial concert favorite.

With his next work, *Der Fliegende Holländer* (*The Flying Dutchman*, 1843), Wagner maintained a lyrical Italianate vocal line, but instead of taking a typical grand opera subject from history, he went to an old nautical legend of the Dutch sea captain cursed to sail the earth forever until redeemed by a woman's love, an intimate story with subtle psychological overtones that Wagner expressed in deep and often somber colors. The premiere stirred a controversy because of the revolutionary quality of the music and of the drama. What *was* so revolutionary about an opera founded on an old sea yarn?

Consider that in 1843, the opera world was dominated by the music of Rossini, Donizetti, and Meyerbeer. Verdi was at the start of his career. The musical language of opera was still fairly simple, and the length of scenes relatively short. Wagner's *Flying Dutchman* presented the audience with scenes of unprecedented length and development, and with a powerfully heavyweight musical utterance that had never been known before. His harmony was more adventuresome than anyone else's—what we now enjoy as rich and expressive was heard at the time as unnerving. Wagner's dark-hued orchestration was more complex and more subtle even than Meyerbeer's. And his melody was extremely moving—to some listeners disturbingly so. Moreover, audiences who viewed opera purely as entertainment were not prepared to accept an operatic hero whose chief motivation is his longing for death.

Yet despite his innovations, in *The Flying Dutchman* Wagner was still composing in an Italianate manner. And despite the length of his set pieces, he was writing an advanced form of bel canto, in which a slow *cantabile* movement was followed by a faster *cabaletta* to close the scene.

Tannhäuser (1845), about a minstrel torn between chivalric love for the noblewoman Elisabeth and profane desire for the goddess Venus, continued Wagner's foray into medieval legend. With *Lohengrin* (1850)—possibly the most ethereally beautiful of his Romantic operas—Wagner moved further away from "numbers" linked by recitative, the fundamental structure of opera since the mid-seventeenth century. He strove instead for increased musical continuity to express the drama of a woman whose too-human curiosity costs her the love of her mysterious hero.

In *Tristan und Isolde* (1865), founded on the medieval romance of Sir Tristram and his doomed passion for Queen Iseult (or Ysoude) of Ireland, it is not the musical scene but the entire act that forms a single continuous unit. Instead of separate "numbers" with orchestral introductions and full closes that usually signal applause from the audience, Wagner lets melodic, arialike passages rise where appropriate out of a continuous, symphonically developed orchestral and vocal texture, with the only full closes occurring at the end of the acts. "Endless melody" is the name he gave this style, and instead of "opera," his work from *Tristan* onward is usually termed "music drama."

In music drama, Wagner looked back to the ancient Greeks for his formal inspiration, just as the Florentine Camerata had done. Wagner had described his aim in his manifesto *The Artwork of the Future* (1849): It was to achieve a "complete work of art" (*Gesamtkunstwerk*), in which poetry, drama, music, song, and the visual arts would be wholly unified in a single, entirely novel kind of work. That unity was assured, for it flowed from one source; since the libretto was to be as important as the music, rather than a mere framework for music, Wagner wrote his own verse libretti.

Once he opened his own Festival Theater at Bayreuth, he was able to oversee every aspect of the finished work, from the sets and costumes to the conducting. The theater itself was of a revolutionary design when it first opened in 1876: Instead of a horseshoe of boxes, the Bayreuth auditorium was fan-shaped, with clear sightlines from every seat. The orchestra pit was covered to soften and blend the instrumental sound and to prevent the musicians' reading lamps from distracting the audience or interfering with the stage images. Moreover, at a time when opera was performed with the house lights up (which encouraged the tradition of talking and socializing during the music), the Bayreuth auditorium was darkened before the music began. Thus Wagner worked to ensure that everything would focus attention on the drama itself.

Music drama dispensed with opera's traditional emphasis on vocal display—cadenzas, embellishments, purely lyrical arias aimed at letting the singer shine. For Wagner, no singer could outshine the work itself. Indeed, Wagner placed unprecedented importance on the orchestra: whereas the opera orchestra traditionally accompanied the singers, Wagner's orchestra played an equal part in a complex polyphonic (many-voiced) whole. While the sung text conveyed the action taking place, the orchestra provided a commentary on the psychological underpinning of the events.

In *Der Ring des Nibelungen* (The Ring of the Nibelungs), Wagner also perfected his system of *leitmotifs* (leading motifs), a series of short, easily recognizable musical themes. Each leitmotif is significant of a character, object, idea, or situation in the drama, and played when that subject is referred to either directly or by implication. (Think of the film *Jaws*, where you know the shark is lurking when you hear the thumping soundtrack, though in Wagner's technique that motive would be sounded whenever the shark was merely mentioned.) More than just "signature tunes," the leitmotifs serve an important structural function, their repetition at significant moments helping to unify the vast expanses of Wagner's scores, much the way the repetition of themes unifies a symphonic movement. Equally important, as the drama progresses, the leitmotifs are developed, transformed, combined in counterpoint, and sounded in changing contexts to create a fascinating, narrative instrumental fabric that constantly reflects what the characters are doing, thinking, and recalling.

Wagner took a tremendously long time to create these extraordinary mature works—for example, he wrote his comedy *Die Meistersinger von Nürnberg* (The Mastersingers of Nuremberg) while he was at work on the *Ring* cycle, itself a labor of twenty years, and he completed his last music drama, *Parsifal*, in 1882, forty years after beginning research into the legend of the Holy Grail. But nothing could match the magnitude of Wagner's *Ring* tetralogy, in which four self-contained music dramas—*Das Rheingold* (The Rhine Gold, 1869), *Die Walküre* (The Valkyrie, 1870), *Siegfried* (1876), and *Götterdämmerung* (Twilight of the Gods, 1876)—relate the old Germanic saga of the theft of a hoard of magical gold at the bottom of the Rhine, the disastrous consequences of that theft to the gods of Valhalla and their descendants, and the establishment of a new world order. Nothing like it had ever been completed before, and nothing like it has been achieved since, though other composers have tried.

Wagner's influence was immense and far-reaching. Although lesser composers imitated his specific use of mythology and symbolism, his concept of music drama as a synthesis of all the arts—a serious work of art in which mere entertainment takes second place to the significance of dramatic purpose—affected the evolution of opera well into the twentieth century. Wagner's luxuriant, often blurred chromatic harmony fostered the eventual breakdown of classical tonality. From *Tristan* onward, the traditional idea that certain chords led unfailingly to other chords because of their relative importance within a specific tonality (or key, such as C-major or A-minor) was increasingly abandoned. Thus Wagner opened the way to the atonal writing of Arnold Schoenberg in the twentieth century, in which there is no one key central to a piece of music.

At the risk of oversimplification, many of Wagner's favorite literary themes were rooted in his own personal longings. For example, the figure of the outsider who is a mystery or an irritant to the rest of society—such as the Dutchman, Senta, Tannhäuser, and Lohengrin—is essentially Wagner himself: His revolutionary attitudes often put him at odds not only with the conventional world of opera production in his day but with the law. The purification of society through the upheaval of a corrupt old regime, a primary theme of the *Ring* cycle, is founded in Wagner's constant wish for a new social order in which social and professional rank would be based on actual merit, not birth. The theme also implied his longing for a society that would understand and support his grand artistic schemes.

Then there is his favorite idea, that of a man redeemed by the love of a woman, which forms the backbone of *The Flying Dutchman*, *Tannhäuser*, and *Tristan*, and is one of many interwoven themes of the *Ring*. This conceit had its roots in Wagner's rocky first marriage to an actress who had no insight into his artistic needs, and to his habit of forming relationships with other men's wives. First there was Mathilde Wesendonck, wife of one of his wealthy patrons, immortalized in his "Wesendonck Songs." Then he met Cosima Liszt von Bülow, daughter of Franz Liszt and wife of his ardent supporter, the eminent pianist and conductor Hans von Bülow. Their adultery became the talk of

Munich society, and ended when Cosima divorced her husband to marry Wagner. It is a sign of Wagner's personal magnetism that von Bülow actually forgave Wagner, and blamed himself for not being worthy of Cosima.

The question of whether love or might has the greater power to rule the world is a central theme of the *Ring*. In fact, even the comedy *Die Meistersinger* can be looked at as a study in the exercise of power over love: The respectable Herr Pogner, a pillar of Nürnberg society, is outwardly a loving father to his daughter Eva. Yet he is quite ready to give her in marriage to the winner of a song contest, regardless of her own feelings in the matter. Fortunately the contest is won by the man she loves. In the real world of Wagner's time, however, arranged marriages were still commonplace, and despite the nineteenth century's espousal of romantic love, the all-powerful *paterfamilias* still ruled the roost where his children's matrimony was concerned. Money and social standing spoke louder than feelings of the heart. To some degree, romantic operas filled an emotional void in many a household where duty substituted for passion.

Because Wagner's music dramas have so many implications, both deliberate and those added later by interpreters, and because works like the *Ring* and *Tristan* are so musically and dramatically complex, the best way to approach them for the first time is to forget the ancillaries. Simply treat them as the most wonderful adventure stories ever created for the opera house. Familiarize yourself with the plots, and let the music cast its spell. Once you have come to know Wagner's richness, you can delve increasingly further into the manifold layers of meaning and symbolism, if you wish.

Of Wagner's innumerable disciples and followers

who brought elements of music drama into the operatic milieu of every country, the two best-known figures are Engelbert Humperdinck (1854–1921) and Richard Strauss (1864–1949). Humperdinck, who had assisted Wagner at Bayreuth during the preparations for the premiere of *Parsifal*, mingled the symphonic and thematic complexities of the Wagner style with the tuneful quality of German folk song. But instead of tackling epic mythological themes, Humperdinck chose the simpler, more accessible realm of German fairy tale. The result, *Hänsel und Gretel*, is beloved throughout the world. Not only does it vividly express the simple directness of childlike imagination in the form of a music drama, but it miraculously appeals to children as well as to the most sophisticated adults.

The Once and Future Richard Strauss

The music of most great composers usually bespeaks a constant forward development of their chosen idiom (the later works of Verdi and Wagner, for example, show a tremendous advancement of technique over their earlier efforts). The career of Richard Strauss takes a somewhat different path: After starting at the avant garde, he became a notable conservative. He first secured his reputation as an iconoclast with a series of symphonic poems—large-scale, single-movement orchestral works illustrating philosophical and literary subjects. For instance, *Death and Transfiguration* (1889) and *Thus Spake Zarathustra* (1896) are relatively abstract treatments of ideas, the former tracing the progress of a soul from earthly suffering to heavenly deliverance, the latter using Friedrich Nietzsche's prose-poem on the doctrine of the Superman as a springboard for a dazzling musical commentary. Strauss's *Till Eulenspiegel's Merry Pranks* (1895) and *Don Quixote* (1897) were more obviously descriptive of actual deeds and characters.

Strauss's employment of massive orchestras and often "advanced" harmony offended conservative musicians and audiences. And he continued to pursue his iconoclastic path when he turned to opera, applying increasingly modern trends to the Wagnerian form of music drama, and quietly enjoying the uproar his works incited. His first mature opera, *Salome*, a lush, intoxicating setting of Oscar Wilde's one-act biblical drama, was declared immoral after its premiere in Dresden in 1905. The story is Wilde's hypothetical elaboration of the brief biblical episode surrounding the murder of St. John the Baptist. Admittedly the play itself was scandalous stuff when Wilde wrote it—in French—in 1891. Moreover, the fact that Wilde's very name was anathema following his imprisonment and exile for sodomy put his work beyond the pale in many quarters. Banned in England (not because it was risqué but because it broke an ancient law against depicting biblical characters on the stage), the play had first been produced in Paris in 1896, triumphantly so, while the author was still serving time in Reading Gaol. Its cast of characters—the neurotic King Herod of Judea, his bitter wife Herodias, and his nubile stepdaughter Salome—form the most decadently dysfunctional family since Lot and his incestuous daughters.

By setting Wilde's play to music, Strauss was characteristically ahead of his time, and the uproar he engendered only boosted his notoriety. At the North American premiere, at the Metropolitan Opera in 1907—a public dress rehearsal on a Sunday morning—Salome's "Dance of the Seven Veils" (which Wilde envisioned as a striptease ending in nudity) and her ecstatic lovemaking to the severed head of John the Baptist so scandalized the high society boxholders that J. P. Morgan, who then held the lease on the Metropolitan Opera House, forbade further performances (after the second, on Tuesday). Happily the opera is well entrenched there now, and is equally popular throughout the world.

Strauss's next opera, *Elektra* (1909), to a libretto based on Sophocles by Hugo von Hofmannsthal, was thought to be unendurably savage and dissonant—"Elektricution," in the words of one contemporary humorist. The story is certainly violent: Elektra's mother, Clytemnestra, having murdered her husband, now lives with a lover. Elektra seethes with hatred for Clytemnestra, who has put her under house arrest, where she deliberately lives in filth and degradation. Meanwhile Clytemnestra is insane with guilt over her crimes. Is it any wonder that these two women should express themselves in the harshest of music?

At the climax of the opera, however, Elektra meets Orestes, the long-lost brother for whose return she has prayed all her life. Strauss expresses Elektra's joy by switching into a romantic melodiousness positively erotic in its warmth and ardor. Orestes is her hero, come to avenge their father's murder. He is also the first man since her childhood to show her any compassion. Scholars are still unsure whether Hofmannsthal or Strauss had read Freud's writing at the time, but the music makes no bones about implying that Elektra's love for her brother is a little more than it seems to be.

Upon listening to a performance of *Elektra* when he was

an old man, Strauss is reputed to have exclaimed in astonishment that he himself could no longer understand how he came to create such a "difficult" score. "I went to the extreme limits of . . . what ears of today can accept," he wrote. Given all the musical developments that have occurred since then, our ears have become a lot more open to "advanced techniques," and nearly half a century after Strauss's death we accept with pleasure the opera's blend of explosion and lyricism.

Nonetheless, after *Elektra*, Strauss applied the brakes to his modernism, partly because he felt he had taken it as far as he wanted to, partly because he felt that having tackled two obsessed female characters in a row, he would invite criticism if he did so again. His next opera with Hofmannsthal, *Der Rosenkavalier* (The Knight of the Rose, 1911), is a delectable comedy of manners nostalgically set in the rococo Vienna of the empress Maria Theresa. With its waltzes and soaring love music, its arias, duets, and sublime trio in the last act, it is one of the most beloved of all operas.

Strauss continued to write operas well into old age, producing his last one, *Capriccio*, in 1942. Of the post-*Rosenkavalier* works, only two others are regularly staged: *Ariadne auf Naxos* (Ariadne on the Isle of Naxos, 1912; revised 1916), based on Molière's comedy *Le Bourgeois Gentilhomme* (The Bourgeois Gentleman), calls for relatively small forces along the lines of Mozart. Its prologue tells a "backstage" story of what happens when the richest man in Vienna engages both a comedy troupe and an opera company to impress his guests with lavish after-dinner entertainment, and then orders the two groups to perform simultaneously to save time. Thus the opera itself, which forms the second act, successfully combines mythological drama with opera buffa. The music is scintillating.

Die Frau ohne Schatten (The Woman Without a Shadow, 1919) is a complex psychological drama, part allegory, part fairy story, about a mythical empress's quest to achieve fertility. Strauss himself found it hard to grasp some of the elaborate symbolism in Hofmannsthal's libretto, and although the score contains some of his most ardent music, warm and intensely moving, the score as a whole can strike some listeners as cool and detached.

If *Elektra* and *Die Frau* are operas for Strauss connoisseurs, *Salome*, *Der Rosenkavalier*, and *Ariadne* are probably the three best introductions to Strauss's work. In any case, once you accustom yourself to his highly flavorful idiom, you'll understand why some people find it as addictive as chocolate. The secret to enjoying this exceptionally rewarding music is to understand that Strauss—whose idol was Mozart—never abandons the warm, essentially middle-class security of good old-fashioned melody and tonal harmony, no matter how far afield his musical adventurousness takes him. Even in *Elektra*, his most harmonically "modernist" opera, the expressive purpose of the dissonant music (very well, the noisier stuff) is balanced and emphasized by its contrast with the more traditionally beautiful music at the climax, much of it in waltz time.

The Roaring Twenties: Berg and Weill

While Strauss continued to compose in an idiom perfected in his comparative youth, German modernism had other exponents. Of these the two works most often encountered on the international scene are Alban Berg's *Wozzeck* and Kurt Weill's *Threepenny Opera*.

Berg (1885–1935) was a pupil of Arnold Schoenberg (1874–1951), the leading theorist of the abandonment of classical tonality. *Wozzeck* (1925) is based on an early-nineteenth-century drama, *Woyzeck*, by Georg Büchner (1813–1837), about a pitiably downtrodden Austrian soldier, helpless to defend himself against the officers who mistreat him, and cast off by his mistress, whom he ultimately murders. Berg had attended the Vienna premiere of this pessimistic drama in 1914, and was deeply affected by it, especially in light of his own military experiences. His opera, which he worked on between 1917 and 1922, caused a scandal at its premiere, and its notoriety led to numerous performances in Germany and Austria until the Nazis forced its withdrawal as "degenerate art" in 1933.

Admittedly, it requires a certain amount of musical understanding to appreciate the opera. *Wozzeck* is crafted in short scenes that follow the construction of the original play. Each act is written as a self-contained structure based on instrumental music rather than on traditional opera: Act II, for example, is a five-movement symphony, each of the movements comprising a scene. To be sure, Berg himself declared that the listener should not concentrate on the musical structures that underlie the drama, but on the drama itself.

The characters in *Wozzeck* often sing in a style called *Sprechgesang*—halfway between song and speech—while the musical idiom mingles the dissonances of Viennese Expressionism with elements of traditional composition: fugue, hunting song, lullaby, etc. Certainly before attending a performance of *Wozzeck* for the first time, you ought to familiarize yourself with it by listening to a recording and following along with a libretto.

Bitter, expressionistic, but more conventionally entertaining is *The Threepenny Opera* (*Die Dreigroschenoper*) by Kurt Weill (1900–1950). The son of a Jewish cantor, Weill became one of the preeminent composers of the Weimar Republic by the time he was twenty-five. Having begun writing modernist operas, he worked with the socialist playwright of interwar Germany, Bertolt Brecht, on a version of John Gay's classic English satire of opera seria and early Georgian morality, *The Beggar's Opera*, which had been revived in London with immense success in 1920. Their version (1928) updated the action and transplanted Gay's humorously unsavory cast of thieves and whores to the decadent underworld of 1920s Berlin. But where Gay had shot his barbs at the Georgian ruling class, Brecht and Weill took aim at postwar Europe's cautious, complacent middle class.

Weill firmly believed in cultural democracy and saw no difference between "light" music and "serious" music. Moreover, he was committed to writing for his own time. "The great 'classic' composers . . . wanted those who heard their music to understand it," he told an interviewer in 1940. "As for myself, I write for today. I don't give a damn about writing for posterity." Hence, in his own gritty way, Weill was able to write commercially successful works for the musical theater that still maintain the seriousness of purpose characteristic of art music. Because he did not write for traditional "opera singers," and because his music often has the sound of 1920s pop (e.g., the famous "Ballad of Mack the Knife"), *The Threepenny Opera* is often done in musical theater settings rather than opera houses.

Conversely, *Rise and Fall of the City of Mahagonny* (1930), is unquestionably a work for opera singers, and, one hopes, opera singers who can act. Another collaboration with Brecht, the story is an indictment of the decadent self-indulgence that the creators saw around them at the time, but that very much characterizes our own era as well. Mahagonny is a city founded on unrestrained material pleasure, where men are executed for not being able to pay their bar tab. Weill's score brims with catchy music hall songs (including the classic "Moon of Alabama") and rousing marches, all of them raucously underlining the ease with which we can destroy ourselves by giving in to the brutish side of our nature. Yet for all its tunefulness, *Mahagonny* sticks in your throat— and that's just what its authors intended.

Further Adventures in German Opera

Wagner, *Parsifal* (1882) Based on the medieval epic by Wolfram von Eschenbach, the plot of Wagner's last work revolves around the conflict between spiritually chaste Christianity and sinful heathenism. The purehearted fool Parsifal enters a knightly community, and his discovery of sexual temptation as well as the moral strength to resist it endow him with faith.

Aglow with religious symbolism, *Parsifal* is immense in scale, with considerable expanses of slow, spacious, deeply felt music. One of the supreme passages is the "Good Friday Spell" in the last act, during which Parsifal baptizes a tormented woman, and redeems her from the endless life to which she had been condemned for having mocked Christ on the Cross.

Berg, *Lulu* (1935, two-act version; 1974, three-act version)
Here's an opera that makes *Salome* look like *Alice in Wonderland*. The composer himself fashioned his libretto from two plays, *The Earth Spirit* and *Pandora's Box*, by the German dramatist Frank Wedekind (1864–1918). Both examine in lurid detail a society obsessed with sex and sensuality: Lulu, demonically beautiful, climbs the social ladder by means of a series of relationships, only to end up a prostitute murdered by Jack the Ripper. Like *Wozzeck*, the music is technically complex, and its beauty often eludes ears that are not yet attuned to Berg's highly individual idiom. However, the modernist techniques of the music yield to its dramatic expressivity, and you will most likely be swept away by your fascination with the characters and their incredible entanglements.

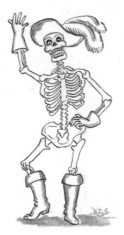

Interlude: Death, Be Not Loud

When listeners define opera as an art form "where everybody dies at the end," they aren't always joking.

Ironically, one of the cardinal principles of Italian opera seria of the seventeenth and eighteenth centuries was that no matter what difficulties faced the protagonists, there had to be a happy ending.

With the rise of Romantic opera, however, the pathos of death and its trappings became a focus of attention. It wasn't just that the nineteenth century was as obsessed with death as the late twentieth is with sex. It was that a good death scene is emotionally fulfilling. After all, wouldn't you feel let down if Romeo and Juliet lived? Or if Macbeth were simply hauled off in chains?

In Romantic opera, as in drama, death often resolves situations that would be otherwise improbable or unsatisfying from a dramatic point of view. For instance, suppose

Puccini's Mimì *did* recover from consumption at the end
of *La Bohème*. What kind of life could she expect as an un-
educated silk flower maker married to a poet—artistic
husbands aren't exactly known for being good providers.
Tragedy and death go happily hand in hand on the opera
stage, and by skimming the surface of the repertoire, you'll
discover that librettists—and the dramatists and novelists
who inspired them—have come up with a remarkable
variety of ways for their heroes and heroines to shake off
their mortal coils.

So, Mimì succumbs to tuberculosis, possibly the most
dreaded disease of the nineteenth century. Chopin died of
it—horribly so, slowly suffocating through the hot Parisian
summer of 1849. So did the younger Alexandre Dumas's
real-life lover Marie Duplessis, the courtesan after whom
he fashioned the doomed heroine of his novel and play, *La
Dame aux camélias*, the source of Verdi's *La Traviata*.
Violetta's death in the last act of the opera, with the rude
noise of Carnival revelers echoing outside her window,
went chillingly and emotionally to the hearts of many in the
audience, for they had probably lost more than one relation
to the same malady.

Admittedly, traditional opera romanticizes death and
disease—we see a representation rather than a repro-
duction. Ugliness must not compromise the original spirit
of the music. Yet while the lyric stage is no place for foren-
sics or intravenous tubes (though it's been tried), the
absence of complete naturalism doesn't mean that opera
lacks sincerity.

The three centuries during which the art form developed
have been as loaded as any with human folly and catastrophe—war, crime, plague. Call it euphemism, call it

platitude, when nineteenth-century audiences wept at opera's relatively sanitized representation of death, they understood that the harsh reality lurked just beneath the greasepaint. It was enough for Violetta to die in a tubercular swoon—Verdi's audience didn't need to see her spit blood, for they could see enough of that outside the opera house. In opera, visual understatement remains more effective than clinical reality. The music conveys the rest.

For all the emotional surge brought on by operatic representations of death by disease, death by misdeed is more in keeping with the lyric stage. Many a male character has met his end at the point of a sword, though often it is a secondary figure whose death spurs on the drama rather than concludes it. In Mozart's *Don Giovanni*, the Commendatore, father of Donna Anna, is killed by the Don's foil while attempting to save his daughter from rape. He returns at the end in the horrifying form of his own statue to drag the dissolute Don to Hell. Mercutio in Gounod's *Roméo et Juliette*, and Valentine, Marguerite's brother in the same composer's *Faust*, both lose their respective duels. In Tchaikovsky's *Eugene Onegin*, Onegin shoots his young friend Lensky in a session of pistols at dawn (preceded by one of the most beautiful of all tenor arias).

With the advent of verismo—opera's great leveler—the elegant duel of the old costume pieces degenerated into something more lurid. Turiddu, the licentious anti-hero of Mascagni's *Cavalleria Rusticana*, dies in a knife fight with Alfio, whose wife has been Turiddu's lover. Duels to the death are for men of honor, but for cuckolds and jilted lovers blinded by passionate rage, only a dagger will do. Hence Don José stabs Carmen when he can no longer stand her taunting rejection, while Canio, the wronged husband of Leoncavallo's *Pagliacci,* murders both his wife and her lover with a similarly impetuous blade. Nor are daggers only men's weapons, as Puccini's Floria Tosca shows when she does in the loathsome Scarpia with a bit of quick thinking and a sharp dinner knife.

Not so messy but equally fatal, poison is an especially good operatic way to dispatch someone because it theoretically allows the poisoned character to go on singing while the deadly potion slowly takes effect. Female characters often resort to this rather than allow themselves to sleep with the baritone: Ponchielli's Gioconda takes a dose to escape making love to the hated Barnaba, but sticks around just long enough to tease him into a lustful frenzy before expiring at his feet. Leonora (in Verdi's *Il Trovatore*) imbibes a similar nip after consenting to submit to Count di Luna in order to rescue her beloved Manrico. When she dies, the Count executes Manrico anyway, only to discover that he has just beheaded his long-lost brother.

There's no doubt that executions make for superb finales: Mario Cavaradossi *(Tosca)* dies before a firing squad (the bullets were supposed to be fake, but that's treachery for you). Verdi's Radamès *(Aida),* condemned to die for treason in ancient Egypt, is sealed into an airless tomb, where he breathes his last in the arms of his beloved Aida (who has secreted herself inside). Bellini's Druid priestess Norma, in atonement for breaking her vow of chastity, joins her Roman lover on a sacrificial pyre. Mention the French Revolution to an opera composer and you're sure to find the guillotine looming in the background; but while Giordano's historic poet, Andrea Chénier, goes to a stirring death that provides the operatic counterpart to the last chapter of *A Tale of Two Cities,* few executions can top the harrowing finale of Poulenc's *Dialogues of the Carmelites,* in which an entire community of nuns marches one by one to lose their heads to the Terror, the thud of the falling blade punctuating their *Salve Regina.*

Suicide comes in many forms on the opera stage. The most famous, and probably most shattering, is that of Madam Butterfly, who ceremoniously uses her father's ritual sword while her blindfolded young son plays nearby with a little American flag she has given him. Wagner's Senta flings herself into the sea to prove her devotion to the Flying Dutchman and thereby break the curse that has kept him wandering the globe for centuries. Both grieving for their lost women, Edgardo (Donizetti's *Lucia di Lammermoor*) and Verdi's Otello stab themselves before anyone can stop them. Verdi's chivalrous outlaw Ernani takes an oath to commit suicide when he hears Don Ruy de Silva blow his hunting horn: With malicious timing, Silva calls in his pledge at Ernani's wedding!

Puccini's Tosca chooses a more spectacular end, flinging herself into the Tiber from the ramparts of Rome's Castel Sant' Angelo. When the composer pointed out to Victorien Sardou, author of the original play, that the Tiber is too far from the Castel to make such a jump feasible, Sardou told him not to quibble. He was right. When Tosca jumps in a burst of melody, no one really worries whether she lands on water, pavement, or a backstage pile of mattresses.

On a more superhuman level, Wagner's Brünnhilde (*Götterdämmerung*) heroically rides her horse onto Siegfried's funeral pyre, bringing the power of the old gods, and the entire *Ring of the Nibelungs* to an end. And, of course, Saint-Saëns's biblical hero Samson plunges architects into cold sweats when he pulls the heathen temple down on the

Philistine horde, sacrificing his life to pay for his dalliance with Dalila—not to mention paying her back for the awful haircut.

Finally there are the mystical deaths that provide a popular conclusion for many an opera. (Medical examiners would only confuse the issue.) Wagnerian heroines often take this path to the infinite beyond, as in Isolde's Love-Death, Elsa's mortal swoon when Lohengrin leaves her after a pretty awful wedding night, and Kundry's Good Friday release when Parsifal restores the Holy Grail to its temple.

Gounod's perennial, *Faust*, has been critically out of fashion (though not out of public favor) for some time. But in its heyday it offered at least four generations one of the most popular of all mystical deaths. Condemned for drowning the baby she had with Faust, and driven mad by grief and fear, Marguerite is visited in her cell by Faust and the devil, Méphistophélès, who promise to rescue her if she'll join them in the Underworld. She comes to her senses, however, and calls on Heaven to help her. Heaven does so, in high Victorian style. To a resounding choir of angels, organ, and brass fanfares, she ascends to her reward while Faust is left cringing below. If you are in a receptive mood (and if the production is sympathetic and intelligent), they'll have to carry you out in a bucket when it's over.

Interlude: Sheer Madness!

From Shakespeare to Cole Porter, poets, playwrights, and musicians have acknowledged the close relationship between love and madness. Indeed, the numerous allusions throughout literature to "midsummer madness" refer to the traditions surrounding Midsummer Eve, June 23, a night when those in and out of love were believed to be at the mercy of fairy tricks and amorous fantasies.

Opera, like spoken drama, is often concerned with the madness of love. To the opera composer, the irrational behavior symptomatic of mental derangement, the abnormal stream of thought, the visions and hallucinations offer myriad opportunities to employ an intensity of language and music that would be considered inappropriate in another dramatic context. From the singer's point of view, the depiction of madness is not just a cue to chew a bit of scenery, but frequently to set the audience on its ears with elaborate vocal ornamentation. Hence, almost as soon as there was opera there were mad scenes—and not just in rehearsals.

Audiences in the Baroque period craved exceptional characters in fantastic situations, and Baroque opera is filled with hissing witches and ranting sorcerers, whose behavior would immediately label them as off-center in real life. But there is a difference between the rage of an angry witch and the raving of a maniac: The true mad scene offers a dramatic twist on eccentricity, because the maddened protagonist is the victim rather than the perpetrator of madness. And where the witch or sorcerer most often flies off in defeat at the end of an opera, ready to wreak havoc another day, the pitiable character in a mad scene is often on the way to greater tragedy, especially in a Romantic opera.

The earliest mad scenes occur in seventeenth-century Venetian opera. Francesco Cavalli became a master of mad scenes, such as those in his *Egisto* (1643), in which Egisto goes mad with despair when he discovers that his beloved Clori, captured by pirates, has fallen in love with another captive. In Cavalli's partly historical comedy *Xerse* (1655), King Xerxes of Persia flies into passing madness when his orders to execute his rival Arsamene are confused, and instead Arsamene is married off to Romilda, Xerxes' intended bride.

Meanwhile, in Restoration England, where Italian opera had yet to make significant inroads, Shakespeare had nonetheless prepared the way in *Hamlet* with the plaintive folk ditties Ophelia sings as she dallies beside the fatal stream. Instead of operatic mad scenes, there was a great vogue for "mad songs," self-contained ballads that related the wild delusions of men and women whose sad condition was usually the result of unhappiness in love. Henry Purcell's "Bess of Bedlam" and John Eccles's "Love's but the frailty of the mind" are two self-explanatory examples of these pithy and often very affecting vignettes. To be sure, the fascination with madness that yielded such haunting and often troubling songs was rooted in a rather callous society that also regarded the mentally ill as objects of derision; many a seventeenth-century Londoner thought it fashionable to drop in at Bethlehem Hospital (Bedlam) from time to time to mock the antics of the inmates.

Mad scenes maintained their popularity in eighteenth-century opera seria. In Handel's *Orlando* (1733)—one of many operas based on Ludovico Ariosto's sixteenth-century epic poem, *Orlando Furioso* (Mad Roland)—the titular hero's madness manifests itself in a terrifying vision of Hell. Handel suggests Orlando's mental unbalance by writing his music in what is possibly the earliest use of quintuple meter (five beats to a bar instead of the usual four or three, lending an unstable feeling). The eighteenth-century musical commentator Charles Burney declared that such a meter would have been intolerable if sung by a sane character.

In nineteenth-century Romantic opera, the mad scene became something of a dramatic cliché. Audiences could tell they were in for vocal fireworks if the soprano appeared onstage dressed in a nightgown with long, uncombed hair and a vacant expression. Donizetti and Bellini were masters at such mad music, with the Mad Scene in Donizetti's *Lucia di Lammermoor* the most famous of them all: Having killed the new husband she has been forced to marry, Lucia appears before her wedding guests in a white shift stained with blood. Donizetti graphically suggests Lucia's confused state in the introductory recitative, where the accompaniment flits through altered fragments of significant themes heard earlier in the opera, until she dwells on the broad theme of her Act I love duet in which she swore fidelity to Edgardo. As the scene unfolds, Lucia imagines that she and Edgardo are being married, while the horrified guests listen to her description of the ceremony enacted in her broken mind.

Throughout this scene Donizetti achieves a perfect balance of vocal fireworks and extremely plaintive melody to create a truly dramatic statement rather than a mere showpiece. A solo flute (called the flute *obbligato*) plays in close relationship with the singer; its airy, disembodied timbre not only complements the high female voice, but suggests an unhinged mind afloat on the crosscurrents of irrational thoughts and emotions.

In addition to *Lucia*, Donizetti wrote mad scenes in several other operas, of which *Linda di Chamounix* (1842) was among the most popular. Here the heroine, a farmer's daughter living the high life in Paris, loses her mind when she hears that the painter whom she loves (and who has been paying the bills without demanding any hanky-panky in return) is to marry another woman. In the end, he restores her reason by singing his love theme from their Act I duet. Recovered, she accepts his proposal of marriage.

Another case of temporary insanity is demonstrated by Elvira in Bellini's *I Puritani*, who loses her mind when she is abandoned at the altar on her wedding day. As soon as the tenor, Arturo, returns in the second act, Elvira snaps out of it, and the opera ends happily.

Shakespeare provided major composers with two mad

scenes of particular substance. For Ophelia in his *Hamlet*, Ambroise Thomas not only wrote showy music but implied the wandering mind of his poor maiden by chromatic shifts through a tricky series of changing keys.

In the Sleepwalking Scene in Verdi's *Macbeth*, a vivid dream produced by guilt-ridden torment has brought Lady Macbeth to the point of madness. Verdi's nightgown-clad soprano is a dramatic one rather than a coloratura, trying desperately to wash the fancied bloodstains off her hands. Instead of vocal fireworks, Verdi captured this Scotswoman's tormented mind by writing brief declamatory phrases that expand at important moments into broad *cantabile* melody. Interestingly, Verdi wanted to get as far away as possible from the idea of madness as a vocal show. During rehearsals of a production of the opera in 1848, he wrote to a colleague of his dismay over the casting of a soprano whose voice and appearance he felt too beautiful for the role: "I want Lady Macbeth to be ugly and evil," he declared. ". . . I want Lady Macbeth's [voice] to be diabolic. . . ."

How different the intentions of his predecessor, Bellini, who strove for complete picturesqueness in the Sleepwalking Scene that forms the climax of his *La Sonnambula* (The Somnambulist). Like Lady Macbeth, Bellini's Adina is not mad but only sleeping; however, the tension is heightened by the fact that she sleepwalks over a rickety bridge, while her fiancé and the other villagers watch in terror. This note of suspense adds a dramatic sharpness to the sweet purity of her aria, "Ah! non credea mirarti."

By the late nineteenth century the operatic mad scene was an obvious target for parody, and at London's Savoy Theatre, Gilbert and Sullivan spoofed the genre in their operetta *Ruddigore* (1887). In Act I, Mad Margaret appears in "picturesque tatters," with bits of milkweed stuck in her windblown hair, "an obvious caricature of theatrical madness," in Gilbert's own stage directions. She reveals, however, that her outward madness actually conceals her lonely heart—shades of the Restoration mad song.

Operatic madness isn't limited to high-flying sopranos. At the opposite end of the vocal spectrum, Verdi wrote a powerful set of baritone mad scenes for the title role of his first great success, *Nabucco*, in which the all-powerful King of Babylonia is struck down by a thunderbolt after he declares himself a god. In this case it isn't florid vocal writing, but an almost whispered melodic line that imparts the sense of wild-eyed abandon and pathos to the portrayal of fallen might.

Even more powerful is the chilling scene in Mussorgsky's *Boris Godunov* wherein the guilt-ridden Tsar Boris, alone in his Kremlin study, succumbs to visions of the dead Tsarevich Dmitri, whom he is suspected of having murdered. A clock chimes the hour—suggested with diabolical persuasiveness by the orchestra—and with each stroke, Boris collapses further into a state of frigid horror as the bloodied features of the dead boy haunt him.

Stark depictions of madness become increasingly common in early-twentieth-century opera, especially as the study of psychology raised interest and understanding in the variety of forms derangement could take. In Richard Strauss's *Salome*, the beautiful princess's murderous obsession with John the Baptist is hardly your ordinary teenage crush, and her ecstatic soliloquy with the Baptist's severed head raised the traditional mad scene to new heights of abnormality.

Twentieth-century opera has also provided the repertoire with some eloquent mad scenes for tenors. At the end of Stravinsky's *The Rake's Progress*, the downwardly mobile Tom Rakewell is left insane after gambling successfully for his soul with the devil. Locked up in Bedlam, he imagines he is Adonis; after his beloved Anne Truelove takes her leave of him for the last time, he sings a lament, "Mourn for Adonis," as he apparently dies of grief.

But Benjamin Britten contributed what are possibly the two greatest tenor mad scenes. Near the end of *Peter Grimes*, the lonely fisherman Peter stands by his boat. Crazed by the death of yet another of his apprentices, and the fear of the villagers who are hunting him down, Peter repeatedly babbles his own name in imitation of the chanting mob, and his mind remains clouded until his friend Captain Balstrode takes him in hand and firmly tells him that his only escape is to drown himself at sea.

In Britten's church parable, *Curlew River*, a madwoman—written for tenor—is desperately seeking her kidnapped child. She weeps at hearing the tale of a boy whom the villagers cared for after he was abandoned by a heathen warrior. The child died, and is regarded as a saint by the locals. Realizing by her pitiful reaction to the story that the woman is the child's mother, the villagers bring her to his burial site. There, she prays for him. His spirit appears, and delivers her from her madness before returning to his grave with the words, "Go your way in peace, mother." It is a moment of transcendent tenderness.

Russian Opera: East Meets West

Once an amateur succeeds in composing a single song ... he considers himself a composer ... goes on composing songs without noticing that they are all repetitions of the same melody ... and will end by composing an opera.

—ANTON RUBINSTEIN

To many people, Russia means the Bolshoi Ballet and balalaikas. To others, it represents one of the most exotic of all opera categories.

How would we get through a morning rush hour without the overture to Glinka's *Ruslan and Ludmilla* or the March from Prokofiev's *Love for Three Oranges*? And how would we make it home again without at least one dose of

Polovtsian Dances from Borodin's *Prince Igor*, the "Song of India" from Rimsky-Korsakov's *Sadko*, or the Waltz from Tchaikovsky's *Eugene Onegin*?

We know, of course, that the hot-blooded art of opera first sprouted in the warmth of sunny Italy. But whether or not climate was responsible, opera took a remarkably long time to take root in the land of endless winter.

The first obstacle to its progress was the overwhelming size of the Northern Colossus, with the resulting vast distances between its major cities. Until the development of railways, distance played an enormous part in separating Russia from the rest of Europe. St. Petersburg is over a thousand miles from Berlin and Vienna, the two main political and artistic capitals of Central Europe, which meant a week or more travel time by horse and coach. Even in the late nineteenth century the fastest trains took almost two days to make the journey, and longer from points like Paris, Milan, and Rome. Russia's isolation was cultural as well. The Victorian diplomat Lord Frederick Hamilton, who had spent considerable time in tsarist St. Petersburg, observed that "to grasp the Russian mentality, it must be remembered that ... Russia is not the most Eastern outpost of Western civilization; it is the most Western outpost of the East."

Nonetheless, Tsar Peter the Great (reigned 1682–1725) opened Russia to the West, and was determined to bring his country into line with Western developments. Yet for all his zeal to import Western art and architecture, Peter seems to have been relatively uninterested in contemporary Western music. So, while there were musical plays and other such entertainments in Peter's Russia, opera had to wait.

It arrived at last thanks to Peter's brooding niece, Empress Anna Ivanovna, whose generally undistinguished reign (1730–40) was at least momentarily brightened by the first visit to Russia of an Italian opera troupe in 1731. Anna's successor was Peter's illegitimate daughter, the vivacious Empress Elisabeth (reigned 1741–61), who spoke French from childhood, and loved Italy with a passion. Under her patronage, the first Russian-language opera was performed in 1755. However, although *Cephalus and Procris* (or, to give its Russian title, *Tsefal i Prokris*) was *sung* in Russian, it was in every other way a straightforward Italian opera seria derived from familiar Greek mythology.

Italian opera, French opéra comique, and even English ballad opera flourished in Russia during the long and brilliant reign (1762–96) of Empress Catherine the Great. A transplanted German princess, she not only encouraged major foreign composers to undertake extended residences in Russia but also wrote several opera librettos herself, usually with political underpinnings—Great Kate was nobody's fool.

From the Middle Ages on, Russia's Orthodox Church boasted a distinctive brand of devotional music: incredibly haunting unaccompanied choral music, with its minor modes, rumbling bass lines, and wailing tenors. Moreover, with Empress Catherine's blessing, operas on Russian subjects, with Russian texts and increasing amounts of folksy, nationalistic-sounding music, were written. Nevertheless, Russian opera did not gain a true Russian musical identity until the extraordinarily successful premiere of Mikhail Glinka's *A Life for the Tsar* in 1836.

Glinka: Father of It All

Mikhail Glinka (1804–1857) had lived in Italy for three years before returning home fired up to write a genuinely Russian opera. He took to the seventeenth-century story of Ivan Susanin, the heroic peasant who sacrificed his own life to save the new tsar, Mikhail Romanov, from warring Polish troops. Glinka had originally named his opera after its hero, but the stir caused by the rehearsals led Tsar Nikolai I himself to suggest the new and obviously flattering title.

Although it is strongly influenced by French grand opera and Italian bel canto, *A Life for the Tsar* is regarded as the bedrock of Russian opera for several reasons. Not only did Glinka base it on an episode from national history, he also incorporated authentic elements of Russian music into his score—balalaika timbres in the orchestra, melodic turns based on Russian folk tunes, choral movements that evoke the textures of peasant choirs. Most important, Glinka infused his recitative with a strong Russian color by paying close attention to the inflections of the Russian language. Indeed, in composing this first Russian opera without spoken dialogue, Glinka hit upon a particularly melodic kind of recitative that was to influence later Russian composers like Mussorgsky and Tchaikovsky.

For his second opera Glinka turned to a magical adventure, *Ruslan and Ludmilla*, by Alexander Pushkin, one of Russia's supreme Romantic authors. The story seemed tailor-made for an opera: To rescue his beloved princess Ludmilla, the doughty warrior Ruslan conquers wicked magicians, a love-starved witch, a gigantic talking head, and finally, an immensely powerful dwarf. Glinka had hoped to collaborate with Pushkin himself on the opera, but as luck would have it, Pushkin was killed in a notorious duel. So Glinka had to rely on a succession of amateur writers to clap together a libretto; the resultant drama-by-committee was equivalent to a painting-by-numbers. To make matters worse, Glinka was an incredibly disorganized worker who started writing the music before he had even received any text. He composed his score willy-nilly over a span of five years, and when *Ruslan* finally premiered in 1842, it was generally considered a dramatic mess.

Thereafter, *Ruslan* managed to cling to the repertoire in Russia, but in the West only the marvelously energetic overture became a concert staple. Interestingly, recent productions of *Ruslan* by the Kirov Opera in St. Petersburg and the San Francisco Opera have made a convincing case for its opulent, primal colors and its rough-hewn dramatic quality as anticipating the kind of highly seasoned fantasy operas that the next generation of Russian composers would make a specialty.

Fundamentally self-taught, Glinka tended to compose by the seat of his pants, yet his freedom from academic conventions—indeed, his ignorance of them—endowed him with a vigorous naïveté, a willingness to experiment, to go out on a limb and create music that to our ears is imaginative, colorful, and often extremely beautiful. Ironically, Glinka's example inspired the two camps of composers that were at loggerheads during the second half of the century.

Essentially, the debate was carried on between the "Slavophile" proponents of Russian musical nationalism, and the academically, sometimes foreign-trained "Westernizers." The latter group saw themselves as no less Russian in spirit, but they aimed not to establish a distinctly Russian nationalist school so much as to develop a sophisticated musical life equivalent to that which flourished in Germany, France, and Italy. Moreover, in their compositions they strove to match the technical polish of Western European music, thus carrying on the cosmopolitan tradition of Peter the Great.

In the Slavophile camp was a circle of part-time composers known as the *moguchaya kuchka* (the mighty handful) or the Russian Five: Mily Balakirev, a railway freight agent who organized the group, and was its only professionally trained member; Nikolai Rimsky-Korsakov, a naval officer; Modest Mussorgsky, a government drudge; Alexander Borodin, one of Russia's leading chemists; and an army engineer named César Cui (rhymes with "Louie"). On the Westernizer front the leading figures were Anton Rubinstein, founder of the state-supported Imperial Conservatory at St. Petersburg, and his most important pupil, Piotr Ilych Tchaikovsky.

To be sure, the German-trained Rubinstein (1829–1894), probably the greatest pianist of his time next to Franz Liszt, was an indefatigable composer of concertos, symphonies, chamber music, some really beautiful songs, and the once-ubiquitous "Melody in F." But of his nineteen operas only one managed to achieve lasting success in Russia, and marginal success elsewhere: *The Demon* (1875), about a fallen angel who pursues the beautiful Tamara to a convent in the hope that she will love him and thus redeem him. She doesn't. Rarely performed in the West, *The Demon* was recently revived, and the resultant live recording (on Marco Polo) provides a splendid opportunity to draw your own conclusions about Rubinstein's score, its Gothic darkness illuminated by splashes of Oriental color.

The Mighty Kuchka

Of the Mighty Handful, Mussorgsky, Rimsky, and
Borodin are the most important to opera audiences.
Balakirev, an extraordinary character who collected ene-
mies like butterflies, wrote magnificent piano music but
no operas, and Cui's ten operas are ignored even in his
homeland.

Modest Mussorgsky (1839–1881), an untidy bear of a man,
possessed one of the keenest dramatic minds of the century.
Like Glinka, he was primarily self-taught. Human speech
was his passion, and he strove to capture its inflections and
its infinite shades of meaning in vocal lines that avoided
conventional tunefulness. Yet the result is often profoundly
melodic and wonderfully expressive: In Mussorgsky's songs
we hear the authentic voices of Russian people of all ages—
from children and their nannies to rural peasantry and the
urban down-and-out, in moods that range from comical to
grotesque to tragic.

Unfortunately, reversals in his family's income forced
Mussorgsky to work part time in the civil service, which
depressed him, and eventually drove him to drink. Worse,
his shambling lifestyle often undercut his creativity. He
embarked repeatedly upon ambitous opera projects, only to
leave all but one of them incomplete. However, that single
work, *Boris Godunov,* is a masterpiece from any angle.

Mussorgsky based his opera partly on history and partly
on Pushkin's historical drama of the notorious tsar who
was suspected of murdering the rightful heir to the throne
in order to usurp it. In fact, Tsar Boris (reigned 1598–1605)
was a strong, able leader whose power was undermined by

famine and by a popular uprising engendered by a young imposter—the "False Dmitri" who, with Polish backing, marched on Moscow claiming to be the dead heir. Though Mussorgsky's opera assumes that Boris was responsible for the murder, Boris is portrayed as a ruler who has accepted the crown with great foreboding. In the second act we see him first as a loving father, aware of the responsibilities of power, but tormented by creeping guilt. When he learns of the existence of the pretender who calls himself the resurrected Dmitri, Boris starts to crumble. During the Clock Scene, one of the most graphic psychological sketches in the whole of nineteenth-century music, the ticking and chiming of a clock in Boris's study conjures up horrible visions of the dead prince, until Boris collapses in terror.

In *Boris Godunov*, the story of a tsar becomes an episode in the greater story of a tragic nation. Boris is not the chief figure of the opera, for opposite him Mussorgsky has ranged the relentless mass of the Russian people. It is the people who are forced by police to persuade Boris to accept the throne, the people who acclaim Boris in the great Coronation Scene, and the people who rally around the false Dmitri after Boris's death. Even when they are not onstage, the people make their presence felt, like an unshakable force of destiny. And while they march inexorably forward at the end of the opera, a solitary Idiot sadly—and chillingly—prophesies the coming time of troubles, troubles that were to grip the Russian people to the present day.

Mussorgsky wrote music of extraordinary power and originality—his orchestration often sounds strangely lean, his harmony often stark and modernistic compared to most music of his time. Though the opera was an audience success at its premiere in 1874, the critics thought otherwise, and their hostile reviews plunged the composer into the severe alcoholism that was to kill him at forty-two.

Fearing that *Boris Godunov* would be shelved because of its strangeness, the efficient and technically proficient Rimsky-Korsakov undertook a complete revision of Mussorgsky's score in 1896. In his effort to bring it in line with the operatic conventions of his time, Rimsky "corrected" the harmony and filled out the orchestration. To turn the opera into a more straightforward story about Boris himself, Rimsky cut material out and changed the order of the scenes, so that the opera would end with Boris's death. Nowadays it is fashionable to sneer at Rimsky's "tampering," while forgetting that Rimsky did in fact accomplish what he set out to do: His version not only kept *Boris Godunov* alive in Russia but helped make it a standard part of the international repertoire. Rimsky himself understood that *Boris* was never intended to be a conventional nineteenth-century opera, and that his editorial labors were only temporary measures for a work that was ahead of its time. As he himself had foreseen, his edition has now been superseded by Mussorgsky's original version in the major opera centers.

Nikolai Rimsky-Korsakov (1844–1908) overflowed with that industrious zeal to refine and polish that was characteristic of the nineteenth century. Moreover, he had a positive compulsion to complete other people's unfinished business. As his Russian colleagues often left plenty unfinished, Rimsky continually had a full plate. In addition to composing sixteen operas, symphonic music (including his most famous work, the tone poem *Scheherazade*), and teaching (Igor Stravinsky was his last and most important pupil), Rimsky held down a naval career, and later a post as Inspector of Russian Naval Bands.

In his approach to opera, musical considerations were more important to Rimsky than dramatic ones, and as an avid collector of Russian folk melodies he was so deeply inspired by the national style that it is often difficult to discern his own melodic invention in the folk style from indigenous folk material he had picked up in the course of his research. Rimsky excelled at vast fairy-tale epics as colorful as an Oriental carpet, and most often wonderfully melodic. *Sadko* (1898) is a perfect example.

Based on an eleventh-century epic, *Sadko* relates the amazing tale of the poor Novgorod minstrel Sadko. When Sadko leaves his wife for a life of adventure after falling in love with Princess Volkhova, daughter of the Sea King, his subsequent adventures take him to foreign lands and even to the sea floor. Ultimately Sadko is deposited on dry land, Volkhova is turned into a river, and—the greatest miracle of all—Sadko's abandoned wife takes him back again, no questions asked! The score is full of gorgeous numbers, the most famous of which is the Song of the Indian Merchant, even more familiar as the "Song of India."

For the tragic *Snegurochka* (The Snow Maiden, 1882), Rimsky adapted his own libretto from a dramatization of the well-known fairy tale of the Snow Maiden who learns the meaning of love, only to melt when a ray of sun strikes her just before her wedding. The characters in this pagan story flit between the spirit and human worlds; to dramatize them, Rimsky composed music in which authentic folk tunes and original melodies are seamlessly interwoven upon an orchestral tapestry of incredibly dazzling instrumental color.

Alexander Borodin (1833–1887) Many listeners often discover the music of Borodin through the classic Broadway musical, *Kismet* (1953), a pastiche of Borodin melodies. And it doesn't detract from the Arabian Nights glories of *Kismet* to note that the melodies are even finer as Borodin wrote them, more subtle and better developed. For instance, those who don't already know the source of "And this is my beloved" are in for a surprise when they hear it as the gentle slow movement of Borodin's String Quartet No. 2, while "Stranger in Paradise" has a host of additional colors in its original form as the Dance of the Polovtsian Maidens in the opera *Prince Igor*.

Like Mussorgsky, Borodin was an amateur musician. An internationally recognized scientist, he composed in his spare time, not that he had much of it. The fact that Borodin was a self-styled "Sunday composer," learning as he went, had a lot to do with his snail's pace—he took five years to complete his First Symphony.

In our own age of intensive professional specialization, we can marvel at a major scientist not only having the energy to pursue composition as a hobby but receiving international recognition for doing so. And despite certain technical flaws, Borodin's best works are among the finest produced by the Five: especially the two string quartets, the two symphonies, and that shaggiest of dogs, *Prince Igor*, on which he worked sporadically for eighteen years.

Borodin had taken his subject from the medieval epic of Prince Igor of Seversk, who tries to show his strength by waging war on the Polovtsi, a fierce tribe of Turkish nomads who frequently attacked what is now the modern Ukraine. In battle Igor's troops are virtually wiped out, and Igor is captured by the enemy, whose leader, Khan Konchak, treats him lavishly, even organizing an entertainment—the Polovtsian Dances—to banish Igor's depression. In the end, Prince Igor escapes and is reunited with his overjoyed wife.

At his death Borodin left *Prince Igor* in a sorry state. Because he wrote his own libretto, and worked on the text along with the music, even that element was never finished. Rimsky to the rescue again, this time with his pupil, the young Alexander Glazunov (composer of the popular ballet *The Seasons*). They toiled for months, shaping the welter of fully orchestrated numbers and sketchy fragments into a cohesive whole.

Prince Igor was finally premiered at St. Petersburg in 1890. To appreciate it best, we have to indulge the composer's theatrical naïveté, and luxuriate completely in the music. Borodin was not interested in a strong dramatic narrative, but rather in creating a magnificent tissue of evocative color. Not for him the stark realism or detailed character development of a Mussorgsky. "I am a melodist and symphonist by nature," he declared.

For Borodin, lyricism was paramount in opera, and his lyricism, so richly imbued with Eastern flavor, evokes a Russian never-never land of eternal springtime, of strawberries growing on peasant rooftops, and of lavish Tartar pleasure domes lined with Oriental rugs. To listen to this music is to understand the romantic Russian spirit that never quite throws off the wonderment of childhood. Like Rimsky's operas, *Prince Igor* represents the musical counterpart to the folk-inspired "pan-Slavic" style in nineteenth-century Russian decorative arts, which yielded the fantastically beautiful enameled silver tea services and punch bowls that now command such astronomical prices at Christie's and Sotheby's. Working with melodies the way the tsar's jeweler Karl Fabergé worked with precious metals and gemstones, Alexander Borodin produced an antiquarian fairy tale based on primitive motifs, but exquisitely fashioned with a modern hand.

Tchaikovsky: French Wine in Russian Bottles

Faced off against the Mighty *Kuchka*, militant and outspoken in their Russian nationalist cause, was the elegant, genteel, and desperately neurotic Piotr Ilych Tchaikovsky (1840–1893). Where Mussorgsky looked like a sleepless dipsomaniac conjured up by Dostoyevsky, Tchaikovsky presented to the world the well-groomed appearance of a diplomat. But under his neatly cropped beard and well-tailored clothes he was a quivering mass of insecurity and self-loathing. Devoted to his mother, who died when he was an impressionable fourteen, Tchaikovsky developed into a classic closet case, forced to deal with his homosexuality in one of the most cruelly intolerant of all nineteenth-century societies. His brief marriage to one of his pupils at the Moscow Conservatory was a disaster. Apart from his beloved sister, his only other intimate relationship with a woman was with a wealthy, reclusive widow, Nadezhda von Meck, his patroness for almost fourteen years. Yet they carried on their relationship entirely by letter, and even when they were both residing in Moscow or vacationing in Florence, they never met. Though Tchaikovsky confided his sexuality openly to his brother Modest (who was also gay), the pressure of his longings eventually proved too great to endure, and despite conflicting details that his biographers have yet to sort out, Tchaikovsky almost certainly committed suicide.

Most audiences are familiar with Tchaikovsky's symphonies, his celebratory "1812" Overture (which even the composer himself deemed bombastic), and certainly with his ballets—*Swan Lake*, *Sleeping Beauty*, and *The Nutcracker*. Yet almost from the start of his career, his chosen field was opera. Tchaikovsky, whose favorite non-Russian operas were Mozart's *Don Giovanni* and Bizet's *Carmen*, eventually completed nine operas, two of which are international standards, *Eugene Onegin* and *The Queen of Spades*, both based on Pushkin stories.

In *Onegin* (1879), the shallow young title character attracts the love of Tatyana, but he condescendingly dismisses her declaration as immature. Some years later he meets Tatyana again, at a grand ball given by her elderly husband, Prince Gremin. Now smitten by her elegant beauty, he frantically proposes that she run away with him. This time, however, it is Tatyana who refuses. Reminding him of his past cruelty, she admits that she still loves him, but that he has missed the boat. She orders him to go, as the curtain falls on his misery.

A number of Pushkin's themes appealed to Tchaikovsky here, especially the contrast between the simplicity of bourgeois country life and the empty decadence of high society, and the emotional pain that results when these two worlds collide. Moreover, the opera is rich in character studies subtly underscored by Tchaikovsky's music: Tatyana develops from a naive teenager into a self-assured but unhappy woman. The Letter Scene, during which she spends a sleepless night examining her feelings while writing to Onegin, is one of the greatest soliloquies in the whole opera repertoire. The country squire Lensky, who acts as the catalyst in the futile relationship between Tatyana and Onegin, is at first a fairly ordinary young swain; however, his aria before the duel with Onegin in Act II strikes a level of profound anguish uncommonly vivid even by Tchaikovsky's own emotive standards. Finally Onegin's cool façade of posh sophistication crumbles to reveal his impotence when he confronts his first genuine emotion.

Like Mussorgsky's *Boris Godunov, Eugene Onegin* is episodic rather than a smoothly flowing narrative. Indeed, Tchaikovsky styled this work "lyric scenes" rather than "opera" in an effort to distance it from the conventions of the time. *The Queen of Spades* (1890, also known by the French equivalent, *Pique Dame*) comes closer to those conventions, though this is hardly a liability.

Pushkin's melodramatic story is a study of obsession: Hermann, an army officer obsessed with gambling, secretly loves Lisa, but she is above his social station. Lisa, betrothed to a prince, is secretly obsessed with the brooding Hermann. Lisa's elderly grandmother, the Countess, makes no secret of her obsession with her lost beauty. When Hermann learns that the waspish Countess knows the secret of winning at cards, he pursues Lisa with wild ardor. She subsequently slips him a key, telling him to come to her room the next day when her grandmother will be out. Instead, he comes that night, but when he confronts the Countess and demands her secret at gunpoint, the old woman dies of fright. Lisa realizes that Hermann has only used her, and drowns herself. Hermann later receives the secret from the Countess's ghost; but when he plays, the winning card turns out to be the queen of spades instead of the ace. Seeing the Countess's ghost again, Hermann kills himself.

Tchaikovsky's brother, Modest, had written the libretto for another composer in 1887, at which time Tchaikovsky claimed to have no interest in the subject. But when two years passed with little progress by the rival, Tchaikovsky became interested. Vacationing in his beloved Florence, he wrote *The Queen of Spades* at white heat between January and June 1890, in order to have it ready for production by the end of the year.

Just as he had identified closely with the protagonists of *Eugene Onegin*, Tchaikovsky was deeply affected by the plight of his central character in *The Queen of Spades*, admitting he had wept painfully while composing Hermann's death scene. His dark, brooding music is as highly charged as a powder keg, especially the diabolical scene in the Countess's bedroom, in which he conveys the terror that finally chokes the old woman with a vividness that keeps you at the edge of your seat. At the same time, the textures of the work are brightened by the passion of his love duets, and the scintillating quality of his dances and ceremonial scenes.

Both *Eugene Onegin* and *The Queen of Spades* have a recognizable Russian flavor—the peasant scenes at the opening of *Onegin* and the melancholy melodic poignance of Lensky's aria contribute to it. So do the mazurkas and other dances in the party scenes of both works.

How, then, do Tchaikovsky's operas differ from the operas composed by the Slavophiles? Without getting technical, let's observe that the Conservatory-trained

Tchaikovsky was always influenced by the recitative and aria textures of French and Italian opera. Apart from the throbbing emotional quality that is as much a personal trait as a Russian one, the Russianness in his operas is often confined to set pieces with particular dance rhythms or conscious imitation of folk styles. In fact, Tchaikovsky's opera *The Maid of Orleans*, based on Friedrich Schiller's drama about Joan of Arc, contains almost no Russian flavor apart from that provided by the sound of the words, because the French locale allows for no Russian genre scenes. Moreover, though Tchaikovsky was attentive to the sound of the Russian language, his arias often beguile us by the gracefulness of their melodies rather than any nationalist quality.

On the other hand, because Mussorgsky, Rimsky, and Borodin were essentially amateurs, relatively untrained in German and Italian techniques of composition, they were obliged to invent their own methods of writing opera, even of setting words to music. Hence instead of setting essentially Italianate or Germanic music to Russian words, they went to their favorite sources—folk music—for guidance. The result was a distinctly Russian musical style: recitative that follows the aural qualities of Russian vowels and intonation, melodies that follow the profiles of Russian folk song, often avoiding conventional Italianate lyricism and measured symmetry, harmony that has its roots in the exotic and frequently Oriental modality of native peasant bands rather than the orthodox key relationships of Germanic textbooks.

For the modern listener, it is important to keep in mind that nationalist and Westernizing influences in nineteenth-century Russian music shouldn't be taken as qualitative assessments. At their best, Tchaikovsky, Mussorgsky,

Rimsky, and Borodin are equally fine. They just went about their work in their own respective ways.

Seeing Red: The Soviet School

Following the revolution, opera in Russia was on shaky ground. First, Lenin felt that badly needed money ought to be spent on more urgent social problems. Second, opera's long-standing identity as an aristocratic entertainment put its very existence in jeopardy. Fortunately, the positive view was taken that native Russian opera, which included native music and themes taken from the culture of the Russian people, could make a valuable contribution to the new regime. This in turn led to the development of a distinctive Soviet school of opera, of which the two towering names are Sergei Prokofiev (1891–1953) and Dmitri Shostakovich (1906–1975). Each is more widely known for his nonoperatic work, and of their respective operas, only a relative handful are produced with anything approaching frequency. In fact, neither had an easy time as an opera composer during the Stalinist era because of the Soviet belief that opera had to toe the Communist Party line, which meant that the stories had to encourage audiences to love their country and its government, and to keep their noses clean. Musically, conservatism was the rule: Be tuneful in the traditional sense, and don't upset the audience with too much dissonance.

Prokofiev, a formidable pianist, counted Rimsky-Korsakov among his teachers, and wrote four operas by the time he was sixteen. His most familiar scores are, of course, his First ("Classical") Symphony (inspired by the elegance and formal clarity of Mozart and Haydn); his wonderfully evocative score for Sergei Eisenstein's film *Alexander Nevsky*; and his immensely popular ballets, *Romeo and Juliet* and *Cinderella*. Of his numerous mature operas, *The Love for Three Oranges* (1921) is probably the one you'll have the best chance of encountering in an opera house.

Prokofiev wrote this modern opera buffa for the Chicago Opera, which gave the premiere in 1921. He based it on an unsentimental fantasy by the eighteenth-century Venetian writer Carlo Gozzi (another of whose "fables" inspired Puccini's *Turandot*). The story concerns an Arabian prince who must be made to laugh if he is to survive a life-threatening bout of melancholia. When he finally does succumb to laughter at the pratfall of the evil Fata Morgana, she casts a spell over him that has him falling in love with three fabulous oranges. After searching the four corners of the earth, he finds the oranges, and within one of them he finds the beautiful Princess Ninetta (they're *very* big oranges). After a series of further adventures, he and Ninetta finally marry. Prokofiev's brilliantly orchestrated score is often extremely funny itself, and the deliberate unreality of the whole concept gives stage directors a chance to flaunt their most flamboyant theatrical ideas.

Prokofiev's junior by fifteen years, Dmitri Shostakovich wrote in a variety of genres, including symphony, chamber music, and film scores. He also wrote in a number of styles when compelled to do so by circumstance: For example, his lushly melodic "romance" from the film *The Gadfly*, in the style of a nineteenth-century French ballet movement, is far removed from the unmistakable twentieth-century idiom of his fifteen symphonies, and it became very popular when it was used as the theme music for a British television series, *Reilly, Ace of Spies*.

Shostakovich's opera *The Nose*, based on Gogol's satire about the sudden disappearance of the nose of a government official, set off a storm of controversy when it was first produced in 1930. The score includes such rousing, and clearly satirical, novelties as an interlude written only for percussion instruments, an obvious jibe at operatic conventions. Although the audience greeted it warmly, several critics attacked the piece as "bourgeois decadence," and it was hastily retired from the stage.

The storm reached a peak upon the production of Shostakovich's extraordinary *Lady Macbeth of Mtsensk* (1934). The opera is founded on a sordid tale by the nineteenth-century writer Nikolai Leskov: Beautiful, intelligent Katerina Ismailova, married to a weakling, finds pleasure in the arms of a handsome farm laborer, Sergei. After Sergei involves her in the murders of her husband and her lecherous father-in-law, they marry, only to be arrested at their wedding. En route to a Siberian prison camp, she drowns herself when she discovers that Sergei has taken another woman convict for a lover. Leskov's story combines the bleak fatalism of Thomas Hardy with the steamy sexual tension of Tennessee Williams. Indeed, this Russian tale contains what were to become classic elements of the backwoods American novel: the beautiful woman imprisoned in a man's world, bored to death and bursting with sexual need; the husband who cannot satisfy her; the overbearing "Big Daddy" figure; and above all, a vengeful destiny.

No one is certain whether the inscrutable Shostakovich composed his operas in line with Communist Party ideology (i.e., as an indictment of the evils of the pre-revolutionary landowning class) or if he was actually taking aim at Stalinist oppression. He himself styled the opera a "tragedy satire," which has left it open to many varied interpretations.

In any case, Shostakovich created an array of unforgettable musical characterizations in an idiom full of beguiling paradoxes: Into this essentially tragic opera he wove music redolent of operetta, music hall, and slapstick film. Yet in the song of the Old Convict in the final act, a veritable hymn of the oppressed, it is hard not to feel that Shostakovich is finally allowing the audience into his heart of hearts. Years later he added yet another layer to the mystery, declaring in his reputed memoir *Testimony* (1979) that "I dedicated *Lady Macbeth* to my bride, my future wife, so naturally the opera is about love, too, but ... it is also about how love *could* have been if the world weren't full of vile things." In short, Shostakovich's opera is an enigma. And like all enigmas, it is endlessly fascinating.

Further Adventures in Russian Opera and Czech Opera, Too

Mussorgsky, *Khovanshchina* (1886) Avidly studying the upheavals caused by Peter the Great's dogged transformation of "old" Russia into a "new" Westernized state, Mussorgsky worked on this opera for years, but Rimsky-Korsakov, Shostakovich, and others had to finish it posthumously. The complex plot concerns the clash between the old Russian orthodoxies and the tsar's progressive retainers, and the violent repression of the "Old Believers by the modern church." Mussorgsky's score contains powerful music, as well as some of his most beautiful work, especially the gorgeous Prelude, "Dawn Over the Moscow River," and the "Dance of the Persian Slaves," both of which are often played in orchestral concerts.

Prokofiev, *War and Peace* (first version, 1946; second [shorter] version, 1955) Based on Tolstoy's epic novel, this twentieth-century grand opera is vast and extremely moving, with spacious choruses and profoundly lyrical melodies. In treating key episodes of Tolstoy's original, Prokofiev is gratifyingly successful at focusing on intimate human stories against the tumultuous backdrop of Napoleon's Russian campaign in 1812. Though performances of this work aren't everyday occurrences, there have been several fine recordings, most recently one by the Kirov Opera, St. Petersburg (Philips).

Prokofiev, *Betrothal in a Monastery* (1946) Based on Richard Brinsley Sheridan's comedy *The Duenna*, and with a tuneful score that happily evokes the manner of Rossini and Donizetti, this Russian opera buffa is one of Prokofiev's most delicate creations, and his most popular opera next to *A Love for Three Oranges*.

Czech opera is definitely growing in popularity, and the three names to know are Bedřich Smetana (1824–1884), Antonín Dvořák (1841–1904), and Leoš Janáček (1854–1928).

Smetana, *The Bartered Bride* (1866, revised 1870) is the best-known Czech opera. The comedy revolves around the machinations of a wily marriage broker, and from the opening measures of the overture, Smetana's music sparkles with the colors of rural life, especially in the drinking chorus (Act II), and the dance numbers—the polka and furiant—which have long been popular orchestral pieces on their own.

Dvořák, *Rusalka* (1901) is Dvořák's best-known stage work, and perhaps the finest Czech contribution to the genre of *Märchenoper* (fairytale opera), which had become a German specialty after the appearance of Humperdinck's *Hänsel und Gretel* in 1893. In order to marry her beloved Prince, the water nymph Rusalka is turned into a human with the help of the witch Jezibaba. However Jezibaba demands that Rusalka remain silent on land, and that the Prince be faithful to her. The Prince tires of her silence and is unfaithful, with dire results all around. Though there are several distinct numbers, among them Rusalka's passionate "Hymn to the Moon" at the beginning of Act I, the music is mainly continuous, richly flavored with poignant melodies, infectious dance rhythms, and scintillating instrumentation.

Janáček, *Jenufa* (1904) is a counterpart of provocative social dramas like Ibsen's *Hedda Gabler* and *A Doll's House*. It combines the violent, grassroots emotions of Italian verismo with a difficult moral question that probes the traditional double standard for men and women: In a Moravian farming village at the turn of the century, Jenufa, pregnant by the loutish Steva, is abandoned by him. Following the secret birth of the illegitimate child, Jenufa's stepmother, called the Kostelnicka (the sexton), is mortified by the disgrace. After Steva refuses to take responsibility, his half brother asks to marry Jenufa, despite being shocked to learn of the baby. Desperate to cinch the union, the Kostelnicka tells him the baby has died. Then, to back up her lie, she drowns it in a stream while Jenufa is asleep, lying afterward that the baby died while Jenufa was in a fever. When the body turns up—during Jenufa's wedding—the Kostelnicka confesses her crime to save Jenufa from being accused. Musically, the opera flashes with a new kind of Czech color, for Janáček mingles the traditional lyrical approach to opera with a visceral, forward-looking sense of harmony and orchestration that approaches the musical bite of the young Richard Strauss.

Janáček, *The Cunning Little Vixen* **(1924)** deals not so much with humans as with an anthropomorphic band of forest animals. The captive vixen, Sharp-Ears, escapes back to the woods to mate with a handsome fox and raise a litter. Ultimately she dies as part of the continuing regeneration of life. Janáček's opera abounds with nature music, forest scenes, ensembles of birds and insects, a joyous chorus of woodland life in celebration of the vixen's wedding, and dances for all kinds of critters. By no means cute or kitschy, *The Cunning Little Vixen* is an amusing, beguiling, and intensely humanistic opera.

And to End, a Hungarian Opera

Béla Bartók, *Bluebeard's Castle* **(1918)** is in one act, with only two singing characters, Duke Bluebeard and Judith, his seventh and newest wife. She opens the doors of his castle one by one, piecing together the awful secrets of his past and realizing it is her turn to enter his world of darkness, blood, and tears. The uninitiated may need time to acclimate themselves to Bartók's towering music. Once again, approach it on record first, following the libretto. And if the opera doesn't grab you at first, you may respond to its shattering splendors as your taste matures and deepens. Bartók never intended to compose music for easy listening, but that's no reason to avoid it.

English Opera? It's Actually Jolly Good

My meaning is, that you would be resolute enough to deliver us from our Italian bondage; and demonstrate that English is soft enough for Opera.
—AARON HILL, LIBRETTIST, TO G. F. HANDEL, 1732

The history of English opera poses a curious problem. If we were only to consider the standard repertoire today, it would be easy to accept received knowledge and say that in the period between the death of Henry Purcell in 1695 and the first production of Benjamin Britten's *Peter Grimes* in 1945 there was no English opera worth considering in this book—the sole exceptions being the comic operas of Gilbert and Sullivan (see the next chapter, "Operetta, or Sleeping Beauties"). But as the byway of nineteenth-century British music has always been a particular interest of mine, I'm going to take the liberty of touching on a few of the parts worth noting, just to complete the picture.

Masques and Marvels

From earliest times, the stouthearted Briton liked music as much as anyone, and musical diversions were a valued part of court life. Ancient Welsh courts were famous for their musical and bardic activities. King Henry VIII, when not busy replacing his wives, thoroughly enjoyed playing the organ and lute, singing, and composing—thirty-four of his own works still survive.

Henry's daughter, Elizabeth I, demanded her share of musical entertainments, and whenever she visited the stately homes of her aristocracy, she always expected to be entertained royally. Her successor, James I, made far fewer visits to his nobles, but preferred to have spectacular revels mounted at his own court.

By the early seventeenth century eight public theaters had been built in London. The most famous of them, the Globe, where most of Shakespeare's plays were presented for the first time, was erected in 1599. Songs and dances, of course, were an important part of British drama, exemplified by the many lyrics in Shakespeare's plays. Prior to the arrival of opera on Shakespeare's "sea-girt isle," however, the most popular form of stage entertainment in sixteenth- and seventeenth-century England was the masque (or "mask").

Rooted in the sixteenth-century French court ballets, English masques combined poetry, music, song, dance, and stage action. Typically, the plots were founded on mythological subjects and the scenery was elaborate. The poet and dramatist Ben Jonson (1572–1637) was among the earliest and best writers of court masques, and between 1605 and 1612 he supplied eight of them to the court of King James I, for which the scenery and costumes were designed by the celebrated architect Inigo Jones.

Some masques were sung throughout, like operas, and some English operas contained spoken dialogue, like masques. Nevertheless, if we agree that there are exceptions to every rule, let's say that in a masque the songs and dances tend to play a more or less incidental role within a spoken play. In the late-seventeenth-century "semi-opera" there is a closer union between the drama and the music; however, the primary action of the piece moves forward in the spoken part rather than in the musical portions. In an opera, the entire text is set to music, whether recitative or aria.

Because of the looseness of the terminology, it is difficult to pinpoint the first English opera. The music to the masque *Lovers Made Men* (1617), by Ben Jonson and Nicholas Lanier, is lost, but the libretto implies that it was sung entirely in recitative, which would make it the earliest English opera. Parliament's closure of theaters on the outbreak of the Civil War in 1649 put a damper on the further development of opera as a public entertainment. Nonetheless, masques were still produced in private during Oliver Cromwell's protectorate. Moreover, theater managers also found ways to get up occasional dramatic performances for royalist audiences. Most notable of these was the dramatist-manager Sir William Davenant, who produced his own *The Siege of Rhodes* in 1656. With music written by several composers, it was given ten times, and was also noteworthy as the first work to include the appearance of a woman on an English stage.

The Restoration, in 1660, inaugurated the reign of Charles II, the "Merry Monarch" whose love of the theater extended to his bed: Among his mistresses was the curvacious and clever actress Nell Gwynn. British delight in spoken drama—especially in the raffish high jinks of Restoration comedy—overshadowed all interest in opera at the time, though the musical stage was not without its attractions. Among the best was the pastoral masque *Venus and Adonis*, with music by John Blow (1649–1708), whose score is sufficiently well integrated with the action to count as a genuine opera. *Venus and Adonis* was the model for the subsequent work that most authorities consider the earliest English operatic masterpiece, *Dido and Aeneas* (1689), by Blow's pupil Henry Purcell, the greatest English composer of his time.

Purcell: Interrupted Melody

A Londoner to the core, Purcell (1659–1695) had been a chorister of the Chapel Royal, and according to documentary evidence he was composing at the age of eight. In the course of his brief life, Purcell was a composer under four monarchs in relatively quick succession—Charles II, James II, and William and Mary. He wrote a considerable amount of sacred and ceremonial music, and also composed an extraordinary body of instrumental music and songs for one or more voices.

Like his contemporary, the diarist Samuel Pepys, Purcell was drawn to the theater, and from 1680 until his death at thirty-six he contributed music to no fewer than forty-four plays. Most of Purcell's incidental music consisted of songs and instrumental movements inserted into the action, the number varying from play to play. But four of the works contain enough music, and enough of it well integrated with the actual drama, to be called "semi-operas." *King Arthur* (play by John Dryden, 1691) comes closest to actual opera in this regard, while the famous Incantation Scene in *The Indian Queen* (1695) employs recitative and aria in a completely operatic manner. Nonetheless, only in the earliest of these richly musical works, *Dido and Aeneas* (1689), did Purcell compose a true opera, sung throughout.

Purcell's librettist, Nahum Tate, based the libretto on the Roman author Virgil's chronicle of the Trojan prince Aeneas and his doomed romance with Queen Dido of Carthage. In Virgil's account, Aeneas abandons Dido when the gods urge him to continue on to Italy, where he is to found Rome. His departure causes Dido to die of grief. Tate replaces the gods with a wicked Sorceress, who hates Queen Dido for the sheer pleasure of it, and tricks Aeneas into leaving her. Certainly the Sorceress adds a supernatural, almost comedic note, to the predominantly elegiac mood of the piece. The Cave Scene in which she and her band of witches prepare their spell is a wonderful piece of Baroque hocus-pocus, and you can't help but smile as they later rejoice at the tragedy they have wrought ("Destruction's our delight, Delight our greatest sorrow"). However, Purcell's musical control of the various situations of drama, grotesque magic, and tragedy is so assured that the final scene never fails to move listeners deeply.

Purcell's recitatives in this opera are extraordinarily expressive settings of the English language, and they convey the elasticity and nuance of speech. Surprisingly, he never wrote another opera, and the works that followed *Dido* were all in the semi-opera category. Had he lived longer, Purcell might have written more operas, and possibly consolidated the establishment of a genuine English operatic school. Although his early death prompted genuine grief within the musical community, it wasn't long before the Italian opera craze was ignited in London.

Eighteenth-Century Developments

For the record, the first full-length Italian opera to be performed complete in London was Antonio Maria Bononcini's *Il Trionfo di Camilla* (Camilla's Triumph), which was produced in 1706, in an English translation. Four years later, London audiences were regaled by *Almahide*, by Bononcini's brother, Giovanni Bononcini, performed complete and in the original *Italian*. By this time the first castrato had made his London debut, setting off the fashion for high-flying male singers whose voices were surgically preserved, and setting the stage for the arrival of George Frideric Handel from Germany. Handel bowed in London with the production of his *Rinaldo* in 1711, the first of nearly forty Italian operas he was to compose for his English audience over the next three decades. (See the chapters on Italian opera and German opera for more details on Handel and his work.)

Though Handel was to experience a series of ups and downs with his aristocratic London audience, the most telling blow to Italian opera was the first production of John

Gay's scathing satire of the genre, *The Beggar's Opera*, in 1728. The title tells it all. Gay, a popular playwright and theater manager, took aim both at the conventions of Italian opera and at the current state of British politics.

Instead of Olympian gods and heroes pondering questions of love and morality, Gay focused on the London underworld of thieves and prostitutes. The hero of the piece is neither Hercules nor Perseus, but one Macheath, a highwayman who finds himself in hot water when he marries Polly Peachum, whose irate father heads a clearinghouse for stolen goods. Eventually Macheath lands in Newgate Prison, pursued both by Polly and by the jailer's daughter, Lucy Lockit, and the two women's battling provided a lively send up of the famous rivalry between the two real-life Italian prima donnas, Faustina and Cuzzoni. The piece was as topical as it was funny. Instead of elaborate arias, the music of *The Beggar's Opera* consists of songs in which Gay's pointed and sometimes risqué lyrics are set to popular tunes of the time.

The Beggar's Opera was an immediate success that wits said made Gay rich and Rich (his producer) gay. During the first season alone, it was performed 62 times, and was played almost annually in London for the next 150 years. In the twentieth century it has been produced in a number of versions, most notably by Frederic Austin and Arnold Bennett (London, 1920, which ran for 1,463 consecutive nights, a record for any opera), and by Benjamin Britten (at Cambridge University in 1948). The composer Sir Arthur Bliss edited a screen version, which starred Sir Laurence Olivier as Macheath (1953). In 1928, Berthold Brecht and Kurt Weill produced an entirely recomposed German version of Gay's work, *Die Dreigroschenoper* (*The*

Threepenny Opera), which has enjoyed a life of its own (see the chapter on German opera).

Most importantly, *The Beggar's Opera* established a new genre on the English musical stage—ballad opera—which was to spur the development of singspiel in Germany and operetta in France (see the chapters on German opera and operetta).

Meanwhile, Handel produced his last Italian opera, *Deidamia*, in 1741, by which time he had embarked upon the string of English oratorios that would keep his name alive to the present day. In fact, between 1754 and 1920 not one of Handel's operas was staged, while his oratorios—*Israel in Egypt* (1739), *Judas Maccabaeus* (1747), and of course *Messiah* (1741)—became perennial favorites in the concert hall.

Throughout his career, Handel never lost his theatrical instincts, and when the upper-crust market for his Italian operas dried up, he was able to transfer those instincts to serving the middle-class taste for biblical stories, while shifting his musical focus from showy virtuoso opera arias to majestic choral movements. The result was a body of music whose vigor has remained undiminished for over two centuries.

Ballad operas (some utilizing existing folk songs, others newly composed with songs in a folk-ballad style) and Handelian oratorio dominated the English scene after 1750, but in the next generation at least one other figure made a lasting, if lesser, mark on musical posterity: Thomas Augustine Arne (1710–1778).

Like Handel, the London-born Arne was a man of the theater, who contributed incidental music to numerous plays as well as composing masques, English-language operas in the florid Italian manner, and several ballad operas. Even those who don't know his tuneful Shakespeare settings—songs such as "Orpheus with his Lute," "Where the Bee Sucks," and "Blow, blow, thou Winter Wind"—are probably familiar with at least one aria by Arne, "Rule Britannia." Originally styled a "grand ode," it formed an imposing and rousing finale to his masque, *Alfred* (1740), about King Alfred the Great's victory over the invading Danes.

Nineteenth-Century Operas: Too Long Overlooked

Though ballad opera had given Handel a run for his money in mid-eighteenth-century London, foreign composers continued to flock there later on. Johann Christian Bach (1735-1782, the youngest son of Johann Sebastian) revived the taste for Italian opera seria, while Domenico Cimarosa (1749–1801) and other Italians fueled the new fashion for opera buffa that was firmly consolidated by the comic works of Rossini.

Much of the current Italian repertoire was performed in the original language for that part of the public that wanted it. At the same time there was an audience for operas (in English translation) by Mozart, Rossini, and other foreign composers; however, the prevailing fashion was not only to translate the libretto but to dish up the music in editions concocted for the "English taste." For example, a version of Mozart's *Marriage of Figaro* produced at Drury Lane in 1826 had the roles of the Count, the Countess, and Figaro played by straight actors, while their arias were assigned to

other performers. In addition, popular English songs were
wedged in here and there to make the piece more accessible
to less sophisticated listeners. This musical hash was one of
many similar "arrangements" of major operas made by Sir
Henry Rowley Bishop (1786–1855), the first composer to
receive a knighthood. But Bishop's chief claim to immortality is the simple ballad "Home, sweet home" ("Be it ever
so humble"), which he used as the primary theme of his
opera *Clari, or The Maid of Milan* (1823).

Of the many ballad operas and other English works produced during the early nineteenth century, the most substantial one was not by an English composer, but by the
German Carl Maria von Weber. *Oberon* (1826) proved to be
Weber's last opera: Stricken with consumption, he had
undertaken it to provide for his family after his death, and
died in London a few weeks after the premiere.

Weber's librettist, James Robinson Planché, was a gifted
stage designer, author, authority on heraldry, and a compe-
tent musician. For all his accomplishments, however, his
plays and opera libretti were pretty thin gruel, popular at
the time because they fed the unsophisticated romantic
appetite for "Gothick Revival" atmosphere and spectacular
visual effects. He freely based his libretto of *Oberon, or the
Elf-King's Oath* on a translation of a German drama
founded on the thirteenth-century French romance *Huon
de Bordeaux*.

Medieval chivalry, fairy magic, and Arabian Nights
exoticism mingled cheek by jowl in the adventures of Sir
Huon and the Caliph's daughter Reiza, whose mutual
fidelity is tested through a series of adventures to end the
argument between the Elf-King Oberon and his queen,
Titania, over whether man or woman is less faithful in love.

There are some obvious parallels with Shakespeare's *Midsummer Night's Dream*: Planché realized that it couldn't hurt to evoke one of the most popular of the Bard's comedies, and Shakespeare himself probably derived his Oberon character from the same French source.

Oberon has clung to the edge of the standard repertoire because of the power and appeal of Weber's score, though its utter lack of dramatic structure has militated against frequent stagings. Nonetheless, the overture, with its "magic horn" motif, is a popular concert piece, and Reiza's magnificent aria, "Ocean, thou mighty monster," is standard issue for all dramatic sopranos.

Victorian Opera: Dead, or Just Sleeping?

It is surprising that whereas nineteenth-century English literature has been widely popularized by television and film dramatizations, and nineteenth-century British decorative arts and painting have become extremely popular among collectors—especially all things Victorian—the music of the period remains unfamiliar outside academic or specialist circles. The development of native opera in Great Britain was hampered by several obstacles, most important of which was that a majority of Britons were less interested in opera than in spoken theater or choral music. Moreover, as in Handel's day, those who did like opera preferred Italian opera, and among upper-crust opera devotees opera *in* English was regarded as plebeian. To complete the vicious cycle, the English language was widely thought to be unsingable, especially by the Italian performers who dominated the scene throughout the century.

At Covent Garden, which was officially known as the Royal Italian Opera from 1847 until 1892, standard French and German works like Gounod's *Faust*, Mozart's *Magic Flute*, and Wagner's *Flying Dutchman* were sung in Italian. Even the occasional English work fortunate enough to make it to London's leading opera house had to be translated into Italian or French so that the English-speaking audience would be protected from the outrage of actually hearing the words in their native tongue.

To make matters worse, until the present century, or at least until the advent of the brilliant wordplay of Gilbert and Sullivan, English librettists and translators usually wrote an amazingly stilted kind of language, deliberately and self-consciously archaic, and often soaring to laughable heights of word twisting in order to fit a chosen meter or rhyme.

In 1835, the Irish composer Michael William Balfe (1808–1870) embarked upon a string of operas that included some of the most popular British works of their time. Of these, *The Bohemian Girl* became his calling card when it was produced in 1843. The plot concerns the young daughter of an Austrian count, who is kidnapped by Gypsies and raised as one of their own. Years later she falls in love with a member of the tribe, who ultimately reveals that he is an exiled Polish aristocrat, and therefore worthy of asking for her hand when she is reunited with her father. (Even in the most romantic English opera, class distinctions count.)

Balfe's librettist was the theatrical entrepreneur and self-styled poet Alfred Bunn. As a manager, Bunn's penny-pinching skulduggery included making artists appear at two of his theaters on the same night. As a writer, his efforts made him the laughingstock of the theatrical profession: He is "the presiding genius of dramatic humbug," wrote the *Theatrical Times*, his lyrics, "the twaddle that any lack-a-daisical young gentleman might scribble in the albums of a feminine sentimentalist." But he persevered, making and losing fortunes with the regularity of clockwork.

Despite the awful text, Balfe's tuneful score made *The Bohemian Girl* the most famous English opera before Gilbert and Sullivan, and one that represents the easy, likable musical style that prevailed at the time. In fact, "Bo Girl" was still sufficiently familiar in 1930 to serve as the basis for Laurel and Hardy's eponymous film.

Balfe enjoyed one of the most successful careers of any Victorian composer, and it was thanks largely to him that romantic English operas began to make their way to non-English speaking audiences

However, the one Victorian who achieved genuine immortality was Sir Arthur Sullivan (1842–1900). Though Sullivan's fame now rests on the operettas he wrote with Sir William S. Gilbert (1836–1911)—*The Mikado, HMS Pinafore, Iolanthe*, etc.—Sullivan himself regarded these as secondary to his real mission, which was the composition of oratorios and even a grand opera. In fact, Richard D'Oyly Carte, Gilbert and Sullivan's business partner, built a theater specifically to house Sullivan's only "serious" opera, *Ivanhoe*, which enjoyed a remarkable run of 153 consecutive performances when it opened at the spanking new Royal English Opera House in 1891. Unfortunately, due to Carte's shortsightedness, he had no other new English opera to produce after Sullivan's, and after some stopgap measures, Carte sold the house (now the Palace Theatre, owned by Sir Andrew Lloyd Webber), and got out of the grand opera business. So did Sullivan.

With the reassessment of Victorian music, Sullivan's serious works are increasingly ripe for revival, at least as representative period pieces that reveal a composer attuned to the demands of his audience for dignified music that could be spacious as much as sentimental. If you should come across one on record, or in concert, don't be afraid to sample it.

Twentieth-Century Masters

The dawn of the new century still didn't find enthusiasts for native opera amongst the bejeweled audiences of Covent Garden, where Italian, French, and German opera remained the regular fare. Nonetheless, British music received a shot in the arm with the so-called folk music revival that began around that time. In a nationalist vein that somewhat paralleled the enthusiasms of Russia's "Mighty Handful" (see Russian Opera), British composers sought to create a distinctly English musical idiom by going back to authentic folk songs and to the music of the Tudor and Elizabethan ages for inspiration.

Among the most successful of these younger composers was Sir Ralph (pronounced "Rafe") Vaughan Williams (1872–1958), whose orchestral Fantasias—one on a theme of Thomas Tallis, the other on "Greensleeves"—are among the most familiar results of this vital movement. With *Hugh the Drover* (composed in 1911; premiered 1924), Vaughan Williams created a true English folk opera equivalent to Gershwin's *Porgy and Bess*, with a score that has the modal tang of genuine folk music, warm and earthy, and tinged with a certain twilight melancholy.

The story is as English as Stilton cheese, about a drover (a man who drives cattle or sheep to market, on foot, of course) who wins the hand of his beloved in a boxing match, only to be accused of being a spy for Napoleon by his vanquished rival. A study in mob hysteria (the whole village attacks Hugh because of one man's hasty acusation), the work ends happily with Hugh's vindication.

Another opera in a similar vein is Gustav Holst's one-act "musical interlude," *At the Boar's Head* (1925). Holst (1874–1934) wrote it while recovering in the country from the effects of a head injury he had suffered in a fall as he conducted. He was reading Shakespeare's *Henry IV* and looking over a volume of English folk songs, and he noticed that one of the melodies fit the Shakespearean passage he had read, whereupon he was inspired to write an opera utilizing texts mainly gleaned from the Falstaff scenes in Shakespeare's *Henry* plays. For his score Holst created a finely orchestrated synthesis of old folk melodies, resulting in a brilliant, amusing, ultimately touching opera.

The work of Vaughan Williams and Holst paved the way for the two composers regarded as the leaders of postwar British opera, Britten and Tippett. Benjamin Britten, Lord Britten of Aldeburgh (1913–1976), the first composer to be raised to the British peerage, remains the preeminent British opera composer of the century. Without a doubt, the continuing popularity of several of his works made him the most visible British stage composer on the international scene, a position he still holds two decades after his death.

Britten shot to the front rank of British composers in

1945 with the production of his first full-length opera, *Peter Grimes*. The libretto was adapted by the playwright Montagu Slater from *The Borough*, by the flinty Georgian poet George Crabbe. Set in Britten's beloved Aldeburgh in East Anglia (where he was to found an international music festival), the story revolves around the bleak life in a fishing community, and the intolerance of conventional society. Peter Grimes, a brutish fisherman disliked by his gossiping neighbors, is suspected by them of killing his apprentices. His only two friends, the retired merchant captain Balstrode and the schoolteacher Ellen Orford, try in vain to persuade Grimes to leave the village, the former suggesting he join the merchant marine, the latter dreaming of possible marriage. Grimes shares her dream— despite his violent nature, he is a romantic who could do with a bit of TLC. But it ultimately proves futile. When his new apprentice is accidentally killed, the village sets off to hunt Grimes down. Driven mad by the situation, Grimes follows Balstrode's advice to sail his boat out to sea and scuttle it.

Peter Grimes was premiered in London at the reopening of the Sadler's Wells Theatre in June 1945, and was an instant triumph. Britten's lifelong companion, the tenor Peter Pears, sang the title role. An artist of consummate gifts, Pears thereafter created Britten's major tenor roles, his voice and sensitivity to language inspiring and influencing much of Britten's vocal writing. Apart from its powerful expression of the bleak drama, the music of *Peter Grimes* is redolent of the sea. Each of the six scenes in the opera is introduced with an atmospheric Interlude, of which four are often played in orchestral concerts as a suite of "Sea Interludes."

Billy Budd (four-act version, 1951; revised two-act version, 1960) is another seaborne Britten opera, with shanties and choral passages that evoke the freshness of salt air and stiff breezes. Its libretto, adapted by E. M. Forster and Eric Crozier from Herman Melville's story, *Billy Budd*, examines the destruction of the innocent Billy by the power of evil on board the eighteenth-century warship HMS *Indomitable*.

In addition to their nautical themes, *Peter Grimes* and *Billy Budd* also focus on outsiders victimized by intolerance or misunderstanding. It was a motive that appealed to Britten as a gay composer at a time when homosexuality was still a forbidden way of life, and as a pacifist during World War II. Similarly, his *Owen Wingrave* (written for television, and premiered by the BBC in 1971) dramatizes Henry James's story of a pacifist who dies under paranormal circumstances while trying to prove his personal courage to his hawkish father. Even Britten's village comedy *Albert Herring* (1947) shows the humorous side of smug provincial conventionalism: A mamma's boy is elected "King of the May"—to his mortification—after the stuffy pillars of the community judge all the village girls to be undeserving. A cup of spiked punch at the May Day celebration releases Albert from his inhibitions, and he returns from a bender the next morning a new man, and a real one.

Britten's final opera, *Death in Venice* (1973), confronts both issues. Based on Thomas Mann's novella about a middle-aged man's obsession with a beautiful boy, the work languidly hovers in the sultry air of the Venetian lagoon. Britten's orchestration evokes atmospheric effects as well as the street sounds, the decadence, and the sickly decay of a Venice stricken by cholera.

Britten wrote two extremely demanding roles in the opera, the writer Aschenbach (tenor) and the seven nemesis characters, played by the same baritone. Peter Pears created Aschenbach at the 1973 Aldeburgh Festival, and in 1974 at the American premiere at the Met. At the close of the first act, Aschenbach, alone onstage, realizes his feelings for the boy Tadzio, and cries out, "I love you." Two decades ago this produced a more startling effect than it does on today's more enlightened audiences. However, those who heard Pears in the role (as I did) could not have ignored the impression that as the opera itself was the ailing Britten's final tribute to Pears, so this passionate outburst was underpinned by Pears's feelings for Britten.

Britten's career as a composer had taken off with relative speed, and he had received international attention while still in his twenties. For his friend Sir Michael Tippett (b. 1905), the road was considerably longer, and though he is, at this writing, the grand old man of English opera, it wasn't until around 1960 that Tippett's music achieved wide recognition. In fact, he was a late starter—where Britten started composing at five, and was already studying composition privately at fourteen, Tippett didn't begin formal training in music until he was past eighteen, and didn't produce his first truly individual composition (the first String Quartet) until he was thirty. Nonetheless, he was prepared for a long haul. Early on in his career, when he was beginning to compose his oratorio *A Child of Our Time* (1944), inspired by the inhumanity of rising Nazism, Tippett was advised by T. S. Eliot to write his own text, to ensure the closest possible union of words and music. Tippett followed this advice, and has since written all his own libretti.

As a dramatic composer Tippett has been motivated by a probing sensitivity to the problems of human interaction, and by the idea of resolving them not by force but by reconciling the conflicting elements. Of his five operas, *The Midsummer Marriage* (composed 1946–52; U.K. premiere 1955, U.S. premiere 1983) is probably the best known. Superficially, the plot, which combines mythic fantasy with observations of everyday life, echoes Mozart's *Magic Flute* in that lovers undergo separation and a series of trials before they achieve sufficient enlightenment to marry successfully. Tippett's exuberant score scintillates with instrumental color and warm lyricism that flows upon a vivacious undercurrent of Renaissance dance rhythms. Dance plays an integral role in the action, and the four Ritual Dances from the second and third acts are sometimes programmed in orchestral concerts.

And what has the Russian-born Igor Stravinsky, pupil of Rimsky-Korsakov and composer of the ballets *Petrouchka* and *The Firebird*, to do with English opera? Indeed, Stravinsky is probably the hardest of all major composers to pigeonhole nationally. *Petrouchka* and *The Firebird* do have their basis in Russian folklore and literature, as does the rarely performed opera *Mavra*, based on Pushkin. But Stravinsky's career was really launched in Paris—thanks to the impresario Sergei Diaghilev, who arranged the world premieres there of a string of the composer's major stage works, beginning with *The Firebird* in 1910. Thereafter, Stravinsky pursued his career as an international composer, living successively in Switzerland, France, and the United States (where he became an American citizen in 1945), gleaning his musical and cultural influences from the world at large.

It was in America, in 1947, that he began work on his opera *The Rake's Progress*, which received its premiere in Venice in 1951. Stravinsky's librettists were W. H. Auden, who had migrated to the United States from England in 1939, and his close associate Chester Kallman.

National boundaries aside, what makes *The Rake's Progress* an English opera rather than an Anglo-Russo-American one is the quintessentially English spirit that informs every note. Inspired by the eponymous series of eight engravings by that most English of painters and social commentators, William Hogarth, the libretto follows the lamentable career of Tom Rakewell: After declining a responsible city position offered by the father of his sweetheart, Tom latches onto the sinister Nick Shadow, who leads him through a life of vice and corruption, and at the end of a year reveals himself as the devil. Tom gambles for his life and wins, but is left mad, and in Bedlam.

For this morality play, Stravinsky wrote music that echoes the eighteenth century, especially Gay's *Beggar's Opera* and Mozart. The small orchestra is of Mozartean dimensions; the action is carried on in *secco* recitative accompanied by harpsichord, and punctuated by arias and ensembles based on traditional operatic forms with straightforward melodies. A definitive example of Stravinsky's neoclassical phase, *The Rake's Progress* exemplifies eighteenth-century methods distilled—and sharpened—through the imagination of a twentieth-century genius. And it is significant that although the 1951 world premiere in Venice was unsatisfactory, after its first production at England's Glyndebourne Festival (1953), Stravinsky's opera was revived there during at least five more seasons.

Further Adventures in English Opera

Britten, *A Midsummer Night's Dream* **(1960)** The libretto was adapted by Britten and Pears from Shakespeare's comedy. A masterpiece that captures the humor and fairy fantasy of the original through one of the most attractive of all Britten scores.

Oliver Knussen, *Where the Wild Things Are* **(1984)** With a libretto by the children's author and illustrator Maurice Sendak, this is a one-act opera for children and adults. A naughty boy is sent to bed without supper, whereupon his room becomes the scene of an anthropomorphic fantasy. But given Sendak's brand of unsentimental humor, the boy turns the tables on the monsters. Knussen allows himself ample opportunity for musical humor, including quotations and parody.

Operetta, or Sleeping Beauties

Operetta is a daughter of the opéra comique, a daughter who went bad; not that daughters who go bad are lacking in charm.

—CAMILLE SAINT-SAËNS

"Operetta." Just let the word trip off your tongue and send a host of images dancing across the mind's stage: Debt-ridden dukes lose their hearts to clever servant girls; fairy queens dictate parliamentary legislation; Olympian gods take a holiday; soldiers of fortune make love to disused princesses; Gypsies play, pirates skulk, the Danube flows. The audience chuckles, sways to the waltzes, and leaves the theater with a spring in its collective step.

So much for the spirit of operetta. Now that shows by Stephen Sondheim and Andrew Lloyd Webber have grown increasingly operatic, now that major opera companies are adopting classic American musicals like *Show Boat*, *Carousel*, and *Of Thee I Sing* into repertoires that already include genuine operettas like *Die Fledermaus* and *The Merry Widow*, people often ask, What exactly *is* operetta? How is it different from opera, or Broadway musicals?

The *Oxford English Dictionary* defines operetta as "a short opera, usually of light and humorous character...." *The Oxford Dictionary of Opera* takes the definition a bit further, calling operetta "a play with an overture, songs, interludes and dances." The word "play" is important, for while opera is usually entirely sung, operetta contains spoken dialogue. Opera usually deals with heroic or tragic situations, operetta with frivolity. In its heyday, operetta was very much the pop version of the operatic art form, and whereas opera composers like Verdi and Wagner were often placed on a pedestal, an operetta composer like Offenbach was regarded by "serious persons" as a corrupter of public morals.

Most important, opera began as the scholarly pursuit of the Florentine Camerata (whom we met earlier in the section on Italian opera). Operetta has less exalted roots: the bawdy *vaudevilles* and similar entertainments played at the Paris fairgrounds during the eighteenth century. Ephemeral, and often short-lived, these pieces were usually cobbled together utilizing existing popular songs. Both featured topical lyrics, operatic parodies, and an overriding sense of irreverent fun. The arrival in 1752 of the Italian troupe that ignited the so-called War of the Buffoons had a tonic effect on the incipient development of French operetta. Although the purveyors of native French entertainments defended their turf, they noted the comparative polish of the Italians' work, and strove to develop a home-grown product of equivalent *finesse*.

After a few false starts, French *opéra comique* was established in its own theater, the Salle Favart. Although Italian opera buffa remained exclusively sung, the French, who traditionally valued drama and dance over opera, generally opted for the mixture of song and spoken dialogue in their comedies.

By 1850, however, opéra comique had also embraced serious plots, which gave at least one fellow composer pause for thought. "I told myself that the [Théâtre de l'] Opéra-Comique was no longer the home of true comic opera, that really gay, bright, spirited music . . . was being forgotten," wrote Jacques Offenbach. "Composers working for the Opéra-Comique were simply writing small 'grand' operas."

Offenbach took the plunge in 1855 by leasing a tiny theater on the Champs-Elysées that he called the Bouffes-Parisiens. Initially his government license limited his productions to one act and a maximum of four singers, but in 1858 came permission to produce two-act works, the first of which was the masterful *Orphée aux Enfers* (Orpheus in the Underworld). He scandalized critics by quoting an aria from Gluck's sacrosanct opera *Orfeo ed Euridice* in a humorous context. Here he gave the world the irrepressible gallop melody that was to evolve into the "can-can," the veritable anthem of Parisian nightlife.

Offenbach was often regarded with a jaundiced eye by

serious musicians. "[He] possesses the warmth that Auber lacks," wrote Richard Wagner, ever ready to kill two birds with one stone. "But it is the warmth of the dung heap." Wagner aside, Offenbach owed his success to his phenomenal melodic and rhythmic invention, and to a genuine sense of humor. The foibles of electroplated Second Empire society were an easy target for the barbs of his gifted librettists. More important, however, the music itself is funny.

In many instances operetta humor is based on burlesque or parody of popular grand operas of the day. In some cases Offenbach would parody the heroic style, such as the hilarious ensemble in *La Belle Hélène*, in which he builds an extended mock-melodramatic set piece for soloists and chorus on the single line, "O ciel, c'est l'homme à la pomme" (Oh Heaven, it's the man with the apple). In many instances, however, he parodies the big boys by quoting them directly. Meyerbeer, doyen of the Paris Opéra in Offenbach's time, is the most frequent target, and snatches from his operas pop up humorously in many Offenbach works, alongside bits of Donizetti, Fromental Halévy, and other "serious" composers. (Copyright posed no problem in those days.) Offenbach also had a keen ear for funny mock-instrumental or natural effects—for example, the tenor's imitation trumpet fanfares in the duet "Ah, C'est un fameux régiment" (*La Grande-Duchesse de Gérolstein*), or the buzzing duet in *Orphée*, sung by Euridice and Jupiter (hot to make love to her while disguised as a fly).

In 1858, Offenbach first visited Vienna with his Bouffes-Parisiens repertoire and created a furor. "*You* ought to write operettas," he said to the Waltz King, Johann Strauss (1825–1899), on another visit to Vienna in 1864. The remark,

worthy of a screenwriter, was casual, and Strauss probably
laughed it off. In fact, Strauss was completely unsuited to
compose for the theater. Functionally illiterate, he
admitted that "words are intractable stuff to me." Hence he
was a poor judge of a libretto. But Strauss had his ego, and
when his wife and several theatrical conspirators persuaded him that a Strauss operetta would demolish all
competition, he found himself to the manner borne. He was
to regret his acquiescence again and again, for while *Die
Fledermaus* and *The Gypsy Baron* were immediate classics, other efforts like *The Queen's Lace Handkerchief* or
Blind Cow sank from sight.

The problem was usually libretti that proffered tasteless
silliness instead of French farce, and childish verses instead of
wit. In the case of *A Night in Venice*, Strauss set the musical
numbers without even reading the whole book through. However, the operetta survived, albeit with some literary touch-
ups, because of Strauss's enchanting score, which remains a
glorious piece of sun-drenched deliciousness.

A generation later Victor Herbert's similar lack of literary acumen was to mar many of the operettas he wrote
for New York. Like Strauss, Herbert (1859–1924) was a
melodist whose chief concern with words was that they provided enough singable vowels. Hence the kind of tosh supplied by a collaborator such as Harry B. Smith makes books
like *The Fortune Teller* and *Sweethearts* laughable rather
than funny today. Nonetheless, the tuneful appeal of Herbert's music is genuine.

The quintessential Victorian composer, Sir Arthur
Sullivan, had the better fortune to work with W. S. Gilbert,
a librettist whose best books provide as much pleasure
as the music because of their funny plots and extra-

ordinarily entertaining language. Sullivan was one of the best-trained musicians to take up operetta, and his inventiveness lends his music a distinctive style that is immediately apparent. Sullivan's parody is usually more technically refined than Offenbach's. Rather than offer direct quotations, he writes original music in the recognizable "style of" to get the point across, and those parodies range widely, from Handel to Bellini to American minstrel shows.

Like Offenbach, Sullivan exploited the topsy-turvy juxtaposition of characters or situations with incongruous musical idioms—a hallmark of operetta style. For instance, in the Act I finale of *Iolanthe* a stage full of English peers in full parliamentary regalia faces down a band of Wagnerian fairies (the Fairy Queen's original costume was inspired by the Valkyries). At the climax, everyone breaks into a skipping tune with oom-pah accompaniment worlds away from either Valhalla or the House of Lords.

Patter, the rapid-fire delivery of as many words as possible in the briefest possible time, is the element most often identified with G&S (though they adopted it from Italian opera buffa). Yet Sullivan's romantic muse can soar movingly in love duets and numbers like "Oh, goddess wise" (*Princess Ida*), "Oh, Mercy, thou" (*Yeoman of the Guard*), and the duet "Sweet and low" (*Utopia Limited*). The romantic sentiment exploited by the Viennese school is even more pronounced, typified by the swooning climax of the *Fledermaus* Ball Scene, and in the amorous languor cultivated by Franz Lehár in the *Merry Widow* love duets.

Contemporary with operetta developments in France, Austria, England, and America was the development of the Spanish form of operetta, *zarzuela*. Its name derived from

the palace of La Zarzuela, near Madrid, where spectacular plays were first performed in the seventeenth century. This extraordinarily beautiful repertoire has remained
almost unknown outside Spain until recently, but thanks to
the energy of Plácido Domingo, who has been instrumental
in the production of recordings and videos, works by such
composers as Tomas Bretón, Ruperto Chapí, and Amadeo
Vives are now widely available. They reveal that zarzuela
music is as tasty as paella, full of characteristic swirl-
ing rhythms (habañera, seguidilla, jota), castanets, and
melodies that range from languid romance to high-spirited
hilarity. Among the most appealing examples of the género
chico (or "little genre," as it is known) are Francisco Barbieri's El Barberillo de Lavapiés, a delightful parody of
Rossini's Barber of Seville; Vives's Doña Francisquita;
and Bretón's La Verbena de la Paloma (The Festival of
the Dove), a popular Madrid religious feast that serves as the
background of the comedy about the misunderstandings that
arise when a randy old pharmacist, Don Hilarion, decides to
do a little flirting.

Back in the operetta mainstream, the new century and
the heady aftermath of World War I created a dichotomy
between fluffy works closer to what we know as musical
comedy, and more serious subjects in which a bittersweet
denouement anticipates the musical plays of Rodgers and
Hammerstein: Sigmund Romberg's The Student Prince
(1924) and Lehár's Paganini (1925) are just two operettas
of the period that end with duty or philosophy parting the
lovers.

Because operetta as a genre was inspired by a fairly
refined brand of middle- and late-nineteenth-century
popular culture, it faded from active perpetuation once

styles shifted to something jazzier and more democratic. Lighthearted as they were, operettas were increasingly shunted into the classical sphere as newer popular styles superseded them, and it is significant that the waltz-song "Wunderbar" in Cole Porter's *Kiss Me Kate* is a deliberate parody of a manner deemed outmoded in 1948.

The secret of enjoying operetta's manifold pleasures today is to approach the genre on its own terms. Tender sentiments aren't exactly fashionable these days; however, beneath our "cool" exteriors, most of us still have a secret soft spot. Therefore, instead of being embarrassed by the lilac-scented emotions of more sentimental operettas, just approach them without apology. They are, after all, based on feelings we can enjoy experiencing if only we give ourselves the chance. To paraphrase composer Francis Poulenc, himself a master of *raffiné* musical charm, don't analyze operetta too much. Just love it.

American Opera: Cinderella Was a Stepchild, Too

> *[America] is full of melody, original, sympathetic and varying in mood, color and character to suit every phase of composition. It is a rich field. America can have great and noble music of her own, growing out of the very soil and partaking of its nature—the natural voice of a free and vigorous race.*
>
> —ANTONÍN DVOŘÁK, LETTER TO THE EDITOR, *NEW YORK HERALD*, 1893

Ask most American opera lovers to name their favorite works, and the answer will probably be something Italian, German, Russian, or French. As for American opera, there's Gershwin's *Porgy and Bess* and there's, well ... After two hundred years, American opera is still pretty much unfamiliar territory, lumped in with other things that we are told are good for us but that we think will be a bit tough to swallow.

Why? First of all, since the early nineteenth century, when the first Italian opera troupe visited the United States, American audiences have enjoyed a love affair with Italian opera. Later came the Wagner craze, as well as periods during which French works enjoyed tremendous vogue. All the while, homegrown operas by American composers went begging. From the earliest time to the present day it seems we Americans have never decided if we really want our own operas or not.

In 1607, the same year that Jamestown, Virginia, the earliest permanent settlement in what is now the United States, was founded, Claudio Monteverdi brought out his first opera, *Orfeo*, in Mantua. But even in the unlikely instance that a member of the original Virginia Colony was aware of Monteverdi nearly 4,000 miles away, the task of survival in the North American wilderness left scant time for courtly pastimes of any sort. The cultivation of opera, like that of slow-growing grapes or olives, requires economic and social stability. Thus, despite the fact that opera went public in mid-seventeenth-century Italy, it didn't begin to sprout in America for another hundred years.

In 1767, the first native American opera was published in Philadelphia. It was never produced, and its title, *The Disappointment*, presaged what American composers would experience down the line. Among the first obstacles faced by colonial opera composers were religious objections to nearly all theatrical projects. They were raised not only because theater audiences tended to be fairly rowdy, or because of the licentiousness of seventeenth-century Restoration drama, but more seriously because of the traditional link between playhouses and prostitution. Moreover, actors and actresses had a reputation for intemperance and promiscuousness—which they still enjoy. Well into the nineteenth century many "proper" folk shunned the theater, with or without music.

As the American colonies girded themselves for rebellion, the Continental Congress passed a resolution in 1774 discouraging "every species of extravagance and dissipation"—opera and theater were at the top of the extravagant heap. With victory in 1781, the restrictions were sufficiently relaxed to allow the production of a musical comedy, *The Temple of Minerva*, with music by the Philadelphian Francis Hopkinson, a signer of the Declaration of Independence. George Washington himself was in the audience.

Italian Opera Emigrates to America

At the beginning of the nineteenth century, America's opera community did boast one figure of international stature. Mozart's collaborator, Lorenzo da Ponte (1749–1838), emigrated to the United States in 1805, leaving behind a web of intrigue and bankruptcy that stretched across Europe. After arriving in New York, the librettist of *Don Giovanni* set up shop as a grocer in Elizabeth Town, New Jersey, a venture that didn't take him long to run into the ground. Several years later, he was invited to join the faculty of Columbia College (later Columbia University) as professor of Italian language and literature in 1825.

That year he also helped to bring the first Italian opera company to New York, led by an elegant and fascinating

Spaniard, Manuel Garcia, one of the most famous singers of his time. Garcia, whose gifted family constituted much of the troupe, had sung the first Count Almaviva in Rossini's *Barber of Seville* in 1816, and both *The Barber* and Mozart's *Don Giovanni* were in the company's New York repertoire.

By the time Garcia's troupe left to tour Mexico the following year, they had established New York as America's opera capital, and forged a solid link between opera patronage and high society that was to last into the present century. And to those gilded patrons, opera meant *Italian* opera. Rossini, Bellini, Donizetti, and Verdi were the overwhelming favorites of the boxholders at New York's old Academy of Music on 14th Street, the city's opera center from 1854 until the opening of the Metropolitan Opera House in 1883. Because the most popular singers were Italian, and because Italian was generally considered to be the language of opera—except in French-oriented New Orleans—even French and German operas were usually performed in Italian translations.

The Italian influence on early American opera was so pervasive that when the outspoken *New York Tribune* music critic William Henry Fry set out to prove that an American could write as good an opera as any European one, he composed a straightforward bel canto score with tuneful music that sounds like Bellini and Donizetti. First performed sixteen times in Philadelphia in 1845, Fry's *Leonora* was composed in English, but when it was finally brought to New York in 1858, it was sung in Italian! Then *Leonora* sank from view, like so many American operas to come.

Americanism

While the landscape painters of the Hudson River School succeeded in creating a visual idiom that was distinctly American next to the work of their English and French counterparts, the progress of American opera was continually hobbled by composers unable to decide whether they should write like Europeans or strike out after something indigenously American.

Moreover, the titles of most nineteenth-century American operas bespeak an urge to blend romantic Old World grandeur with something—anything—American. But whereas American audiences continually doted on foreign imports like Verdi's *Il Trovatore* and Gounod's *Faust*, they ignored native operas like George Frederick Bristow's *Rip Van Winkle* (1855) and Henry Hadley's *Azora, Daughter of Montezuma* (1917). And when our composers tried to attract the public with operas on European subjects—for example, *Zenobia, Queen of Palmyra* (1882) by Silas Gamaliel Pratt—they still got the cold shoulder.

If Americans truly wanted homegrown opera, it might have flourished, but its first offerings faced problems that have doomed many a product—marketing and distribution. In Italy, where opera was in the blood, nearly every town had at least one opera house, producing a regular season of old and new works. Hence the leading Italian music publisher, Ricordi, had a ready-made circuit on which to send the latest operas by Verdi and his colleagues. America, huge enough to boggle the imagination of the most sophisticated European, had no comparable system. Even though most American towns boasted an "opera house," hardly any actually housed opera, certainly not on a regular basis.

These buildings were called opera houses primarily because the silver kings and cattle barons who built them preferred the term to the more prosaic "theater," which still carried a nasty connotation in the heartland. And in the major cities like Chicago, Philadelphia, and New York, where opera was regularly played, audiences generally felt that the only good opera was a foreign one.

The perseverance of American composers finally began to pay off in the twentieth century. During the 1930s several American scores enjoyed at least a temporary vogue after their premieres at the Metropolitan Opera, which was *the* preeminent native venue in those days. Louis Gruenberg's *The Emperor Jones* (after Eugene O'Neill's spooky drama about a murderous Pullman porter who becomes despot of a Caribbean island) gave the great baritone Lawrence Tibbett a meaty role (albeit in blackface). Surprisingly, though the Met produced Gruenberg's opera in 1933, it turned up its nose at George Gershwin's *Porgy and Bess* two years later, despite the fact that the composer had the Met in mind when he wrote it.

In 1985, Gershwin's "American folk opera" finally bowed on the Metropolitan Opera stage. By this time it had been eagerly adopted into the repertoire of other companies throughout the nation.

American Opera Takes Wing: Virgil Thomson

Since the post–World War II era, American opera composers have built up an impressively large repertoire of works that range from the surrealism of Virgil Thomson's

Four Saints in Three Acts (1934) to the cheeky antics of Leonard Bernstein's *Candide* to the minimalism of Philip Glass's *Einstein on the Beach,* and beyond.

In *Four Saints in Three Acts* (composed 1927–28), and in his second opera, *The Mother of Us All,* Virgil Thomson (1896–1989) wedded his appealing, often Baptist hymn–like music to essentially plotless librettos by Gertrude Stein, earth mother to the "lost generation" of expatriate Americans who flocked to Paris between the world wars. There are actually four acts in the first opera, and the saints number eleven (not counting the unnamed ones in the chorus). Thomson himself proclaimed the theme of *Four Saints* as "the religious life—peace between the sexes, community of faith, the production of miracles." Those who fancy the surrealistic, mystical, even humorous references in Stein's free-associative wordplay (for instance, "If a magpie in the sky on the sky can not cry if the pigeon on the grass alas can alas and to pass the pigeon on the grass alas . . .") will have a glorious time. Others may not be amused.

The Mother of Us All concerns the life of Susan B. Anthony and her struggle for women's voting rights. In a moving epilogue, Anthony's ghost haunts the United States Capitol, pondering her martyrdom—"not to what I won but to what was done"—and exhorting future generations to follow her example.

Premiered at Columbia University in 1947, *The Mother of Us All* has chalked up over one thousand performances in the past three decades through its popularity among university opera workshops.

Thomson's final opera, *Lord Byron* (1972), appeals to more traditional palates—at least it would if it were performed more frequently, as it deserves to be. Librettist Jack Larson (whom baby boomers will possibly recall as Jimmy Olson on the 1950s *Superman* television series) supplied a fascinating drama about the defeated effort to obtain a grave for Byron in Westminster Abbey. Set shortly after the poet's death in 1824, the opera quotes passages from Byron's writings, and uses flashback episodes concerning his wretched marriage and his love affair with his half sister to evoke the tempestuous life of the notorious Romantic poet. For the curious, the 1992 recording of *Lord Byron* (Koch International Classics) is well worth the price.

Great American Classics

Americans may love new cars, new gadgets, and new fashions, but in the annals of American opera, the works that have achieved the best performance record tend to be those that have preserved the good old-fashioned conventions; in opera, as in fly-catching, honey is a lot more effective than vinegar, and the compelling story and the melodic, harmonious score have a better chance of getting beyond the first hearing.

Of this group, some of the most consistently revived operas are by the Italian-born Gian Carlo Menotti (b. 1911), founder of the Festival of Two Worlds in Spoleto, Italy, and Charleston, South Carolina. A brilliant theatrical inventor, he wrote his first opera at eleven, and after a long and successful international career, he still remains active. Of Menotti's numerous operas, the best are the earlier ones, some of which were produced on Broadway, and which come as close to standard repertoire as any American work. *The*

Medium (1946) is a powerful two-act thriller in which Mme. Flora, a phony medium, shoots her harmless servant boy in a drunken terror after she begins to think that the spirits have actually touched her. Because *The Medium* is relatively short, Menotti later wrote a curtain-raiser, *The Telephone* (1947), a sprightly contemporary opera buffa about a woman whose endless chain of phone calls keeps her boyfriend on pins and needles, waiting to propose to her.

Menotti's *Amahl and the Night Visitors* (1951) was the first opera written expressly for television, and the touching Christmas tale of the crippled boy healed when he offers his crutch as a gift to the Holy Child became a great favorite from the start. *The Saint of Bleecker Street* (1954) continues the Italian verismo tradition with an emotional story set in New York's "Little Italy." Lauded by critics, the work netted Menotti the Drama Critics' Circle Award, the New York Music Critics' Circle Award, and a Pulitzer Prize.

Menotti, author of his own libretti, also wrote the libretto for *Vanessa* (1958). A study of obsessive love, the score was composed by Menotti's lifelong companion, Samuel Barber (1910–1981), another American neo-Romantic, whose lush music is currently enjoying a serious re-evaluation.

Like Menotti, Dominick Argento (b. 1927) has roots in the Italian tradition, and his operas successfully communicate an emotional impact. Moreover, he is adept at both comedy and drama. Of his comedies, *The Boor*, based on Chekhov's *The Bear*, has enjoyed numerous performances in the United States and abroad since its premiere in 1957. Of his dramas, *The Aspern Papers* (1987) is a splendidly atmospheric work based on Henry James's novella. Argento's most popular opera is the quizzical *Postcard from Morocco* (1971). A one-act chamber extravaganza for seven singers and eight instrumentalists, which investigates a chatty group of eccentric travelers gathered at a Moroccan railway station in 1914, each concealing an odd secret. Argento's score is great fun, brimming with delightful flashes of color and musical humor, all of which are evident in the Minnesota Opera's 1972 recording, now re-released on CD on the CRI label.

In addition to the previous operas, the following have earned their status as American classics. Each is richly rewarding as music and as drama. All are well worth getting to know whenever and wherever the oportunity presents itself.

Carlisle Floyd's *Susannah*, a modern version of the biblical story of Susannah and the Elders, was first produced in 1955. Floyd (b. 1926), who wrote his own libretto, relocated the story to the southern backwoods. Susannah, gentle, generous, and morally straight, is cursed with the sort of beauty that excites men to lust and women to jealousy. When a group of church elders peer on her bathing naked in a stream, they report to the town what they could only fantasize, that Susannah tempted them to sin. From here the drama builds to an explosive climax. Recently recorded with Cheryl Studer (Virgin Classics), *Susannah* is as melodramatic as Puccini's *Tosca*, and just as gripping.

Douglas Moore (1893–1969) took the story of *The Ballad of Baby Doe* (1956) straight from the rumbustious history of the Colorado silver boom of the 1880s, and set it to a beautiful score that glows with the warmth of American folk music. Having stolen her husband, the wealthy Horace Tabor, away from his first wife, Augusta, Elizabeth "Baby Doe" Tabor remains faithful to him even after he loses his fortune. The action culminates in an unforgettable finale, in which Baby Doe comforts her dying husband with a tender lullaby and takes up her vigil at his silver mine as snow begins to fall. Appropriately, the 1956 premiere took place at Central City, Colorado, close to where the historical Tabors lived and died. Because of the affecting quality of the music, and the strength of John Latouche's libretto, the opera has enjoyed regular revivals (though the 1959 Deutsche Grammophon recording is unfortunately out of print at present).

Aaron Copland (1900–1990), widely regarded as the most American of American composers, is best known for his popular ballets *Billy the Kid*, *Rodeo*, and *Appalachian Spring*. His opera *The Tender Land*, commissioned for television but rejected by NBC, was premiered by the New York City Opera in 1954. The setting is characteristically rural American. The teenaged Laurie, aching to escape the confinement of her grandfather's farm, falls for Martin, a drifter, and sees elopement with him as her key to freedom. After Martin jilts her, Laurie decides to leave home anyway. Admittedly the story is a bit *too* relaxed to make a truly gripping opera. However, the score boasts some glorious Copland set pieces, especially the soaring quintet "The promise of living," the toe-tapping party dance "Stomp your foot upon the floor," and the tender love duet "The world seems still tonight." (All the homespun poignance of the score and story are captured eloquently on the Virgin Classics 1990 recording under Philip Brunelle's direction.)

Marc Blitzstein (1905–1964) was commissioned in 1946 to write a work for musical theater and chose Lillian Hellman's play *The Little Foxes*, about a scheming family in the turn-of-the-century South whose members stop at nothing to outwit one another. (The play had made a superb film vehicle for Bette Davis in 1941.) When Blitzstein's version, *Regina*, premiered on Broadway in 1949, however, the audience thought it too operatic to be a musical, and vice versa. After Blitzstein reworked it, *Regina* was produced by the New York City Opera, at which time Hellman, who had initially been skeptical about a musical treatment of her play, declared it "the most original of American operas, the most daring." It remains one of the most successful operatic adaptations of a modern play, with a score that gets under your skin and stays there, as you can hear on the 1992 London recording.

Equally memorable, Lee Hoiby's *Summer and Smoke* is an adaptation by playwright Lanford Wilson (*The Hot L Baltimore*) of Tennessee Williams's play about repressed desire. It has enjoyed numerous productions, including a televised one on Public Broadcasting, since its premiere in 1971. Hoiby (b. 1926) writes lush, deeply expressive music, as gratifying to sing as to hear, and his score captures the bittersweetness of a young woman's happiness sacrificed on the altar of Victorian respectability.

Hoiby later opted for the difficult challenge of setting Shakespeare directly from the original blank verse, and composed a very effective version of *The Tempest*, full of arching melodies and well-tailored ensembles that capture the essential magic and mystery of Prospero's enchanted isle.

On the Cutting Edge with Philip Glass

Philip Glass (b. 1937), one of the most successful and most highly debated American composers, made his splash with *Einstein on the Beach* in 1976, in collaboration with the American director-designer Robert Wilson. *Einstein*, non-narrative in the conventional sense, but nominally concerned with the violin-playing formulator of the theory of relativity, proved the first in a trilogy of works concerned with figures who left their mark on history. *Satyagraha* (1980), to a libretto in Sanskrit by Constance DeJong and Glass, treats Mahatma Gandhi's early years in South Africa. *Akhnaten* (1984) uses the Egyptian pharaoh as the central figure in an examination of reaction to religious orthodoxy; the libretto, by Glass and several associates, incorporates texts in Egyptian, Akkadian, and Hebrew, narrative passages in "the language of the audience," and for local color, excerpts from Fodor's and Frommer's guides to Egypt.

Though controversial, Glass's operas have won him an international following. His music has appealed to trend watchers, not only because of the enormous hype he can stir up (he is among the world's most widely performed composers), but because the minimalist patterns of his music—seemingly endlessly repeated bits of simple melody and harmony with subtle shifts of rhythm—don't sound "ugly" to those who fear the discords' atonality. With his finger on the pulse of public fashion, Glass also has a keen sense of a subject's timeliness, as well as the enviable ability to attract collaborators who have made headlines themselves. *Hydrogen Jukebox* (1990) has a libretto by the veteran "beat" poet Allen Ginsberg. For *The Voyage*, commissioned by the Met to mark the five hundredth anniversary of Columbus's arrival in America, Glass worked with librettist David Henry Hwang, author of the play *M. Butterfly*.

Taking Glass's own premise of man's never-ending quest for discovery, Hwang devised a libretto of chic references to history and pop culture, which treats the professed study of civilization in a series of quick image bites. In *The Voyage*, Glass moves well away from the deadly deedly-doodlings of fundamental minimalism to a more conventionally melodic manner, which he has continued to explore in his subsequent works, among them an operatic treatment of Cocteau's *La Belle et la Bête* (Beauty and the Beast.)

Another recent Met commission prompted John Corigliano (b. 1938) to compose his first opera, *The Ghosts of Versailles*, which sold out the house during its first season in 1991–1992. Inspired by *La Mère coupable* (The Guilty Mother), the final play in Pierre Beaumarchais's "Figaro" trilogy, it takes up where Rossini's *Barber of Seville* and Mozart's *Marriage of Figaro* leave off, and relates what happens when the household of Count Almaviva finds itself at the mercy of the French Revolution. As a successful composer of film scores, Corigliano has created an entertaining homage to the operas we all love. His score is completely modern, but memorably accessible, including quotations from Mozart and Rossini, as well as music that deliberately recalls the styles of composers like Richard Strauss and Puccini, and even the operettas of Offenbach and Gilbert and Sullivan. Since its Met triumph, *Ghosts* has been produced by the Lyric Opera of Chicago, and recorded both on CD and video (Deutsche Grammophon), which makes it readily available to a wide public.

For fans of American opera, the problem remains that, apart from *Porgy and Bess*, relatively few American operas are regularly performed. In fact, most of them rarely make

it to a second season. On one hand, the dynamics of the
opera business favor the production of world premieres to
achieve publicity and funding for regional companies
around the country. After the critics have gone home, however, most other company managers would prefer to produce a different new work rather than take on something
already premiered by another company. On the other hand,
history is littered with operas, old and recent, that are
infrequently revived because they lack musical or dramatic
staying power.

Cases in point are the two operas by John Adams, *Nixon
in China* and *The Death of Klinghoffer*. Both have librettos,
by Alice Goodman, that are essentially "ripped from the
headlines" of current events. But more important, both
were initially suggested by the controversial stage director
Peter Sellars. The difficulty here is that the stuff of television docudramas doesn't readily lend itself to the heroic
nature of opera. It's one thing for Verdi's insomniac King
Philip of Spain (*Don Carlos*) to brood at midnight that his
young wife has never loved him, and that he will only find
sleep in the tomb; it's another for Richard Nixon to muse at
bedtime about the end of his public career (*Nixon in
China*).

Like Glass, Adams began as a minimalist, and his music
shares with Glass's the virtue of not sounding raucous or
"difficult" to ordinary listeners. Moreover, it is well orchestrated, and brims with stimulating instrumental color. But
the repeated patterns, despite their rhythmic vitality, often
sound like accompaniments to an unwritten melody, so that
the listener eventually grows impatient waiting for tunes
that never present themselves.

Rubbing Elbows with Broadway

Given the contemporary cross-pollination between opera and musical theater, we ought to note that although Stephen Sondheim writes for Broadway rather than the opera house (and primarily for Broadway vocalists rather than opera singers), most of his works are virtual operas. For example, the scores of *Sweeney Todd, the Demon Barber of Fleet Street* (1979), *Sunday in the Park with George* (1984), and *Passion* (1994) are primarily continuous in texture, the musical numbers often flowing into one another, with a minimum of spoken dialogue. In *Sweeney Todd*, Sondheim deploys several musical motifs (some based on plainchant from the Requiem Mass) with a dramatic purpose that evokes Wagner. The chorus plays a major role, as commentator and as active participant in the drama, while the ensemble writing is often highly complex. Moreover, Sondheim's lyrics are among the cleverest since Gilbert and Sullivan.

Finally, no discussion of American opera would be complete without touching on Leonard Bernstein, whose importance to the repertoire looms larger as the line between opera and musical theater grows increasingly faint. *West Side Story* needs no explanation—is there anyone who isn't familiar with "Maria," "Somewhere," or the irresistible "America"? Though it is still often considered a non-operatic Broadway show, the recording with Kiri Te Kanawa and José Carreras under Bernstein's own baton (Deutsche Grammophon) proved where the composer himself felt it was heading.

Bernstein's *Candide*, originally billed as "a comic operetta" and later revised into an opera proper, is based

on Voltaire's hilarious satire: Instructed by Doctor Pan-
gloss that this is "the best of all possible worlds," the opti-
mistic Candide and his beautiful Cunegonde overcome
banishment, war, rape, and a host of other trials while wandering the world (in company with the uproarious Lady
with One Buttock). Ultimately they realize that happiness
comes of making the best of reality if they "make their
garden grow."

Getting Your Feet Wet: An Introduction to the Opera Experience

Because it's much the shortest.
—KING GEORGE V OF ENGLAND,
ON WHY *LA BOHÈME* WAS HIS FAVORITE OPERA

In the introduction to this book, I briefly recounted my gradual discovery of opera, a process that extended from my early childhood through adolescence. Some people catch on much earlier, especially if they grow up in homes where opera is already loved. Others come to it suddenly, and later.

My wife, for example, made the discovery when she was a college student. One day her brother came home with a recording of Mozart's *Magic Flute*, told her he was about to listen to it, and, offering her a copy of the libretto, invited her to join him and follow along. From *The Magic Flute*, she took on Wagner's *Ring of the Nibelungs* (four operas) and was hooked by the majestic combination of myth and music.

Still, most people discover opera by hearing an aria, or perhaps a scene, divorced from the complete work. This

initial exposure can take place at a concert or on a public
television broadcast, or by chance encounter on the radio.
Madison Avenue's love affair with opera has also had its
effect, and snatches of arias now soar regularly over the
airwaves to pitch everything from wine and pasta to fast
cars. And certainly the film world has found in opera a
treasure trove of music that creates an immediate mood.
How many people have discovered opera through hearing
the melting phrases of Puccini's "O mio babbino caro"
(from *Gianni Schicchi*) at the start of the Merchant Ivory
film *A Room with a View*; or by the love duet from Bizet's
The Pearl Fishers in *Little Women*; not to mention the
various arias used in films like *Guarding Tess, Philadelphia, The Bridges of Madison County,* and *The American
President.*

The best way, therefore, to increase your knowledge of
the music of opera is to begin with what you know already.
Let's say it's a single aria. If you don't know what opera it
comes from, you can begin by finding out. Recordings of the
highlights used in film and TV have been produced in
myriad "theme" albums, such as the Deutsche Grammophon
label's *Mad About Opera* discs, or the EMI series *Movies
Go to the Opera.* So, you buy that recording (or borrow
it from the public library, or a friend) and play your favorite aria until you know the music by heart. Now you
want more.

The next step is to hear the entire opera. You can take
the plunge in several ways: You can buy tickets for a performance. You can wait for a radio or television broadcast—
not only are the Metropolitan Opera Saturday matinee
broadcasts a tradition throughout the world, but other
major companies like the San Francisco Opera and Chicago

Lyric Opera are regularly broadcast and telecast as well. You can get hold of a complete recording, which usually includes a synopsis and a libretto in the original language with an English translation so that you can follow along. Or you can get hold of a video of the opera, which usually has subtitles to let you follow the text while viewing.

But suppose the complete opera is more than you feel able to swallow at once. It may be quite a jump from a four- or five-minute aria to a complete opera in a single bound. Those whose hearts race every time they hear Wagner's "Ride of the Valkyries" might well blench at the prospect of taking in the whole of *Die Walküre*. Very well, why not try just the whole act in which the seductive aria occurs?

As a professional critic, I review a great many operas, live and on records and videos. On my "off" time I frequently get a hankering to hear this or that act of an opera rather than the whole opera. There's no crime in that. In fact, just as opera lovers have favorite operas, and favorite arias, they also have favorite acts.

Therefore, try the following plan to ease yourself into whole operas. First, obtain a complete recording of the opera in question. In the libretto, which comes with the recording, find that favorite aria. For argument's sake, let's say that it's "La donna è mobile," from Verdi's *Rigoletto*. You'll find it in Act IV, sung by the Duke of Mantua. Then go to the plot synopsis in the libretto, and read the story of the whole opera. You'll learn that the Duke, for all the splendid music he gets to sing, is a male chauvinist pig of the first swill. He sleeps with any woman in sight—his latest conquest has been Gilda, the beautiful, virginal daughter of his court jester, the hunchback Rigoletto. Rigoletto seeks revenge by hiring an assassin, Sparafucile, to murder the Duke. Sparafucile uses his tarty little sister, Maddalena, as bait. The Duke has bitten and come to spend the night with Maddalena at the dilapidated inn run by Sparafucile.

As the Duke waits in his room, he sings, with characteristic male chauvinism, that "La donna è mobile, qual' piume al vento" (Women are as fickle as a feather in the wind).

Meanwhile Rigoletto has brought his ravished daughter to show her what a skunk the Duke is before he arranges the Duke's murder. They lurk outside the inn, peering through cracks in the walls. Inside, the Duke cozies up to Maddalena, cooing sweet words into her ears: "Bella figlia dell' amore" (Beautiful daughter of Love). He is ardent—and randy; Maddalena plays at being as coy as a wanton can be; Rigoletto thirsts for vengeance; and Gilda weeps to see the handsome Duke with another woman. Unfortunately, naive Gilda loves the Duke, despite his being a cad.

Out of this mixture of emotions Verdi has created one of the greatest ensembles in the whole operatic repertoire, the *Rigoletto* Quartet.

Now play the recording and follow along with the libretto. By the time fifteen minutes have passed, you will not only have heard your favorite aria in its dramatic context, but you'll have listened to yet another blue-ribbon piece from the same opera. Verdi's glorious melodies will have taken on a new and richer meaning for you, beyond their superficial appeal as catchy tunes.

Having acquainted yourself with the whole scene built around "La donna è mobile," you're ready to take in the complete act. First you read the rest of the plot—the ensuing storm, Maddalena's request to her brother not to kill the Duke, Sparafucile's decision to trick Rigoletto by killing the next person who comes to the inn instead of the Duke, and concealing the body in a sack, Gilda's decision to sacrifice herself, and the final horrible moments, when Rigoletto opens the sack expecting to gloat over his master's corpse, only to discover it's his dying daughter.

Now play the entire act (or go to the videotape). Thereafter you may want to listen to the act a few more times, or go on to the rest of the opera from the beginning. *Rigoletto* is ideal for this kind of familiarization. The melodrama—founded on *Le Roi s'amuse* by Victor Hugo, author of *Les Misérables*—is powerful, and the story uncomplicated. Moreover, each of the opera's four acts is relatively brief, and packed with extremely melodious music.

Puccini's *La Bohème* is another good opera for whetting your appetite because so many of its musical high points are well known as excerpts. For example, as separate arias, Rodolfo's "Che gelida manina" and Mimì's "Mi chiamano Mimì" have always been tremendously popular; however, when you listen to them in the course of the first act of the opera, they make an even greater musical impact.

Dramatically, each aria allows the two characters to introduce themselves to one another, and to introduce themselves to us, the audience, in some detail: Rodolfo tells us that he is a poet, and describes himself in deliberately poetic language: "I live in happy poverty, but in terms of dreams of love and castles in the air, I've the soul of a millionaire." Mimì's language is far simpler: "They call me Mimì, but my name is Lucia. . . ." She describes her life as an embroiderer of silk flowers, living alone, dreaming in her own way of the real flowers that blossom at winter's end, when the sun shines at last and warms the cold world. She is, after all, consumptive, and though this is not emphasized, the soaring warmth of her music as she describes "the first kiss of April sun" implies how much the return of springtime can mean to someone in her fragile condition. Admittedly, the words are most often ignored by listeners as they focus on the melting beauty of Puccini's melody. But how much more moving these pieces are when you know what they mean.

On a purely musical level, Puccini's deployment of the two arias is even more subtle. Although by tradition the audience applauds at the end of Rodolfo's aria, a recording of the complete opera reveals how quickly Mimì's aria follows Rodolfo's in direct response to his last line, begging her to tell him who she is. There is no intervening recitative between the two. Just a rest before her first note. Thus the second aria virtually flows out of the first one, creating a balanced musical unit. But Puccini isn't finished just yet; Mimì concludes her aria in an offhanded fashion, trailing away in an apologetic, almost spoken line, saying, "I hardly know what else to say; I'm just your neighbor, and have bothered you at an inconvenient time."

Again the music just halts momentarily, without a full close, and the moment is almost immediately interrupted by Rodolfo's friends calling from the street. Their banter maintains the musical energy of the scene, and serves as a bridge to the real climax, the duet "O soave fanciulla." Here again we arrive at a piece long popular as an excerpt, yet in its dramatic context we can hear the way it sums up what has come before, repeating the climactic melody of Rodolfo's aria, and finally reprising the opening measures of the same aria as the two lovers walk off into the night singing of their "Amor!" Thus the three familiar numbers are in fact the closely integrated parts of a beautifully crafted piece of musical architecture. Whatever aria proves your starting point, by graduating from arias to scene to entire act, you are accustoming yourself to the pace of opera and to its ebb and flow on an increasingly larger scale.

Beginner's Luck

For those who are getting their feet wet, here is a winning selection of additional operas that will leave you asking for more. Not only are they all regularly performed in opera houses everywhere, they are also widely available on CD and on video. Titles with an asterisk (*) are also fine for younger people. Just remember that an opera is a story like any other, and so long as you, and your youngsters, pay attention to what's going on, the music and the drama will do the rest.

For Romantics . . .

Puccini: *Madama Butterfly** When a gentle geisha marries an American naval officer, she thinks it's for life; he doesn't. One of the most irresistible of all operas, and the work that inspired the Broadway show *Miss Saigon*.

Puccini: *Tosca* Pure knuckle whitener. A hot-tempered diva, her artist lover, and the menacing chief of Rome's secret police in a love triangle set against the backdrop of Napoleon's Italian campaign.

Verdi: *La Traviata** The same story of the consumptive Parisian courtesan and her doomed love for a younger man that Greta Garbo filmed as *Camille* in the 1930s. But the opera puts the nonsinging version in the shade because of Verdi's poignant score.

R. Strauss: *Der Rosenkavalier* Both a comedy of manners and a touching story of how a beautiful woman comes to terms with the loss of her younger lover to a girl closer to his own age. Strauss's score is a lilting stream of waltzes and splendid melody.

Gounod: *Faust* His legendary pact with the devil gives the old philosopher Faust his youth, but he misuses it to ruin Marguerite. This opera has gone in and out of fashion, but the warm beauty of its score is undeniable. Try the Kermesse Scene and the Garden Scene for starters.

Tchaikovsky: *Eugene Onegin* A straightforward drama of frustrated romance with soulful music by the composer of *The Nutcracker* and *Swan Lake*.

Donizetti: *Lucia di Lammermoor* Based on Sir Walter Scott's novel, poor Lucy plights her troth to her brother's worst enemy, only to be driven to madness and murder. The Mad Scene and the great Sextet are only two of the high points that have made this a favorite opera for more than a century and a half.

Offenbach: *The Tales of Hoffmann** The only serious opera by the best of all French operetta composers. Based on several of E. T. A. Hoffmann's tales of dreamlike fantasy and romance, the music bursts with joie de vivre, and even an appropriate touch of madness.

Hot and Heavy . . .

Bizet: *Carmen** The Toreador Song and the Habañera nestle spicily in the midst of this highly charged melodrama of a Spanish Gypsy and her fatal effect on a young soldier.

Puccini: *Turandot* In ancient China the icy Princess Turandot sends all suitors to the block when they can't answer her riddles. Prince Calaf's aria "Nessun dorma" (No one is sleeping) is a favorite, and no one possibly could nod off during this most exotic of all Puccini operas.

Great and Grand . . .

Verdi: *Aida** The famous Triumphal March is only one of the high points in this mixture of pomp and trying circumstances set in ancient Egypt.

Verdi: *Otello* The Moor who loved not wisely but too well. No need to brush up your Shakespeare for this towering musical feast.

The Music Says It All . . .

Verdi: *Il Trovatore* Count di Luna loves Leonora, but Leonora loves Manrico; Manrico loves Leonora, too, but loves his old Gypsy mother better. The old Gypsy hasn't told him that she's really not his mother, and that di Luna is his brother. The story is tangled, but the tuneful score hits home. That's why even the Marx Brothers couldn't dampen its appeal when they razzed it in *A Night at the Opera*.

Myths and Fairy Tales for Any Age . . .

Humperdinck: *Hänsel und Gretel* The Grimms' fairy tale ingeniously set to music that warms your heart. No adult is too old for this one, nor any reasonable child too young. Splendid fare at Christmas, or at any time.

Mozart: *The Magic Flute* A prince must rescue a princess from the clutches of the evil Queen of the Night. This is the opera that Ingmar Bergman filmed. It's available on video, and a sheer delight.

Mozart: *Don Giovanni* The proverbial Don Juan has enjoyed 1,003 conquests in Spain alone, but when he kills the father of his latest target, he soon finds time running out. A supernatural Gothic tragicomedy, this masterpiece was widely popularized in Joseph Losey's 1979 film version.

Wagner: *Lohengrin* Possibly the most consistently beautiful of all Wagner scores, this story of knighthood, witchcraft, and a woman's tragic curiosity provides a compelling narrative that embodies the essence of German Romanticism.

Wagner: *The Flying Dutchman* The legendary Dutch captain cursed to sail forever on his ghostly ship until he can find salvation through a woman's love. The earliest and shortest of Wagner's standard operas, it is a truly Gothic yarn set to glowingly melodious music.

Wagner: *Die Walküre* The second part of the *Ring of the Nibelungs* cycle, set in the distant era of Norse mythology. Siegmund discovers the beautiful Sieglinde married to a lout. They fall in love, only to discover they are long-lost twins. But that doesn't stop them! Their elopement causes an uproar on earth and amongst the gods in Valhalla. Some of Wagner's most popular music is in this score; if you follow along with the story, you won't be able to put it down.

Effervescent Fun for All . . . *

Mozart: *The Abduction from the Seraglio* Two Spaniards must rescue their lady loves from the Pasha's harem. Amadeus was in love when he composed this score, and it shows.

Rossini: *The Barber of Seville* Figaro here, Figaro there, deservedly the most famous of all Italian comedies.

Rossini: *La Cenerentola* A delightfully humorous take on the Cinderella story. The fairy godmother is a wise sorcerer in this version, and the musical fireworks never stop.

Operetta*

With its humor, its spoken dialogue, and irrepressible tunefulness, operetta is also a fine way to gain entry into the world of opera. These are just some of the most frequently performed ones:

J. Strauss: *Die Fledermaus* A husband would like very much to cheat on his beautiful wife, but she already has a would-be lover of her own. Music by the Waltz King; need we say more?

Lehár: *The Merry Widow* She's beautiful, she's rich, and her love life is of supreme importance to her country. Would that all widows could be this joyous.

Gilbert and Sullivan With a keen sense of the ridiculous, W. S. Gilbert aimed his barbs at the eternal foibles of society, and has kept society laughing at itself for over a century. Sullivan's music is indescribably delicious:

The Mikado The most popular of all the G&S canon. Even the German kaiser liked it. The Lord High Executioner can't hurt a fly, but he needs to execute somebody before the Mikado arrives for a visit. Japan was never like this.

Iolanthe When the Lord Chancellor of England mistakenly insults the Queen of the Fairies, the repercussions send the House of Lords reeling.

Patience The famous send-up of Oscar Wilde and the English Aesthetic craze of the 1880s. Two rival poets battle for the love of a milkmaid.

HMS Pinafore You can smell the salt and tar on board a British man-o'-war whose crew of hardy seamen are exceedingly polite.

The Pirates of Penzance A Major General who knows more of history and art than of military strategy must call upon a company of fainthearted policemen to rescue his daughters from the clutches of a band of orphaned pirates.

Bernstein: *Candide* Voltaire's uproarious satire of this best of all possible worlds. Dick Cavett used the sparkling "Glitter and Be Gay" for his TV theme. The Lady with One Buttock is "so easily assimilated" when she learns proper Spanish rhythm, and the glorious finale teaches us all the pleasures of a simple life.

Learning What's Around

Once the bug bites, the best way to keep apprised of movings and shakings in the opera world is through the magazines and periodicals that cover the opera and classical music fields. Among the most widely read publications are *Opera News*, *Opera Monthly*, and the British *Opera*, while opera is also covered in *BBC Music Magazine* (distributed in North America). These offer a wealth of useful, often fascinating information on the personalities and events that make opera tick, as well as reviews and recommendations of the latest recordings, videos, and live performances. Those interested primarily in recordings can choose from Britain's venerable *Gramophone* (which publishes a North American edition), or such American heavyweights as *Fanfare, CD Review, American Record Guide, Stereophile,* and *Stereo Review.* Of course, the quarterly *Schwann-Opus,* part catalogue part magazine, is the source to consult on what's available on record. Most are available on better-stocked newsstands, in stores such as HMV, Barnes & Noble, and Tower Records, or by subscription.

And don't overlook classical music radio, commercial and public. Though not broadcast everywhere, several programs are widely available. Two are especially significant. George Jellinek's syndicated program, *The Vocal Scene*, has long investigated every facet of vocal music, through Mr. Jellinek's deep knowledge and love of the art. National Public Radio's program, *Performance Today*, broadcast throughout the country over the NPR network, offers news, live and taped performances, and reviews of recordings by nationally recognized critics. Opera isn't the focal point, but it is part of the mix.

As your knowledge grows, you might find it useful to zero in on critics whose taste mirrors your own opinions about singing voices, musical styles, repertoire, etc. You will then be able to read their writing with a sense of confidence in their opinions about what to see, what to buy, which new singers to notice.

Above all, follow your instincts. If a particular composer appeals to you, investigate more of his works. If you like a particular singer, look into his or her other recordings or performances. Once you find your niche in opera, you will continually make extraordinary discoveries.

When in Rome, or
A Little Bit of Opera Etiquette

The customs and observances of theater- and opera-going have evolved remarkably over the centuries. In Shakespeare's day, theaters were uproarious places, roofless like a modern stadium, with gentry seated on benches along several ranks of balconies, and the common folk, or "groundlings," milling in a boisterous throng on the ground around the stage. Adding to the general noise level was the frequent interplay between the audience and the actors, which could often become bawdy to the extreme. By the Restoration period in England, it was difficult to tell which was more risqué, the licentious comedies or the behavior of the "orange girls," who made their way through the house selling oranges and more fleshly refreshments for ready money.

When the first public opera houses opened in mid-seventeenth-century Italy, they too were fairly lively places, and remained so well into the nineteenth century. Compared to New York's present 4,000-seat Metropolitan Opera House, or the 2,155-seat Bolshoi Theater in Moscow, most older houses were small, seating between a few hundred to a thousand people. Hence members of the audience could see one another and be seen, and social display played as important a part in an opera performance as the opera itself. Moreover, early theaters were lit by candles, which kept the auditorium and its many distractions illuminated through the entire performance and prevented people from keeping their undivided attention on the stage. Audience members often purchased a candle along with their copy of the libretto so they could follow the performance line by

line (modern supertitles actually have a historical prece-
dent). Those candles gave off a lot of heat, which, together
with only rudimentary ventilation and the combined smells
of melting tallow, perspiration, perfume, and greasepaint,
made an evening at the opera fairly ripe.

Because the libretto indicated when the major arias
would be sung by the various characters, members of the
audience often left their seats to socialize in another box
during passages they felt were less important. If a whole
act didn't interest them, they might go out for a bite, and
return for their favorite number. Performances were therefore accompanied by talk, laughter, and as much moving
about in the audience as there was on stage.

Gas lighting was introduced in 1822 at the Paris Opéra,
the chief house in nineteenth-century Europe (located in
the rue Le Pelletier before the building of the great Palais
Garnier a half century later). However, the gaslights in the
auditorium were still kept lit throughout the performance,
so the chatter and social interplay continued unabated.
Then Richard Wagner opened his Festival Theater at
Bayreuth in 1876, and instituted a startling new innovation:
Before the curtain went up, the house lights went down,
dimming the auditorium and turning all eyes on the stage.

Electricity was first used in a theater to light Gilbert and
Sullivan's brand-new Savoy Theatre auditorium on opening
night in 1881, and it improved matters further: Whereas
gaslights required a small flame to remain lit in order to be
turned up again, electric lamps could be turned off completely. Thus, by around 1890 attendance at the theater and
opera had pretty much evolved into the quiet, attentive
activity we know today. Still, as late as 1934 a celebrated
conductor—Sir Thomas Beecham, according to many

sources—felt compelled to turn to the audience just before the curtain rose and shout, "Shut up, you bastards!" Old habits die hard.

So, for that matter, do the old and often picturesque names given to the various locations around an auditorium. Social history comes into play here. Most traditional opera house auditoria are constructed in a horseshoe shape, with rings of boxes and balconies around the floor. The proverbial "diamond horseshoe" got its name from the glittering effect of the elaborate jewelry customarily worn by ladies seated in the boxes of New York's old Metropolitan Opera House—now demolished.

Apart from boxes at the Met and elsewhere, the most expensive tickets in an opera house are usually the orchestra seats, which get their name from being on the floor of the auditorium where the orchestra pit is located. In some theaters these seats are called Parterre, from French for "by the ground." In Britain, they are usually called the Stalls or Orchestra Stalls, a Victorian invention: In eighteenth- and early-nineteenth-century theaters, patrons sat on long wooden backless benches. But with the rise in the taste for luxury, theater managers replaced the benches with the rows of padded seats with backs and arms that separated each from the other like individual stalls. The Dress Circle, usually a level or two above the boxes, gets its name from its early-nineteenth-century antecedent at London's historic Theatre Royal, Drury Lane, where a ring of Dress Boxes was so called because they were reserved only for well-dressed, dignified patrons. When the boxes were later replaced by an open ring of seats, the name "Dress Circle" was coined.

At the top of the house, the seats were traditionally

called the Gallery, or "the gods," a term first used in 1752 in
London houses. Nowadays these seats are usually known as
the Balcony or Upper Circle or the more homey Family
Circle in American houses. Toward the end of the Victorian
age, London and New York theater managers let their
taste for crimson damask and purple mohair furnishings
color their nomenclature for other parts of the house: Even
today travelers to distant box offices can often choose from
seating in grand tiers, royal circles, imperial grand circles,
amphitheatre stalls, and other palatial-sounding locations.
Especially if the house is an old one, before choosing your
tickets, make sure to look at the seating plan to be certain
of the view: If you're seated behind a pillar, the grandest
circle is just a blind alley.

Whether those who haven't gone to an opera are cowed
by the idea of attending a performance in a foreign language, or whether it's just the odd notion that the opera
house is filled with aesthetic snobs, there is often a great
deal of fuss about attending the opera, as if it were some
ritual from another planet. In fact, it is much the same as
going to any theater, and the same rules of courtesy hold.

You should arrive on time for the performance—nothing
is so distracting as latecomers slithering into the middle of
a row. In many houses, latecomers are not permitted to
enter the auditorium until the end of the first act, or possibly the first scene, if the act is a long one. Try to be in your
seats about ten minutes before the curtain, especially if the
opera house is an unfamiliar one, so you can look around and
enjoy being where you are. This will also give you a chance
to read the program, to see who is in the cast, and bone
up on the plot. Many American opera houses today

feature some form of surtitles. Libretti are usually available for sale at the door, however.

Once the lights go down—and *definitely* once the conductor has appeared and bowed—*don't talk*. Admittedly one of the original purposes of the opera overture was to let a noisy audience know that the performance had begun. That's also why many Mozart and Rossini overtures start with a few loud chords (ta-DA). Even so, you should employ the rule of thumb that as long as the houselights are out, you *don't talk*.

If a performance thrills you, contain your gasps of pleasure, however difficult it may be to do so. Wait at least until the end of the aria to applaud, and that includes waiting until the end of any orchestral postlude. Applause brings up the question of booing. European audiences, especially Italian and German ones, boo what or whom displeases them as often as they applaud what they like. Cries of disapproval are not nearly so widespread in America—perhaps because of our sense of fair play. It is a touchy matter, to be sure, and as a rule you probably shouldn't proclaim your negative opinions until you have a substantial amount of operatic experience under your belt. In either case, some operas, especially Wagner music dramas, are customarily played straight through, with no applause until the end of the act. So if you aren't sure just when to applaud, the safest thing is to watch what those around you do, and follow suit if you agree.

And for that matter, don't hum along, or loudly tap your fingers or toes in time to a catchy section. Drumming, tapping, humming, and even conducting are fine in the privacy of your own home. But in the opera house there is nothing more distracting to other listeners than this kind of demonstrative enjoyment. Equally annoying is the lozenge slowly, painfully, noisily unwrapped from its crinkly cellophane. Unwrap it *before* the lights go down.

Above all, going to the opera should be enjoyed as a special occasion. It can be an opportunity for dressing up, though it's not necessary to don tails or tux and evening gowns except on opening nights—and even then, a dark business suit and cocktail dress will do just fine. But always remember that as with any performance, noisy accessories, such as two- or three-bangle bracelets jangling on the wrist, can distract both the performers and your fellow audience members. By the same token, alarm watches, beepers, and cellular phones have no place in any auditorium.

Finally, don't be afraid to ask questions when you don't understand something, about the story, about the music, about the color of the tenor's hat. Frequently the house staff people are very knowledgeable, especially the ushers, who often work in an opera house precisely to be near the operas, and who pride themselves on being well informed. But whether you consult an usher or a fellow patron, whether your question pops up at intermission or at dinner, ask. True opera lovers want to share their enjoyment with others, so by asking questions of someone who knows a thing or two, you stand to increase your knowledge, and with it your enjoyment.

Making a Production of It

You're traveling in Europe, and find yourself in a town with a fine old opera house. Rossini's *Barber of Seville* is on that night. You decide it would be a splendid way to spend the evening. After a pre-curtain dinner, you take your seats in the lovely auditorium, with its elaborate gilt decoration.

The house lights dim. Applause for the conductor. Rossini's overture strikes up and bubbles along, putting you in the mood for the comedy to come. The heavy brocade curtain rises. But what's this? Instead of the familiar Spanish street, with Dr. Bartolo's house, the stage is dominated by an immense female torso, quite anatomically correct. And when Almaviva (in an Armani suit) enters, he directs his serenade toward a lighted window that magically appears in the torso's crotch.

Well, well. The libretto synopsis didn't prepare you for *this*, did it? Nor did your preliminary reading about Gluck's *Orfeo ed Euridice* prepare you for a performance of that opera in which Euridice is killed by a hit-and-run taxicab; nor the *Don Giovanni* that takes place in Brooklyn nor the *Traviata* in which Violetta dies in a modern hospital bed hooked up to a battery of flashing monitors.

Welcome to the world of opera production, where anything goes. Or at least it seems to, now that stage directors (increasingly referred to by their British title, producer) continue to throw off old conventions in search of new ways to look at beloved old operas.

Lest I seem too critical of contemporary opera direction, let me say at once that opera, like any art that has been around for several centuries, definitely needs to be shaken up from time to time.

A new interpretation of a twice-familiar opera doesn't automatically mean trouble. The British director Jonathan Miller, for instance, has produced *Rigoletto* against a Mafia background that has worked splendidly. Several years ago, in one of the finest productions of *Don Giovanni* that I can recall, at the Royal Swedish Opera in Stockholm, all manner of interpretative liberties had been taken with the original, including the Don singing his Champagne Aria while splashing about in a wooden bathtub. After he had been dragged to perdition by the statue, Don Giovanni appeared upstage in the finale, being caressed by several nubile young women, presumably in Hell, but able silently to mock the moralizing of his earthbound friends during the epilogue, thus having the last laugh.

In the modern workings of an opera performance, it is the conductor who presides over the musical end, making sure that the orchestra, singers, and chorus play and sing the right notes at the right time. Likewise, it's the stage director who presides over the dramatic end, though even the most headline-making producer is supposed to be sub-servient to the conductor.

In the history of opera, however, the distinctive role of the stage director is a relatively modern one. From the sev-enteenth through nineteenth centuries, stage direction was largely a matter of moving the chorus and soloists on and off the stage without bumping into anything. The composer was usually in charge of the production, working with the ballet master and the stage manager. Sets for castles, town squares, and forests were often similar in appearance from one opera house to another, and they were in the charge of the scene painter and chief carpenter, who also arranged the hand-winches, trapdoors, and other machinery neces-sary for the various spectacles and effects.

As recently as the turn of the century, smaller opera houses and traveling companies relied on conventional painted flats that could be pressed into service for more than one opera—the ramshackle inn needed for the last act of *Rigoletto* could also do for Lillas Pastia's hostel in the second act of *Carmen*; the monks' cloister used for *La Forza del Destino* could be reused for the cloister in *La Favorita*; a quasi-Egyptian backdrop could serve *Aida* as well as *The Magic Flute*.

Operatic acting was fairly rudimentary. Soloists sang their arias downstage at the footlights, or were arranged in a line for ensembles. Their movements were limited to stereotyped gestures for anger, love, sadness, and so on.

The nineteenth century witnessed increasing complexity in the matter of staging, especially in Paris, where the sumptuous productions at the Opéra involved elaborate sets and costumes. Nonetheless, composers from Verdi and Meyerbeer to Massenet and Puccini oversaw the stage action in their own operas, at least for the first few productions in major theaters. Likewise Wagner, whose primary goal was to transform opera into a completely unified work, took charge of every aspect of his productions.

The decades following World War II saw the rise of a new school of interpretive directors, of whom the most influential figure was Wieland Wagner (1917–1966), grandson of the composer. Having been cleared by a de-Nazification court, and faced with resuscitating the Bayreuth Festival, which had been a focal point of wartime Nazi propaganda, Wieland took a hard look at the Wagner repertoire and decided to make a clean break with the past. Stripping away the romantic pomp and elaborate realism that had characterized Bayreuth productions under the stewardship of his grandmother, Cosima, and his father, Siegfried Wagner, Wieland approached the music dramas in ways that emphasized the mythical element of the stories and their complex psychological underpinning. Instead of relying on traditional representational scenery, Wieland employed his stage as a vast, uncluttered canvas for abstraction, using extraordinarily imaginative lighting to create subtle and revolutionary implications of mood, locale, and relationship between the characters. He also weaned his singers away from conventional and often meaningless stage gestures, replacing them with simple, sparse motions, so that every movement was charged with significance.

Today, opera productions run the gamut from the pictorial opulence of Franco Zeffirelli's work, in which everything down to the candles and curtain rods is designed with meticulous attention to historic detail, through the often outrageous modernism of Peter Sellars and his kindred spirits, who attempt, with varying results, to reinterpret classic operas in terms of contemporary urban life— Wagner's Tannhäuser as a television evangelist, Mozart's *Marriage of Figaro* set in New York's Trump Tower.

Faced with so many choices of what to see and hear— even if you can't scour Europe and America for new productions, many of them are available on video—our chief duty as an audience is not to be complacent. Don't accept in opera what you wouldn't accept in any theatrical production. By the same token, just because a production is traditional in style doesn't mean it is interesting—handsome sets and costumes alone don't create gripping drama. The odd or strange reinterpretation may well offer new dramatic insight into a familiar work. Nonetheless, the ranks of stage directors are full of clothiers in search of gullible emperors, and for every routine traditional staging of an opera, there is an equally dreary modernist staging.

The bottom line, when viewing a production, is that we

must always ask ourselves if the director has been able to make a viable dramatic point by presenting an opera in a novel interpretation. We must ask if the director has been able to inspire and guide his or her singers to portray believable flesh-and-blood characters (the greatest works of Mozart, Verdi, Wagner, and Puccini are concerned with real people and real emotions, no matter how sensational the plot). And we must ask if the visual experience goes against the grain of the music, or really does enhance it and enlighten us.

Why We Say "Bravo!"

Bravo, signor padrone! Ora incomincio a capire il mistero ... (Bravo, my lord! Now I am beginning to understand the mystery ...)
—LORENZO DA PONTE,
THE MARRIAGE OF FIGARO, ACT I

According to the laws of physics, every action results in an equal and opposite reaction. According to the laws of opera, every action results in an equal reaction—but not necessarily its opposite. Because humans are vocal creatures, our first response to things is usually some sort of exclamation—a gasp of surprise, a shout of joy, a roar of anger. On the football gridiron and the baseball diamond, a touchdown or a home run elicits raucous shouts. Likewise, when an opera singer delivers a magnificent rendition of "Mi chiamano Mimì," "Dich, teure Halle," or "Di quella pira," the audience has its own cry of pleasure: "Bravo!"

The word is rooted in the Italian adjective *bravo*,

meaning, among other things, "clever," "capable," and "plucky." Indeed, it takes no small amount of pluck to sing to an audience of hundreds, even thousands, not to mention sing brilliantly. Venerable in its original tongue, "Bravo!" entered the English language over two centuries ago as a similar exclamation for something admirable. "That's right—I'm steel—Bravo!—Adamant—Bravissimo!" declares the hero of the elder George Colman's 1761 comedy, *The Jealous Wife*. In Italian and in English, "bravo" is also an old word for a daring villain, or, as Dr. Johnson's *Dictionary* put it, "a man who murders for hire." Hence not only is the murderous character Sparafucile listed as a *bravo* in the original libretto of Verdi's *Rigoletto*, but the annals of opera include such once-popular titles as *Il Bravo*, by Rossini's contemporary Saverio Mercadante, and *Bianca, or The Bravo's Bride*, by Michael William Balfe, one of the most popular composers of Victorian London.

Getting back to modern times, as an Italian exclamation, *bravo* is sensitive to gender and number. Say, "*Bravo!*" when it's a male singer, "*Brava!*" when it's a female (some enthusiasts like to lay it on thick with "*Brava diva!*"), "*Bravi!*" when there are two or more singers worth crowing about. If you're really feeling generous with compliments and want to encompass a whole group, "*Bravi tutti!*" is your answer (though it's best to reserve this for the final curtain calls of the evening).

And when you've felt the earth move, when you realize that you won't be able to sleep that night for the sheer pleasure the performance has given you, let the artists know it by raising your voice in a superlative shout of "*Bravissimo!*" To an opera singer, there's no greater compliment.

Postlude: If Music Be the Food of Love... Let's Eat!

Though food and opera have long gone hand-in-hand as far as pre-theater dinners and after-theater suppers are concerned, singing and chewing are obviously incompatible. So on the lyric stage, eating scenes are far outstripped by drinking or toasting scenes crowned with a *brindisi*, or drinking song.

In fact, those dining scenes that do occur in opera are usually interrupted by more pressing dramatic concerns. For instance, the lavish meal set for the ribald hero of Mozart's *Don Giovanni* comes to a rapid end when the statue of the Commendatore arrives with a poor appetite— at least, for food. In Verdi's *Macbeth*, the guilt-stricken Macbeth would gladly sit at his banquet table in Act II, if his chair weren't already occupied by Banquo's ghost.

Of course there's the traditional, if not always accurate, image of the opera singer whose avoirdupois betrays a fondness for good food. Opera's so-called Golden Age coincided with the so-called Gilded Age, when people lived in blissful ignorance of cholesterol and triglycerides. The

Gilded Age witnessed the zenith of elaborate cuisine. It was the era in which the hotelier César Ritz and the chef Auguste Escoffier were to dining what Gilbert and Sullivan were to music. In fact, Ritz and Escoffier were responsible for the initial success of London's Savoy Hotel, built in 1889 by Gilbert and Sullivan's business partner, Richard D'Oyly Carte: Having erected London's first truly comfortable hotel, Carte engaged Ritz and Escoffier to assure that the guests' experiences would be truly delicious as well.

In those days, Escoffier and other chefs created elaborate dishes to honor leading personalities of the time, and of these dishes, composers, singers and even operas received their ample share of tribute. Escoffier's famous *Cook Book* (first published as the *Guide Culinaire* in 1903) reveals a tantalizing array of dishes that mingle richness with operatic history. Some, like Spaghetti Tetrazzini, Pear *Belle Hélène*, and Peach Melba—not to mention their ascetic counterpart, Melba Toast—have remained part of contemporary gastronomy; others are now only relics of a more opulent past. But when these filling creations were first rolled into the plush dining rooms of the rich and famous, they surely elicited ovations worthy of any opera house.

Pasta and Italian opera have a mutual affinity, and the famous Spaghetti Tetrazzini, with its rich sauce of diced chicken, cream, and Parmesan cheese, was Escoffier's tribute to the coloratura soprano Luisa Tetrazzini. Then there's Spaghetti Caruso, named for one of Tetrazzini's favorite singing partners, the mounds of pasta covered in a marinara sauce studded with mushrooms and diced chicken livers.

Though not an Escoffier invention, one of the most frequently encountered dishes on Italian restaurant menus is Lobster or Shrimp Fra Diavolo, with a spicy red sauce piquant with kitchen diablerie. Its apt name comes from the eighteenth-century Italian bandit, Michele Pezza, known as "Brother Devil," who long eluded his pursuers in the mountains of Calabria. Daniel F. E. Auber and his librettist Eugène Scribe immortalized him in their most famous comic opera, *Fra Diavolo*, which, though composed in French, subsequently became a great favorite when translated for Italian theaters.

Chicken and chicken breasts figure prominently in the operatic pantheon. For example, Poularde Adelina Patti, named for the Victorian diva, can be translated as "Chicken Patti," but that has an unfortunate connotation in the era of fast food. A poached pullet stuffed with rice is served with a paprika-flavored *suprême* sauce (chicken stock, mushroom stock, cream) and surrounded by glazed artichoke bottoms and whole truffles.

Chaud-froid de Poularde à la Gounod honors the composer of *Faust*. A *chaud-froid* is simply a cold dish of cooked meat or poultry. This one combines squares of cold poached chicken breast on slices of chicken mousse, coated first with a cold chicken cream sauce. Then it is decorated with pieces of black truffle in the form of a bar of music, covered with clear chicken jelly—to protect the truffle appliqué—and presented in a silver dish embedded in a block of ice.

Chicken Sautée *Mireille* memorializes a Gounod opera that deserves to be more familiar today. The opera's Provençal setting is reflected in the sauce of tomatoes, onion, sweet red pepper, and garlic added to the sautéed chicken. Saffron-flavored rice completes the dish.

Red meat has its own operatic nature. Next to Beef Wellington (named after the "Iron Duke," whose proverbial toughness is hardly mirrored by this succulent fillet),

Tournedos Rossini is possibly the most celebrated prepara-
tion of the tenderloin: diminutive steaks cut from the
narrow portion between the center cut, or Châteaubriand,
and the tip, or filet mignon. (The latter is *not* named for
Ambroise Thomas's opera, but refers to the tender
(*mignon*) quality of the meat itself.)

The word *tournedos* has an apocryphal history. According
to one tale, Rossini, no mean cook himself, was dining at the
Café Anglais in Paris. Summoning the maître d'hôtel, he
complained that his beef was tasteless and sent it back to
be garnished with his favorite combination of goose liver,
truffles, and Madeira sauce. Assured that this would be unfit
for the composer's eyes, Rossini apparently quipped, "Then
serve it while I turn my back [*tourne le dos*]." Whether
Rossini or Escoffier actually invented the dish, it calls for
sautéed fillets, each on a fried crouton spread with meat jelly,
topped with a slice of goose liver and a slice of truffle, surrounded with truffled Madeira sauce, and accompanied by a
dish of buttered noodles and Parmesan cheese.

Beyond beef we come to a variety of operatic savories.
Selle de Veau à la *Tosca* (named for the Sardou melodrama
that inspired Puccini's opera) calls for braised sliced veal
loins, put back on the bone, over a bed of cut macaroni with
cream and sliced truffles. The whole arrangement is glazed
with a Mornay sauce (béchamel mixed with stock and
Gruyère and Parmesan cheeses).

Ham Soufflé *Carmen* is a cheese soufflé incorporating
ground ham and puréed tomatoes, baked with a garnish of
sweet red pepper strips to suggest the nature of Bizet's
Iberian spitfire.

And what of the German repertoire? If you're in a mood
for *Der Rosenkavalier* or another Richard Strauss opera,

you might consider honoring the composer's memory by serving up mutton chops (or lamb chops for the faint-hearted) with the accompaniment he always demanded when staying at the Savoy: raspberry jam. (It used to send the kitchen staff into fits.)

You can even wax operatic at breakfast—or brunch—if you're willing to forget calories and quick bites in favor of one of the following ample eye-openers.

Eggs Meyerbeer honors the composer of *Les Huguenots.* Two baked eggs are served flanking a grilled lamb's kidney, with a Périgueux sauce of Madeira and chopped black truffles.

Fried Eggs Verdi are hard-boiled eggs, stuffed with an herbed mixture of the yolks, chopped ham, and béchamel sauce, rolled in breadcrumbs, deep fried, and served with a garnish of asparagus tips.

Desserts, the grand finale of any fine meal, have proved a great inspiration to lyrical cooking. Two of the most famous ones are also among the simplest to prepare: Peach Melba and Pear *Belle Hélène.*

Escoffier invented the former for Nellie Melba, although it didn't take its present name and form at first. Though Melba (born Helen Mitchell in Melbourne, Australia) had become the leading soprano of Covent Garden's Italian and French wings, she had a hankering to sing Wagner, for which her bell-like voice was too light. Against everyone's better judgment she undertook the role of Elsa in *Lohengrin* in 1892. Though it wasn't exactly a success, the would-be Wagnerite played hostess the following night at a celebratory supper at the Savoy, prepared, of course, by Escoffier. Unable to choose between an ice cream dessert and fruit, Melba told him to effect a compromise. The result was poached peaches over vanilla ice cream under a strawberry glaze, which, in honor of Melba's

Lohengrin venture, he mounted between the wings of a carved ice swan nestled in a nest of spun sugar and strawberry leaves. He named it Les Pêches au Cygne, or Swan Peaches.

Yet Escoffier was apparently unsatisfied with the strawberry glaze, and several years later he revised the dish, dispensing with the swan and substituting a more sharply contrasting raspberry glaze for the peaches. Having transformed it, he rechristened it Pêche Melba.

Poire *Belle Hélène*, cold poached pear coated with hot chocolate sauce and served on vanilla ice cream, was invented in honor of the beautiful, and comical, Helen of Troy in Offenbach's operetta *La Belle Hélène*.

And after all this richness, what about Melba Toast? Escoffier originally devised it while taking Sunday tea with César Ritz and his wife at their house in suburban north London. Sitting in the garden, Marie Louise Ritz said she wished that their buttered toast could be thinner. Ever ready to oblige a lady in distress, Escoffier popped up and ran into the house, emerging shortly thereafter with a plate of very crisp pieces of toast he had effected by splitting ordinary toast slices in two and returning them to the oven.

On the spot, he named the curled and smoking wafers, Toast Marie in his hostess's honor. However Mme. Ritz modestly protested that such an appellation was "too anonymous." In light of commercial developments this was fortunate, for it relieved Escoffier of blame for inventing a Ritz cracker. In any event, it wasn't long before that warbling trencherman Nellie Melba discovered Escoffier's toast while in the throes of a diet. She took to it immediately, and with typical graciousness, allowed Escoffier to rename it after *her*. Thus was Toast Melba launched upon its *via crunchis*.

BON APPETIT!

in an opera. (For further detail, see "Airs and Graces: What Is an Aria?")

arietta   (ah-ree-EHT-tah) A brief aria,* usually with a simple melody.

arioso   (ah-ree-OH-zoh, Italian: like an aria) A solo passage in a more melodic style than recitative* but shorter and less elaborately structured than a full-blown aria.

arpeggio   (ahr-PEHJ-yoh, Italian: from *arpa*, harp) A chord whose notes are played one after another, as would be done on a harp, rather than simultaneously. Arpeggio accompaniments, with and without an actual harp, are common in nineteenth-century opera arias, especially slow ones, e.g. in the tenor aria "Una furtiva lagrima" in Donizetti's *L'Elisir d'Amore.*

ballet   A dance episode performed during the course of an opera. Ballets play an important part in French Baroque opera, and are also a standard feature of nineteenth-century grand opera.* (For further discussion, see the chapter on French opera.)

basso continuo   See **continuo.**

bel canto   (behl CAHN-toh, Italian: beautiful song) The traditional Italian vocal technique, which emphasizes beauty of tone and brilliance of performance. (For further discussion, see "Romantic Bel Canto Era")

brindisi   (BREEN-dee-zee, Italian: from *brindare,* to toast) A drinking song, often written for solo voices with a refrain for chorus, e.g., "Libiamo ne' lieti calici" in Verdi's *La Traviata.*

buffo/buffa   (BOOF-oh/BOOF-ah, Italian: comic) The term "opera buffa" refers to Italian operatic comedies, e.g., Rossini's *Barber of Seville.* The term "basso buffo" refers to a bass singer who specializes in comedic roles

Coming to Terms with Opera: A Concise Glossary

As with any art form, opera has a language of its ~~own~~ beside the foreign one being sung on the stage. Oper~~atic~~ minology can be bewildering to those just starting ~~out~~ even to old hands. Here are some of the terms t~~hat~~ frequently crop up in operatic conversation. Use ~~this~~ glossary whenever you need a quick explanatio~~n or~~ pronunciation.

Note: Cross-references within the gloss~~ary are marked~~ with an asterisk.

a capella   Choral or vocal music unacc~~ompanied by instru~~ ments.

aria   (AH-ri-ah, Italian: air) The usu~~al~~

such as Dr. Bartolo in Rossini's *Barber*. Buffo basses don't necessarily have beautiful voices (though a fine voice doesn't hurt), but they *must* be good comic actors, and have a facility for singing rapid patter.*

cabaletta (cah-bah-LEHT-tah, Italian: etymology uncertain, possibly from a galloping horse, *cavallo*) In early-nineteenth-century Italian opera, a short, exciting song that forms the final section of an aria or duet. Characterized by a popular melodic style, with a fast tempo and simple repeated rhythms in the vocal line and accompaniment, the cabaletta provides a showy contrast to the slow cantabile* that precedes it. Rossini, Bellini, and Donizetti cast many of their scenes in aria-cabaletta form. Verdi gradually discarded the cabaletta as a formality that impeded dramatic action. Verdian examples do exist, including the brilliant tenor cabaletta "Di quella pira" in *Il Trovatore*, the superb duet, "Si, vendetta" in *Rigoletto*, and the fiery "Sempre libera" in *La Traviata*.

cadenza (cah-DEHN-zah, Italian: cadence) An elaborate, ornamental vocal flourish written at the end of an aria, and sometimes at important points within the aria itself. The cadenza allows the singer an opportunity to display skill at vocal flourish or fioritura,* sometimes in contrast to equivalent showmanship by an instrumental embellishment, or obbligato.* Cadenzas were originally devised by the singers themselves, but by the nineteenth century, Rossini and other composers began to write their own cadenzas in order to limit the liberties singers could take with their music.

cantabile (cahn-TAH-bee-leh, Italian: in a singing manner) A term originally applied to an aspect of bel canto,* emphasizing a smooth, flowing, lyrical, melodious style of singing, or playing (as in Chopin piano music). During the early and mid-nineteenth century cantabile came to refer to the slow opening section of an aria; also to the slow, expressive middle section of a duet, in which case it is preceded by a faster, more declamatory section called the *tempo d'attacco* (attack). In relevant arias and duets, the cantabile is followed by a cabaletta, and the whole unit is referred to as a scena.*

cantilena (cahn-ti-LEH-nah, Italian: singsong or lullaby) A term commonly used to describe either a flowing, melodious vocal part, or a singer's ability to sing in a smooth, flowing manner. A singer needs good cantilena skills to sing a cantabile properly.

canzone (cahn-ZOHN-eh, pl. *canzoni*, from the Provençal *canzo* or folk song) Originally a troubadour song, during the eighteenth century the word came to mean a simple, often folklike song performed *as a song* by one character in an opera to another, e.g., "Voi, che sapete" in Mozart's *Marriage of Figaro*, sung by Cherubino to the Countess while accompanied by Susanna on a guitar. Even if the opera were a spoken play, a canzone would still be sung.

canzonetta (Italian: a little canzone) Usually a light, brief song in a simple style.

castrato A gelded male soprano* or alto.* Now obsolete. (For further discussion, see "Altered States: The Castrato.")

cavatina (cah-vah-TEE-nah, Italian: from *cavata*, carved out, i.e., an epigraph) In eighteenth- and nineteenth-century operas, a brief solo song, simpler in style than a full aria. The cavatina itself is a mere sentence or two set to music and introduced by an orchestral anticipation of the first vocal phrase. In early and mid-nineteenth-century Italian opera, a cavatina is often the first aria sung by a character. Examples include the Countess's "Porgi amor" in *The Marriage of Figaro*, Nemorino's "Quanto è bella" in Donizetti's *L'Elisir d'Amore*.

chest voice/chest register/singing from the chest —See **register**.

coloratura (coh-loor-ah-TOO-rah, Italian: coloring) Brilliant vocal ornaments and ornamental passages, containing rapid notes, runs of scale* and arpeggio* patterns, trills,* and related virtuoso* material. A fundamental element of Italian bel canto* style. Mozart's two arias for the Queen of the Night in *The Magic Flute* are famous examples for soprano. Rossini's operas are characterized by much coloratura writing. See also **fioritura, gruppetto, passagework, trills**.

comprimario (com-pri-MAH-rio, Italian: with the principal singer) In modern parlance, the *comprimario* sings supporting roles such as Lord Arthur Bucklaw, the murdered bridegroom in *Lucia di Lammermoor*. Their voices usually lack the striking individuality, beauty, or size of lead singers, but they often enjoy long and satisfying careers as valued character players, without suffering the intense pressure of international stardom.

concertmaster/concertmistress (called the "leader" in England) The first violinist of an orchestra. Apart from leading the orchestra's violin section, the concertmaster plays any solo violin passages in an opera, acts as the orchestra's chief representative in negotiations with the management and the conductor, or music director, and when necessary substitutes for the conductor in rehearsals and, in a pinch, at a performance.

continuo Abbreviation of the term "basso continuo." In Baroque and early classical music, the instrument or group of instruments that play the bass line of a composition and supply the harmony supporting the melody. The usual continuo group includes a bass string instrument (such as a cello) and a harpsichord or other keyboard intrument, which also plays the bass line and fills in the chords (traditionally guided by numerical figures written over the bass line, in a musical shorthand). Though the basso continuo plays with the full orchestra throughout seventeenth- and eighteenth-century opera, it alone accompanies the recitatives.

counterpoint (from Latin: *punctus contra punctum*, note against note, and thus melody against melody) Music in which two or more melodic lines play at the same time. Most music, from the simplest round (e.g., "Row, row, row your boat") to the most complex Bach fugue,* or a love duet for two singers, involves counterpoint. Such music is called *contrapuntal*.

countertenor A high tenor who cultivates his falsetto* register in order to sing roles in seventeenth- and eighteenth-century repertoire originally composed for a male alto or mezzo-soprano. A countertenor is *not* a castrato.

cycle A series of operas or music dramas* that tells a continuous story. The greatest and most famous cycle is Wagner's *Ring of the Nibelungs*, which comprises four music dramas: *Das Rheingold, Die Walküre, Siegfried,* and *Götterdämmerung* (Twilight of the Gods), all four ideally performed consecutively over four days. (See "Wagner Without Tears" in the German opera chapter.)

da capo aria (Italian: literally "from the head," i.e., the beginning) In Baroque practice, a three-part aria in which the first and third sections are identical (A–B–A form). The melody in the first section of a da capo aria is sung straight, but the singer usually adds elaborate ornamentation when reprising it in the third.

deus ex machina   (DAY-oos ex MAH-keen-ah, Latin: god from a machine) In Baroque and classical opera seria,* the convention whereby a crisis in the plot is resolved happily by the appearance of a god or other divine figure who decrees that all shall end well. The god usually enters from high above the stage and descends in a cloud or chariot operated by some form of stage machinery, hence the term.

divertissement   (dee-vehr-tiss-MOHN, French: diversion) In French Baroque opera, the ballets and other songs or dances not essential to the plot but providing a light moment within the more serious framework. The divertissement could also be a self-contained dramatic entertainment with singing and dancing, and sometimes fireworks or other spectacle, often presented for a special occasion.

duet   A composition for two singers, in which both parts are of equal musical importance, e.g., "O soave fanciulla" in Puccini's *La Bohème*.

dynamic marks   Words or abbreviations indicating how loudly or softly a piece of music is to be played or sung:

pianissimo   (*pp*) extremely soft

piano   (*p*) soft, quiet

mezzo piano   (*mp*) soft, but slightly louder than piano

mezzo forte   (*mf*) somewhat louder than mezzo piano, but not so loud as forte

forte   (*f*) loud

fortissimo (*ff*) extremely loud

crescendo (*cresc.*) an indication to increase the volume from one point to another

decrescendo (*decresc.*) / **diminuendo** (*dim.*) An indication to decrease the volume from one point to another

sforzando/sforzato (*sfz* or *sf*) literally, "forcing," meaning to make a sudden vigorous accent on a single note

entr'acte (French: between the acts) Music, usually instrumental, played between the acts or scenes. In Italian opera such music is sometimes called the intermezzo.* Among the most famous of these pieces are the three entr'actes in Bizet's *Carmen* and the intermezzo in Mascagni's *Cavalleria Rusticana*.

falsetto (fahl-SEHT-to, Italian: *falsa*, false) The highest register* of the male voice, having an unnatural or effeminate sound. It is occasionally employed by tenors to reach high notes above their ordinary chest and head range. See **countertenor**.

finale (fee-NAH-leh, Italian: final, last) The conclusion of an act or an entire opera, often with series of movements contrasted in tempo and mood, and performed by the soloists and chorus. Because much of the dramatic tension is likely to climax at the end of an act, finales tend to be longer and more elaborate than the scenes and arias that precede them.

fioritura (fyor-i-TOO-rah, pl. *fioriture*, Italian: florish) Florid vocal ornament, or coloratura, either written out by the composer or improvised by the singer.

fugue (fyoog, Italian: *fuga*, to chase) An instrumental composition typical of the eighteenth-century Baroque style, in which three or more distinct musical lines (called "voices") begin in succession, then interweave with each other while variously taking up a short melody (called a "subject") and tossing it from voice to voice. Johann Sebastian Bach is the characteristic composer of fugues. Fugues are rarely employed in the vocal portions of an opera (a notable exception: the final ensemble of Verdi's *Falstaff*). But they are an occasional feature of the Baroque French overture. See **overture.**

grand opera Often used as a generic term for serious opera as distinguished from opera buffa or operetta. Historically, grand opera refers to large-scale operas, especially French ones written from the 1830s onward, with elaborate historical subjects dramatized in four or five acts, and calling for a large cast, lavish sets and costumes, and a general emphasis on spectacle. (For further discussion, see "Grand Opera" in the French opera chapter.)

gruppetto (groo-PEHT-toh, Italian: little group) A melodic ornament in which a main note is alternated with two subsidiary notes, the first a whole step above the main note, the second a half step below the main note (e.g., the series of notes C–D–C–B–C). Also called a "turn."

harmony Broadly speaking, several notes sounded at once (i.e., a chord) creates harmony. The term refers, therefore, to the vertical or chordal structure of music, as opposed to the horizontal structure, which is melody* and counterpoint.*

head voice/head tone See **register.**

intermezzo (inter-MET-zoh) In Baroque and early Classical opera, a light, often comedic entertainment introduced between the acts of an opera seria. The eighteenth-century *intermezzi* (e.g., G. B. Pergolesi's *La Serva Padrona* [The Servant (as) Mistress, 1733]) were the predecessors of opera buffa. In the late nineteenth century, the purely instrumental intermezzo (or entr'acte*) became a fixture of verismo opera.

kapellmeister (German: chapel master) Originally the title given to the master of music in a court chapel. Later the term came to denote the conductor of any musical organization, whether ecclesiastical or theatrical. Outside German-speaking countries, however, it has unfortunately come to imply a conductor of integrity and skill who lacks inspiration.

largo See **tempo.**

legato (leh-GAH-toh, Italian: tied, i.e., ligature) Refers to music played or sung in a smooth manner, without any audible break between the notes.

leitmotiv/leitmotif (LITE-mo-tif, German: leading motif) A term not invented by Richard Wagner, nor much used by him, but important in regard to his work. The leitmotif is a basic musical feature in his music dramas.* Leitmotifs are musical motifs, or symbols, linked to specific characters, situations, and recurrent ideas in the drama. As such, they are repeated in the course of a music drama or cycle whenever that character, situation, or idea is referred to or even thought of. (For further discussion, see "Wagner Without Tears" in the German opera chapter.)

libretto (Italian: little book) The literary text of an opera. The word also refers to the printed booklet in which an opera text (often with a translation) is published for sale at the opera house, or to accompany a complete recording of an opera. See **titles.**

lyrics Words or verses written expressly for musical setting. Lyrics imply text for a song or aria* as opposed to the text of recitatives.*

Märchenoper (MEHR-schen-oh-per, German: fairy opera) An opera based on a fairy tale or folk tale, and usually employing some folk melodies or themes imitating folk melodies. The genre was extremely popular in late nineteenth-century Germany, and exemplified by Humperdinck's *Hänsel und Gretel.*

masque (pronounced "mask") A hybrid seventeenth-century English entertainment combining spoken dialogue with musical and dance episodes. (For further discussion, see "Masques and Marvels" in the English opera chapter).

melodrama, melodramatic music A musical genre in which speech or action is accompanied by instrumental music. Melodramas occur most frequently in German operas with spoken dialogue, and the two most familiar examples are the Grave-Digging Scene in Beethoven's *Fidelio*, and the Wolf's Glen Scene in Weber's *Der Freischütz.* The term "melodrama" also refers to a play in which a sensational plot takes precedence over psychologically natural characterizations. Victorien Sardou's *La Tosca*, the source of Puccini's opera, is a classic example of melodrama, while television soap operas are melodrama's simpleminded descendants.

melody Generally speaking, any series of notes in horizontal (or linear) succession forms a melody. When we think of melodiousness or tunefulness, however, we are thinking of melodies with a distinctive quality that appeals to our ears. When two or more melodies are played together so that they sound well, we have counterpoint.*

messa di voce (meh-sah dee VO-cheh, Italian: placing the voice) A characteristic vocal technique of eighteenth-century bel canto in which the singer sustains a single note while gradually increasing and then diminishing the volume. The term should not be confused with *mezza voce*.*

mezza voce (meht-zah-VOH-cheh, Italian: half voice) To sing softly, with restrained volume.

mezzo-soprano The female voice range between soprano and contralto. (For further discussion, see "The Marvelous Middle Ground.")

minimalism Originally a visual arts term, adopted by musicians to describe a style of composition in which extended musical passages are built upon a single, brief musical figure or motif* by continuous repetition with little if any change. Philip Glass's *Einstein on the Beach* is a classic example of musical minimalism applied to opera.

mise-en-scène (meez-on-SEHN, French: put into scene) A term referring to the physical elements of a stage production, i.e., sets, props, costumes.

motive/motiv/motif A short, distinctive musical theme recurring throughout a scene or an entire opera as a unifying element. Related to a leitmotif,* but not necessarily used in the same comprehensive way.

music drama A term significant to Wagner but not actually invented by him. In current usage, music drama is a form of opera in which text, music, and stage action are completely integrated. Most notably, music drama abandoned number opera's* separate arias linked by recitative. Instead, lyrical passages equivalent to arias rise out of a continuous flow of arioso*-like dialogue. Music drama also discards all purely vocal display in favor of purely dramatic expression. (For further discussion, see "Wagner Without Tears" in the German opera chapter.)

musical comedy A musical play with songs, dialogue, and dances, usually in a jazzier, less sentimental vein than European operetta.* Briefly: in an operetta, Ruritanian grand dukes and student princes waltz with merry widows and chambermaids; in a musical comedy, Chicago bankers and Long Island merchant princes fox-trot with waitresses and circus performers. (For further discussion, see the chapter on operetta.)

number opera An opera composed of separate "numbers"—arias, duets, ensembles, choruses, etc., so called because they are actually numbered in the score. Each number tends to end with a full close, which is ordinarily a cue for applause. The numbers are linked by recitative* or spoken dialogue. The number opera was the standard operatic form through the mid-nineteenth century, and most works from Handel's day through that of Verdi followed this format. Wagner moved away from number operas toward the musical continuity of music drama.* Verdi followed suit in his later works, especially *Otello* and *Falstaff*.

obbligato (oh-blee-GAH-toh, Italian: obligatory) In Baroque practice, an instrumental solo played as a duet with the solo voice. The term is derived from the fact that such an instrumental solo was notated by the composer and the player was obligated to play it as written instead of improvising in the manner of the continuo* player. Arias with violin, flute, or other instrumental obbligatos are a characteristic feature of seventeenth- and eighteenth-century opera seria, while such instrumental embellishments became a frequent element in nineteenth-century opera, such as the flute obbligato in the Mad Scene in Donizetti's *Lucia di Lammermoor*. (See "Interlude: Sheer Madness!")

opera buffa   See **buffo/buffa**.

opera seria   (SEH-ri-ah, Italian: serious opera) Term denoting the chief genre of Italian opera during the seventeenth and eighteenth centuries. Distinguished by serious or tragic plots based on ancient history or classical mythology, and composed according to specific conventions and formalities. (For further discussion, see "Opera Seria" in the Italian opera chapter.)

operetta   A theatrical work with spoken dialogue and music, light, comedic, and often sentimental in tone. Offenbach, Gilbert and Sullivan, and Johann Strauss wrote the most famous examples. The ancestor of musical comedy. (For further discussion, see the chapter on operetta.)

ornamentation   See **coloratura, fioritura, gruppetto, passagework, trill**.

overture   (Italian and French: opening) An instrumental composition, comprising several sections in contrasting tempos,* played before the curtain rises, to introduce an opera or related work and set the mood. Often called the sinfonia in Italian operas. Baroque operas often start with a so-called French overture, distinguished by a slow, dignified opening section in duple meter, leading to a fast section in triple meter. Many nineteenth-century operas and operettas begin with a potpourri overture made up of themes from the opera itself, which gives a taste of what lies in store (e.g., the overtures to Verdi's *La Forza del Destino*, Johann Strauss's *Die Fledermaus*, and Gilbert and Sullivan's *Iolanthe*) See **prelude**.

parlando/parlato (pahr-LAHN-doh/pahr-LAH-toh, Italian: speaking/talking) A direction to sing with a light tone of voice approximating speech. Eighteenth-century secco recitative* is often performed in this manner. So is comic patter.*

passagework Sections of an aria that contain brilliant display of coloratura rather than important thematic ideas. One refers variously to "scale passages," and "arpeggio passages." Baroque opera seria arias are often distinguished by passage work, as is the vocal writing of Rossini.

passaggio See **register.**

patter Words sung very rapidly to produce a comical effect. Patter songs, arias, and ensembles abound in Italian opera buffa and in operettas by Gilbert and Sullivan, Offenbach, and other composers.

portamento (por-tah-MEHN-toh) Singing method in which the voice glides smoothly from one note to the next. A particularly expressive stylistic trait employed with great finesse by Caruso and other late-nineteenth- and early-twentieth-century singers, and by string players as well.

preghiera (preh-GYEH-rah, Italian: prayer) In a Catholic nation such as Italy, opera composers, especially during the nineteenth century, fully exploited the emotional implications of prayer scenes in their operas. French and German composers followed suit. The musical style is often quiet, with a simple melody for the solo singer or singers presented in relief against a choral background. *Preghiera* numbers abound in opera: e.g., "La Vergine degli Angeli" in Verdi's *La Forza del Destino* and Desdemona's "Ave Maria" in *Otello*. Sarastro's

"O Isis und Osiris" in Mozart's *Magic Flute* is an earlier example.

prelude A piece of instrumental music, shorter and less elaborate in form than a full overture, written as an introduction either to an act or to a whole opera. Verdi often wrote preludes to his operas instead of complete overtures, in order to set the mood quickly and economically. Of these, the preludes to *Rigoletto* and to the first and third acts of *La Traviata* are memorable examples.

premiere/premier (French: first) The first performance of a work. In Italian, called the *prima* (PREE-mah).

presto See **tempo**.

quartet In opera, an ensemble for four voices, e.g., "Bella figlia del' amore" in Verdi's *Rigoletto*. Other examples include the *brindisi** "E nel tuo, nel mio bicchiero" in Mozart's *Così fan tutte*, and the beautiful "Mir ist so wunderbar" in the first act of Beethoven's *Fidelio*.

quintet In opera, an ensemble for five voices. Comparatively rare in the repertoire, the best-known example is the rapturous "Selig, wie die Sonne" in the last act of Wagner's *Die Meistersinger*.

recitative (reh-chee-tah-TEEV, Italian: *recitativo*, recitation; French: *récitatif*; also referred to by the English pronunciation of the abbreviation, "recit.") Musical setting of speech or dialogue in which the music closely follows the inflection and rhythm of speech as opposed to formal melody. Recitative links the arias and ensembles in an opera and it is in the recitatives that the action of the story advances. *Recitativo secco* (SEH-coh, i.e., dry) is accompanied only by the continuo.* *Recitativo accompagnato* (ah-cohm-pahn-YAH-toh, i.e., accompanied) is accompanied by the orchestra.

register Men's and women's voices are said to have different registers from bottom to top, each with its distinctive tone quality. In men, the registers are called chest, head voice, and falsetto.* In women, the registers are called chest, middle, and head voice. Chest voice gives the most powerful tones, head voice the lighter, and often more flexible ones. Well-trained voices are able to move easily and seamlessly from one register to the next, by controlling muscular tension in the larynx. Nonetheless, most voices have a break between registers—called the *passaggio* (pah-SAHJ-yo, Italian: passage) where difficulties such as "cracking notes" can occur while "switching gears." Attentive composers are careful, therefore, to avoid writing legato melodies across the break, or to ease the difficulties by writing the troublesome notes on an easy vowel.

romanza (ro-MAHn-zah, Italian: romance) An aria, usually amorous, usually slow in tempo, e.g., "Celeste Aida" in Verdi's *Aida*.

roulade (roo-LAHD, French) A florid vocal passage or highly ornamented melody. See **coloratura**.

rubato (roo-BAH-toh, Italian: robbed) A deliberate flexibility of tempo used as an expressive device. Rubato makes use of subtle quickenings and slackenings of tempo at significant points in a piece of music. Rubato has been discussed since the eighteenth century, but became a characteristic feature of nineteenth-century performance.

scale A series of notes arranged in ascending or descending order, as in do-re-mi . . . scales are one of the essential building blocks of music. Vocally speaking,

rapid scale passages are a feature of coloratura,*
passagework,* etc.

scena (SHEH-nah, Italian: scene) Used variously in Italy
to refer to the stage setting, as well as the subdivisions
of an act. Musically speaking, a scena refers to a
solo scene similar to an aria, but more loosely constructed (e.g., Leonore's "Abscheulicher" in Beethoven's *Fidelio*). In nineteenth-century Italian opera,
a scena is a solo scene made up of an introductory
recitative,* followed by a slow cantabile* aria, and con-
cluding with a fiery cabaletta.*

sextet An ensemble for six voices. The most famous operatic example is the sextet "Chi mi frena" in Donizetti's
Lucia di Lammermoor.

sinfonia (sin-FOH-nia, Italian: symphony) An overture.*

soubrette (soo-BRET, French: cunning) In eighteenth-
century Italian convention the stock character of the
quick-witted servant girl. Despina in Mozart's *Così fan
tutte* and Susanna in *The Marriage of Figaro* are soubrette
roles. In common vocal parlance, the soubrette is a light
soprano, adept at comedy, who would sing the roles above,
as well as Adele in J. Strauss's *Die Fledermaus*.

spinto (Italian: pushed) The term used to describe an
essentially lyric tenor or soprano whose voice has sufficient push or power to sing the lead roles in late-
nineteenth-century Italian opera, especially those in
the Verdi and Puccini repertoire.

squillante (squeel-LAHN-teh, Italian: pealing, ringing) A
term often invoked to describe the brilliant sound of a
well-produced tenor voice. One also refers to the
squillo (peal) of a tenor. A tenor whose voice lacks
penetrating brilliance is said to lack *squillo*.

stage director/producer/régisseur   In contemporary usage, the stage director (called producer in Britain; *régisseur* in Germany and other countries) is in charge of the dramatic production of a performance. The stage director decides on the stage action, rehearses the soloists and chorus in their individual characterizations, and works with the set, costume, and lighting designers to determine what the audience will see when the curtain rises. (For further discussion, see "Making a Production of It.")

surtitles/supertitles   See **titles**.

tableau   (ta-BLOW) The French term for scene, referring either to the stage setting or the subdivisions of an act. Also used to describe a deliberate "freeze-frame" effect on stage at the end of a scene as the curtain falls.

tempo   (Italian: time) The relative speed at which a piece of music is to be played. Tempo marks are normally given in Italian and range from slowest to fastest as follows:

largo   broad, very slow

lento   slow

adagio   slow

andante   (ahn-DAHN-teh, literally: walking) an easy pace

moderato   moderate

allegretto   lively but not too fast

allegro   (literally: cheerful) lively or quick

presto   very fast

prestissimo   as fast as possible

accelerando   (ah-chel-eh-RAHN-doh, literally: accelerating) an indication to increase the speed

ritardando   an indication to slow down

tessitura   (teh-see-TOO-rah, Italian: texture) The average pitch or range of a melody, aria, or entire role, relating

to where it lies in a singer's voice. The tessitura of a
piece can be uncomfortably high or low or just right,
depending on the singer.

titles/surtitles/supertitles The running translation of the
text of an opera projected on a screen above the stage.
At the Metropolitan Opera House, the translation is
shown on miniature screens discreetly arranged in
front of every seat in the auditorium.

However controversial, this technological development, based on the subtitles used for foreign films and
operas on video, has proven a great boon to audiences
throughout the world, allowing them to follow the dramatic action closely at actual performances no matter
what language is being sung on stage. Titles are often
employed even when the opera is sung in English
because the sung words of an opera often fail to carry
into the auditorium from the stage.

tonality Music written in a specific key (C major, A
minor, B-flat major) that revolves around a central
pitch is called "tonal." Tonal music represents the
dominant form of Western music from the seventeenth through early twentieth centuries. Though
popular music is still basically written in a tonal idiom,
much serious music in the twentieth century has
explored nontonal idioms ("atonality"), characterized
by generally dissonant harmony and the absence of
conventionally tuneful melody. Operas written in this
idiom can be extremely powerful, expressive, and
even beautiful (Berg's *Wozzeck*, for example), but
many listeners still regard them as an acquired taste.
One of the reasons that minimalism* has achieved
popularity is its simple tonal harmony. Hence it

doesn't sound harsh the way many people expect modern music to sound.

travesti   (French: past participal of *travestir*, to disguise) See **trouser role.**

tremolo   See **vibrato.**

trill/shake   The rapid alternation of a principal note with the note either a whole step or half-step above it. Written as a vocal ornament, primarily for female singers, and for lyric and coloratura tenors, and occasionally for baritones and even the rare bass.

trio   An ensemble for three voices, e.g., "Di geloso amor' sprezzato" in Verdi's *Il Trovatore*; "Anges purs, anges radieux" in Gounod's *Faust.*

trouser role   A male character sung by a female, e.g., Cherubino in Mozart's *Marriage of Figaro*; Prince Orlofsky in J. Strauss's *Die Fledermaus;* Hansel in Humperdinck's *Hänsel und Gretel.* Trouser roles are usually intended to suggest boys or adolescents, and are most often sung by mezzo-sopranos, who combine a lyrical timbre with a suggestive boyish heft to the voice.

turn   See **gruppetto.**

vibrato   (vee-BRAH-toh, Italian: vibration) In violins and other string instruments, a slight wavering of pitch produced by the oscillating motion of the left hand. The natural pulsation or wavering that one hears in the sustained tones sung by a trained adult voice. Produced partly by the throat muscles and partly by the action of the diaphragm and the breath passing over the vocal chords, a fine vibrato adds flavor, color, and expression to the vocal sound. Voices lacking a vibrato (e.g., children's voices) are said to be "white."

When the vibrato is unpleasantly fast, it is called a "bleat" or "goat bleat." When the vibrato is unpleasantly slow, or wide (i.e., it sounds as if the sustained voice is wavering between two distinct pitches), it is called a "tremolo" (TREH-moh-loh) or a "wobble." The wobble is often the result of poor vocal technique, or the unfortunate effect of vocal deterioration.

virtuoso A term used to describe any musician who performs with great technical skill and polish.

wobble See **vibrato**.

zarzuela (sahr-SWEH-lah, Spanish, from the palace of La Zarzuela near Madrid) A traditional, and very appealing Spanish operatic genre related to operetta but also including works in a more serious vein. (For further discussion, see the chapter on operetta.)

Acknowledgments

Writing, especially when one is plowing through in the small hours of the night, seems like the loneliest profession imaginable. But in reality a book and its author could not exist without a little help from their friends. Words are insignificant gratitude for the assistance and encouragement unstintingly given by the following friends and colleagues:

For reading various portions of the manuscript and offering sage and welcome comments I thank: Dr. Judith Burton, F.R.S.A., Chairman of the Department of Fine Arts and Humanities, Columbia University Teachers' College. George Jellinek, broadcaster, author, and one of America's preeminent commentators on opera. James Keller of *The New Yorker*, a writer and thinker of elegance and distinction, and a wonderfully generous spirit. Raymond Sokolov, Arts Editor of the *Wall Street Journal*, and a renowned authority on matters of gastronomy.

Four invaluable colleagues at *Opera News* also took the time to peruse and comment on various portions of the manuscript, despite the daily pressure of reading endless galleys and new copy: Patrick J. Smith, editor-in-chief; Brian Kellow, managing editor; Jane Poole, senior editor; and John Freeman associate editor. To them my additional thanks for permitting me to adapt the chapter on operetta from my article originally published in *Opera News*.

My thanks also to Robert Sandla, editor of *Stagebill Magazine*, and to Fiona Maddocks, editor of *BBC Music Magazine* for permitting me to adapt the material on verismo and on the baritone from articles I, respectively, wrote for those publications.

I further thank: Sir Donald McIntyre, whose portrayals of Wotan and Hans Sachs are amongst my choicest memories, for his perceptive observations on Wagner's dramaturgy, which we have discussed over many a dinner on both sides of the pond. Curtis Brown for helping me unearth a number of elusive facts. Gilbert E. Kaplan, and Marie and Spanton Ashdown, for their observations as truly enlightened members of the great opera audience. Jeanne McCafferty, a splendid mystery novelist and knowledgeable expert on the recording industry, for her advice on getting through the traumatizing experience of putting something between covers while clinging outwardly to a semblance of daily professional life. Gail and William Averill for their valuable comments and good cheer when I needed them. Sonia and George Toubin, whose assistance and eagle eyes kept me from despairing. Deirdre Mullane, my editor at Dutton, whose idea this book was, and whose burgeoning interest in opera helped give it shape and direction. My literary agent Robert Silverstein, who so adroitly shepherded this project into position. And, of course, the sterling baritone Thomas Hampson, who made time in his busy performance schedule to honor this book with a thoughtful introduction. And his tireless personal assistant, Carla Maria Verdino-Süllwold, who kept the channels of communication opened between us to the four corners of Mr. Hampson's peripatetic world.

As colleagues and friends they are all of them priceless.

Without a doubt, my deepest appreciation and love to my wife, Michelle Jacobs, whose delight in opera is boundless. Despite her own professional obligations, she tirelessly acted as a knowledgeable sounding board for a multitude of questions. She read and commented on each chapter and each illustration as it took form. Most of all, she endured with humor and infinite patience my dreadful company during the gestation of this book.

Index

Abbado, Claudio, 54
Abduction from the Seraglio, The
    (Mozart), *see Entführung aus dem*
    Serail, Die
Académie Royale de Musique, 95
Adams, John, 226
Adriana Lecouvreur (Cilea), 89
Africaine, L' (Meyerbeer), 106
Aida (Verdi), 3, 45, 81, 84, 148, 237
Akhnaten (Glass), 224
Alagna, Roberto, 26
Albert Herring (Britten), 199
Alceste (Gluck), 99
Alda, Frances, 5
Aldeburgh Festival, 200
Aler, John, 26
Alfred (Arne), 191
Allen, Thomas, 28
Almira (Handel), 118
alto, 19, 35
Amadeus (Shaffer), 68
Amahl and the Night Visitors (Menotti),
    220
Anderson, Hans Christian, 15
Anderson, Marian, 19
Andrea Chénier (Giordano), 90, 148,
Anna Bolena (Donizetti), 75
Araiza, Francisco, 26
Argento, Dominick, 220
aria, 35
Ariadne auf Naxos (R. Strauss), 139,
    140
Arne, Thomas Augustine, 190–91
Artwork of the Future, The (Wagner),
    131
Aspern Papers, The (Argento), 220
At the Boar's Head (Holst), 197
Atys (Lully), 114

Auber, Daniel F.E., 101, 108, 207, 257
Auden, W.H., 202
Azora, Daughter of Montezuma
    (Hadley), 216

Baker, Dame Janet, 20
Balakirev, Mily, 163, 164
Balfe, Michael William, 194, 254
ballad opera, 160, 190
Ballad of Buby Doe, The (Moore),
    221–22
Ballo in Maschera, Un (Verdi), 82
Barber, Samuel, 220
Barber of Seville, The (Il Barbiere di
    Siviglia) (Rossini), 51, 56, 72, 74,
    210, 215, 239, 248
Barberillo, de Lavapies, El (Barbieri),
    210
Barbieri, Francisco, 210
baritone, 26–28
Bartered Bride, The (Smetana), 179
Bartók, Béla, 181–82
Bartoli, Cecilia, 20
bass, 28–30
Bayreuth Festival, 131–32, 244, 251
Beaumarchais, Pierre, 225
Beauty and the Beast (Glass), 225
Beethoven, Ludwig Van, 12, 56, 124–26
Beggar's Opera, The (Gay), 142, 189–91,
    202
Behrens, Hildegard, 18
bel canto, 65, 130
Belle Hélène, La (Offenbach), 207
Bellini, Vincenzo, 51, 74, 76, 153, 155,
    209, 215
Berg, Alban, 141, 144
Berlioz, Hector, 55, 56, 106–107
Bernstein, Leonard, 218, 227

Betrothal in a Monastery (Prokofiev), 179
Billy Budd (Britten), 199
Bishop, Sir Henry Rowley, 192
Bizet, Georges, 108, 215
Bliss, Sir Arthur, 189
Blitzstein, Marc, 222
Blow, John, 186
Bluebeard's Castle (Bartók), 181–82
Bohème, La (Puccini), 84, 90, 146, 229, 233–35
Bohemian Girl, The (Balfe), 194–95
Boieldieu, François-Adrien, 100–101
Boito, Arrigo, 92
Bolshoi Theater, 243
Bonci, Alessandro, 43
Bonney, Barbara, 17
Bononcini, Antonio Maria, 188
Bononcini, Giovanni, 188
Boor, The (Argento), 220
Boris Godunov (Mussorgsky), 114, 156, 164–66, 172
Borodin, Alexander, 163–64, 168–70, 174–75
Borodina, Olga, 21
Bouffes-Parisiens, 206
Bouilly, Jean Nicolas, 125
Bravo, Il (Mercadante), 254
Brecht, Berthold, 142–43, 189
Bretón, Tomas, 210
Britten, Benjamin, 157, 183, 189, 197–200, 203,
Büchner, Georg, 141
Bumbry, Grace, 20

cabaletta, 73, 130, 263
Caccini, Giulio, 60, 62
cadenza, 263
Cadmus et Hermione (Lully), 95
Caldwell, Sarah, 57
Callas, Maria, 16, 40, 43, 49–53
Camerata, 61, 63, 99, 205
Candide (Bernstein), 218, 227, 241
cantabile, 73, 130, 263–64
Capriccio (R. Strauss), 139
Carmen (Bizet), 108–109, 147, 171, 237, 258
Carolsfeld, Ludwig Schnorr von, 24
Carreras, José, 21, 227
Carte, Richard D'Oyly, 195, 256

Caruso, Enrico, 5, 6, 43–48
Caruso, Spaghetti, 256
Castor et Pollux (Rameau), 114
castrato, 22, 31–35
Cavalleria Rusticana (Mascagni), 86, 88–89, 147
Cavalli, Francesco, 66, 152
Cendrillon (Cinderella) (Massenet), 110
Cenerentola, La (Cinderella) (Rossini), 72, 239
Cesti, Antonio (born Pietro), 66
Chaliapin, Fyodor, 6, 30
Chaud-froid de Ponlarde à la Gounod, 257
Chernov, Vladimir, 28
Cherubini, Luigi, 99–100
Chicken Sautée *Mireille*, 257
Cilea, Francesco, 89
Cimarosa, Domenico, 191
Clari, or The Maid of Milan (Bishop), 192
Clément, Edmond, 43
Clemenza di Tito, La (Mozart), 67
coloratura, 16, 265
conductor, 54–57
Conlon, James, 57
Consul, The (Menotti), 91
Contes d'Hoffmann, Les (Offenbach), *see Tales of Hoffmann, The*
continuo, 64, 266
contralto, 18–20
contratenor altus, 19
convenienze, 41
Copland, Aaron, 222
Corelli, Franco, 25
Corigliano, John, 225
Così fan tutte (Mozart), 69, 70, 71
countertenor, 35
Croft, Dwayne, 28
Crozier, Eric, 199
Cui, César, 163, 164
Cunning Little Vixen, The (Janáček), 181
Curlew River (Britten), 157

da capo aria, 38, 68
Dafne (Peri), 61–62
Dame Blanche, La (Boieldieu), 100–01
da Ponte, Lorenzo, 69, 70, 214, 252
Dara, Enzo, 31

Daughter of the Regiment, The
    (Donizetti), 24, 75
De Stefano, Giuseppe, 53
Death in Venice (Britten), 199
Death of Klinghoffer, The (Adams), 226
Debussy, Claude, 2, 110, 113
Del Monaco, Mario, 25
Delibes, Léo, 115
Demon, The (Rubinstein), 163
Dialogues of the Carmelites (Poulenc),
    113–14, 149
Dido and Aeneas (Purcell), 186, 187–88
director, stage, 248–53
diva, 40–42
doctrine of the affections, 66, 123–24
Doktor and Apotheker (Dittersdorf), 120
Domingo, Plácido, 21, 26, 210
Don Carlos (Verdi), 82, 102, 226
Don Giovanni (Mozart), 69 71, 147, 171,
    214–15, 238, 249, 255
Don Pasquale, 30, 75
Doña Francisquita (Vives), 210
Donizetti, Gaetano, 5, 51, 74–77, 79, 130,
    153 54, 179, 207, 215
Donna del Lago, La (Rossini), 74
dramatic soprano, 17
Dreigroschenoper, Die (Weill), *see*
    Threepenny Opera, The
Drury Lane, Theatre Royal, 245
Duprez, Gilbert Louis, 23
Dvořák, Antonín, 12, 180, 212

Eddy, Nelson, 28
Edgar (Puccini), 84
Eggs Meyerbeer, 259
Egisto (Cavalli), 152
Einstein on the Beach (Glass), 218, 224
Elektra (R. Strauss), 138–40
Elisabetta, Regina d'Inghilterra
    (Rossini), 74
Elisir d'Amore, L' (Donizetti), 5, 45, 75
Emperor Jones, The (Gruenberg), 217
endless melody, 131 (also see: infinite
    melody)
Enfant et les Sortilèges, L' (Ravel),
    112–13
Entführung aus dem Serail, Die
    (Mozart), 120, 121, 239
Ernani (Verdi), 79–81, 149
Escoffier, Auguste, 256, 258, 259, 260

Eugene Onegin (Tchaikovsky), 147, 159,
    171, 173, 236
Euridice (Caccini), 62
Euridice (Peri), 62

Falstaff (Verdi), 80, 82, 92
Fanciulla del West, La (Puccini), 85
Farinelli, 34
Farrar, Geraldine, 46
Faust (Gounod), 44, 107–108, 147, 150,
    194, 236
Fedora (Giordano), 88
Feen, Die (Wagner), 129
Ferrier, Kathleen, 19
Fidelio (Beethoven), 124–26, 127
Fille du Régiment, La (Donizetti), *see*
    Daughter of the Regiment, The
fioritura, 16, 73, 268
Fischer-Dieskau, Dietrich, 28
Flagstad, Kirsten, 17
Fledermaus, Die (J. Strauss), 205,
    208–209, 240
Floyd, Carlisle, 221
*Flying Dutchman, The (Der Fliegende
    Holländer)* (Wagner), 4, 129–30,
    134, 149, 194, 238
Forrester, Maureen, 20
Forza del Destino, La (Verdi), 45, 81
Four Saints in Three Acts (Thomson),
    217–18
Fra Diavalo (Auber), 101, 257
Frau ohne Schatten, Die (R. Strauss),
    140
Freischütz, Der (Weber), 126–28
Freni, Mirella, 17
Fried Eggs Verdi, 259
Fry, William Henry, 215

Galli-Curci, Amelita, 47
Gallo, Lucio, 28
Garcia, Manuel, 215
Gardiner, John Eliot, 57
Gay, John, 142, 189
Gergiev, Valery, 57
Ghosts of Versailles, The (Corigliano),
    225
Gianni Schicchi (Puccini), 92, 230
Gigli, Beniamino, 47
Gilbert, Sir William S., 195, 208–209

Gilbert and Sullivan, 155, 184, 194–95, 227, 240, 244, 256
Giménez, Raúl, 26
Gioconda, La (Ponchielli), 27, 84, 147
Giorno di Regno, Un (Verdi), 78
Glass, Philip, 218, 223–25
Glinka, Mikail, 160–62
Gluck, Christoph Willibald von, 68, 98–99
Gobbi, Tito, 28
Goethe, Johann Wolfgang von, 107, 110, 115
Götterdämmerung (Wagner), 133, 149
Gounod, Charles, 107–109, 257
grand opera, 101–107, 269
Grande-Duchesse de Gérolstein, La (Offenbach), 207
Gruberova, Edita, 16
Gruenberg, Louis, 217
Guarany, Il (Gomes), 25
Guillaume Tell (Rossini), see William Tell
Gypsy Baron, The (J. Strauss), 208

Halévy, (Jacques-François-) Fromental, 207
Hamlet (Thomas), 155
Hampson, Thomas, 28
Ham Souflée Carmen, 258
Handel, George Frideric, 52, 66, 118–19, 183, 188, 190–91, 209
Hänsel und Gretel (Humperdinck) 136, 238
harmony, 133–34, 269
heldentenor, 24
Hellman, Lillian, 222, 223
Hendricks, Barbara, 17
Heppner, Ben, 26
Herbert, Victor, 208
Hérodiade (Massenet), 110
heroic tenor, 24
Heure Espagnol, L' (Ravel), 112
Hippolyte et Aricie (Lully), 97
HMS Pinafore (Sullivan), 195, 240
Hofmannsthal, Hugo von, 138
Hoiby, Lee, 223
Holst, Gustav, 197
Horne, Marilyn, 20
Hugh the Drover (Vaughan Williams), 196–97

Huguenots, Les (Meyerbeer), 102, 104
Humperdinck, Engelbert, 136
Hvorostovsky, Dmitri, 28
Hwang, David Henry, 224
Hydrogen Jukebox (Glass), 224

Incoronazione di Poppea, L' (Monteverdi), 64–65
infinite melody, 39 (also see: endless melody)
Iolanthe (Sullivan), 195, 209, 240
Ivanhoe (Sullivan), 195

Janáček, Léos, 180, 181
Jenufa (Jánaček), 180
Jewels of the Madonna, The (Wolf-Ferrari), 91
Jommelli, Nicolò, 66
Jones, Dame Gwyneth, 17
Juive, La (Halévy), 47, 102

Kallman, Chester, 202
Karajan, Herbert von, 57
Khovanshchina (Mussorgsky), 178
King Arthur (Purcell), 187
Kirov Opera, St. Petersburg, 162, 179
Kleiber, Carlos, 57
Knussen, Oliver, 203
Kowalski, Jochen, 35

Lady Macbeth of Mtsensk (Shostakovich), 177–78
Lakmé (Delibes), 115
Larmore, Jennifer, 21
Larson, Jack, 219
Latouche, John, 222
Lehár, Franz, 209–10
Leitmotif, 132–33, 270
Leoncavallo, Ruggero, 86, 89
Leonora (Fry), 215
Leonore (Beethoven), 125
Levine, James, 54
libretto, 62, 243–44, 270
Liebesverbot, Das (Wagner), 129
Life for the Tsar, A (Glinka), 160–61
Lind, Jenny, 15
Linda di Chamounix (Donizetti), 154
Lobster Fra Diavolo, 256
Lohengrin (Wagner), 130, 150, 238, 259

Lombardi alla Prima Crociata, I
  (Verdi), 5, 79
Lord Byron (Thomson), 218–19
Love for Three Oranges, A (Prokofiev),
  158, 176, 179
Lucia di Lammermoor (Donizetti), 3–4,
  149, 153, 236
Ludwig, Christa, 20
Luisa Miller (Verdi), 82
Lully, Jean Baptiste (born Lulli), 52, 56,
  94–97
Lulu (Berg), 144
Lustigen Weiber von Windsor, Die
  (Nicolai), *see Merry Wives of
  Windsor, The*
Lyric Opera of Chicago, 225, 230–31
lyric soprano, 16

Macbeth (Verdi), 82, 155, 255
Madama Butterfly (Puccini), 85, 90, 149,
  235
maestro al cembalo, 55
Maeterlinck, Maurice, 111
Magic Flute, The (Mozart), 121–22, 127,
  129, 194, 201, 229, 238
Mahler, Gustav, 6, 12, 56
Maid of Orleans The, (Tchaikovsky), 174
Mala Vita (Giordano), 89
Mamelles de Tirésias, Les (Poulenc), 113
Manon (Massenet), 86, 110
Manon Lescaut (Puccini), 84
Maria Stuarda (Donizetti), 75
Marriage of Figaro, The (Mozart),
  69–70, 191, 225, 252
Martha (Flotow), 45
Martinelli, Giovanni, 43, 47
Martón, Eva, 18
Mascagni, Pietro, 86, 89
Masked Ball, A (Verdi), *see Ballo in
  Maschera, Un*
masque, 185–86
Massenet, Jules, 85, 109–10, 251
McCormack, John, 43, 47
McIntyre, Sir Donald, 28
McNair, Sylvia, 17
Médée (Medea) (Cherubini), 51, 53, 99
Medium, The (Menotti), 91, 219–20
Mefistofele (Boito), 92
Mei, Girolamo, 61

Meistersinger von Nürnberg, Die
  (Wagner), 133, 135
Melba, Nellie, 6, 256, 259
Melba Toast, 256
Melchior, Lauritz, 25
melodrama, 271
melody, 35–36, 61, 76–77, 271
Mendelssohn, Felix, 15
Menotti, Gian Carlo, 91, 219
Mentzer, Susanne, 21
Mercadante, Saverio, 254
Mérimée, Prosper, 87, 108
Merrill, Robert, 28
Merry Widow, The (Lehár), 205, 209, 240
Merry Wives of Windsor, The (Nicolai),
  128
Messiah (Handel), 190
Metastasio, Pietro, 66–67
Metropolitan Opera, 5, 137–38, 200, 230,
  243, 245
Meyerbeer, Giacomo, 104–106, 129–30,
  207, 251, 259
mezzo-soprano, 20–21
Midsummer Marriage, A (Tippett), 201
Midsummer Night's Dream, A
  (Britten), 203
Mignon (Thomas), 115
mignon, filet, 258
Mikado, The (Sullivan), 195, 240
Miller, Jonathan, 249
minimalism, 224, 272
Minter, Drew, 35
Mireille (Gounod), 257
Molière (born Jean-Baptiste Poquelin),
  94–95, 139
Moll, Kurt, 31
Monteverdi, Claudio, 63–65, 213
Moore, Douglas, 221
Moreschi, Alessandro, 35
Morris, James, 28
Mother of Us All, The (Thomson), 218
Mozart, Wolfgang Amadeus, 12, 56, 66,
  68–72, 120, 202
Muette de Portici, La (Auber), 101
music director, 57
music drama, 131–34, 272–73
musical comedy, 273
musical theater, 142, 227–28
Mussorgsky, Modest, 163–66, 174, 178
Mustafà, Domenico, 35

Muti, Riccardo, 54
mystery play, 59–60

Nabucco (Verdi), 78–80, 156
Nagano, Kent, 57
New York City Opera, 223
Nicolai, Otto, 128
Night in Venice, A (Eine Nacht in Venedig) (Strauss), 208
Nilsson, Birgit, 17
Nixon in China (Adams), 226
Nono, Luigi, 86
Norma (Bellini), 76–77, 148
Norman, Jessye, 40
Nose, The (Shostakovich), 177
Nozze di Figaro, Le (Mozart), see Marriage of Figaro, The
number opera, 273
Nutcracker, The (Tchaikovsky), 171

Oberon (Weber), 192–93
Oberto, Conte di San Bonifacio (Verdi), 78
Offenbach, Jacques, 205–209
Olsen, Sanford, 26
opera buffa, 29
opéra comique, 98, 103, 119, 160, 206
opéra lyrique, 107
opera seria, 66–68, 73
operetta, 204–11, 239–41
Orfeo (Monteverdi), 63, 213
Orfeo ed Euridice (Orphée et Euridice) (Gluck), 68, 99, 206, 249
Orlando (Handel), 153
Orphée aux Enfers (Orpheus in the Underworld) (Offenbach), 206–207
Otello (Rossini), 74
Otello (Verdi), 80, 82, 92, 149, 237
Otter, Anne Sophie von, 21
Owen Wingrave (Britten), 199

Paganini (Lehár), 210
Pagliacci (Leoncavallo), 2, 44, 86, 90, 91, 148
Paris Opéra, 102, 244
Parsifal (Wagner), 133, 143, 150
Patience (Sullivan), 240
Patti, Adelina, 42, 257
Pavarotti, Luciano, 21, 26, 52
Peach Melba, 256, 260

Pear Belle Hélène, 256, 260
Pears, Sir Peter, 198, 200
Pêcheurs de Perles, Les (The Pearl Fishers) (Bizet), 115, 230
Pelléas et Mélisande (Debussy), 2, 111
Peri, Jacopo, 61–62
Peter Grimes (Britten), 157, 183, 198–99
Pinza, Ezio, 6
Pique Dame (Tchaikovsky), 171–73
Pirates of Penzance, The (Sullivan), 241
Planché, James Robinson, 192
Platée (Rameau), 98
Ponchielli, Amilcare, 84
Ponselle, Rosa, 6
Porgy and Bess (Gershwin), 196, 212, 217, 225
Porpora, Nicola, 34
Postcard from Morocco (Argento), 220–21
Poularde Adelina, Patti, 257
Poulenc, Francis, 113–14, 211
Prey, Hermann, 28
Price, Leontyne, 17
Prince Igor (Borodin), 159, 168–70
Princess Ida (Sullivan), 209
Prokofiev, Sergei, 175–76, 179
Prophète, Le (Meyerbeer), 102, 105
Puccini, Giacomo, 3, 83–86, 109, 251
Purcell, Henry, 153, 186–88, 193
Puritani, I (Bellini), 76, 154
Pushkin, Alexander, 161–62, 164, 171–72, 201

Queen of Spades, The (Tchaikovsky), 171–73
Queler, Eve, 57
Quilico, Gino, 28
Quinault, Philippe, 95

Ragin, Derek Lee, 35
Rake's Progress, The (Stravinsky), 157, 202
Rameau, Jean-Philippe, 52, 97–98, 114
Ramey, Samuel, 31
Ravel, Maurice, 111
recitative, 39, 67–68, 130, 276
Regina (Blitzstein), 223
Rheingold, Das (Wagner), 133
Rienzi (Wagner), 129

Rigoletto (Verdi), 80–82, 84, 231–33, 249, 254
Rimsky-Korsakov, Nikolai, 163, 164, 166–68, 174, 175, 178, 201
Rinaldo (Handel), 118, 188
Ring des Nibelungen, Der (The Ring of the Nibelungs) (Wagner), 132–35, 229, 239
Rinuccini, Ottavio, 60, 62
Rise and Fall of the City of Mahagonny, (Weill), 142–43
Ritorno d'Ulisse in patria, Il (Monteverdi), 64
Robert le Diable (Meyerbeer), 104
Roberto Devereux (Donizetti), 75
Romberg, Sigmund, 210
Roméo et Juliette (Gounod), 108, 147
Rosenkavalier, Der (R. Strauss), 139, 140, 236, 258
Rossini, Gioachino, 72–74, 77, 103–104, 130, 179, 215, 258
Rousseau, Jean-Jacques, 123
Royal Swedish Opera (Stockholm), 250
Rubinstein, Anton, 158, 163
Ruddigore (Sullivan), 155
Ruffo, Titta, 28
Rusalka (Dvořák), 180
Ruslan and Ludmilla (Glinka), 161–62

sacra rappresentazione, 60
Sadko (Rimsky-Korsakov), 159, 167
Saint of Bleeker Street, The (Menotti), 91, 220
Saint-Saëns, Camille, 107, 149, 204
Salieri, Antonio, 69, 104
Salminen, Matti, 31
Salome (R. Strauss), 137–38, 140, 156
Samson et Dalila (Saint-Saëns), 25, 45, 47, 107, 149
San Francisco Opera, 162, 230
Sardou, Victorien, 149, 258
Satyagraha (Glass), 224
Scarlatti, Alessandro, 66
scena, 73, 272
Schikaneder, Emanuel, 122,
Schoenberg, Arnold, 134, 141
Scotti, Antonio, 45
Scribe, Eugène, 100, 104–105, 257
Sellars, Peter, 226, 252
Selle de Veau à la *Tosca*, 258

Semiramide (Rossini), 73
Sendak, Maurice, 203
Serra, Luciana, 16
Shakespeare, William, 80, 126, 129, 152, 154, 184
Shostakovich, Dmitri, 173, 176–78
Siegfried (Wagner), 30, 133
Sills, Beverly, 16
Simon Boccanegra (Verdi), 84
Slezak, Leo, 43
Smetana, Bedřich, 179
Smirnov, Dmitry, 43
Snegurochka (The Snow Maiden) (Rimsky-Korsakov), 167
Solti, Sir Georg, 54
Sonnambula, La (Bellini), 76, 155
soprano leggiero, 16
spinto, 17, 278
Spontini, Gaspare, 100
Sprechgesang, 141
Stade, Frederica von, 20
Stein, Gertrude, 218
Stevens, Risë, 20
Stiffelio (Verdi), 81
stile rappresentativo, 62
Stracciari, Riccardo, 28
Strauss, Johann, Jr., 208
Strauss, Richard, 136, 258–59
Stravinsky, Igor, 167, 201
Student Prince, The (Romberg), 210
Studer, Cheryl, 18, 40, 221
Sullivan, Sir Arthur, 195–96, 208
Summer and Smoke (Hoiby), 223
Suor Angelica (Puccini), 92
Susannah (Floyd), 221
Sutherland, Dame Joan, 50, 52
Sweethearts (Herbert), 208
Swenson, Ruth Ann, 16

Tabarro, Il (Puccini), 85, 91
Tales of Hoffmann, The (Offenbach), 236
Tannhäuser (Wagner), 130, 134, 252
Tchaikovsky, Piotr Ilych, 163, 170–75
Te Kanawa, Dame Kiri, 40, 227
Tebaldi, Renata, 50
Telephone, The (Menotti), 220
Tempest, The (Hoiby) 223
Tender Land, The (Copland), 222
tenor, 21–26
Terfel, Bryn, 28

Tetrazzini, Luisa, 46, 256
Tetrazzini, Spaghetti, 256
Thaïs (Massenet), 110
Thomas, Ambroise, 115, 155
Thomson, Virgil, 217–19
Threepenny Opera, The (Weill), 140, 142, 189
Tibbett, Lawrence, 28, 217
Tilda, La (Cilea), 89
Tippett, Sir Michael, 200–201
Tosca (Puccini), 51, 85, 90, 148, 149, 235, 258
Toscanini, Arturo, 56–57
Tournedos Rossini, 258
Traviata, La (Verdi), 49, 81, 88, 146, 236, 249
Tristan und Isolde (Wagner), 131, 133, 134, 135, 150
Trittico, Il (Puccini), 91, 92
Trovatore, Il (Verdi), 3, 41, 81, 148, 237–38
Troyens, Les (Berlioz), 106
Turandot (Puccini), 85, 237

Utopia Limited (Sullivan), 209

Van Dam, José, 28
Vanessa (Barber), 220
Vaughan Williams, Sir Ralph, 196
Venus and Adonis (Blow), 186
Verbena de la Paloma, La (Vives), 210
Verdi, Giuseppe, 5, 46–47, 58, 77–83, 109, 155, 156, 205, 215, 251, 259
Verga, Giovanni, 89
verismo, 86–92, 109
Verrett, Shirley, 20
Vêpres Siciliennes, Les (I Vespri Siciliani) (Verdi), 81

Vestale, La (Spontini), 100
Vickers, Jon, 25–26
Villi, Le (Puccini), 84
Vives, Amadeo, 210
Voigt, Deborah, 18
Voyage, The (Glass), 224–25

Wagner, Cosima, 134–35, 251
Wagner, Richard, 39, 56, 105, 128–36, 143, 205, 209, 244
Wagner, Siegfried, 251
Wagner, Wieland, 251
Walküre, Die (Wagner), 77, 133, 239
War and Peace (Prokofiev), 179
Weber, Carl Maria von, 55, 56, 126–28, 192
Weill, Kurt, 142–43, 189
Werther (Massenet), 110
Where the Wild Things Are (Knussen), 203
William Tell (Rossini), 74, 103–104
Wilson, Lanford, 223
Wilson, Robert, 224
Wolf-Ferrari, Ermanno, 90
Wozzeck (Berg), 141

Xerse (Cavalli), 152

Yeoman of the Guard, The (Sullivan), 209

Zaide (Mozart), 121
Zarzuela, 210
Zauberflöte, Die (Mozart), *see Magic Flute, The*
Zeffirelli, Franco, 252
Zeno, Apostolo, 66, 67
Zigeunerbaron, Der (J. Strauss), *see Gypsy Baron, The*